P9-CMF-941

Leaders of Religion

EDITED BY H. C. BEECHING, M.A.

THOMAS CHALMERS

THOMAS CHALMERS.

From a Portrait by Thomas Duncan, R.S.A., A.R.A.

THOMAS CHALMERS

BY

MRS. OLIPHANT

SECOND EDITION

METHUEN & CO.
36 ESSEX STREET, W.C.
LONDON
1896

THOMAS CHALMERS.

CHAPTER I.

TOWARDS the end of last century, on the 17th March, 1780, Thomas Chalmers was born, the fourth son and sixth child of a well-to-do and comfortable family occupying a solid and substantial house at the west-end of the village of Easter Anstruther, popularly called Anster, in Fife. His father, John Chalmers, was a "dyer, ship-owner, and general merchant," a man of homely competency, a Scotch burgher, member of the Town Council, and elder in the Church, the most respectable and substantial of rural tradesmen, with links of alliance which attached him to the higher classes, territorial and clerical, in the district. The house still stands, and is more or less an object of curiosity and veneration as the birthplace of the great Dr. Chalmers, and I remember the half-contempt with which my questions about an old tenement once belonging to an ancestor of my own were received in the village. "Ye'll be wanting Dr. Chalmers' house?" the women at their doors said, eyeing with amazement the stranger who sought another shrine. It stands within sight and sound of the sea, not far from the little harbour where the ships of which John Chalmers was part-owner, fishing-boats, or merchant smacks, or perhaps a whaler on its return from Greenland, lay. Anster was not the prosperous town it had been a hundred years before, in the days when Maister James Melville, who has left one of the most graphic of diaries behind him, chronicling many national events, was minister; nor was it an emporium of salted herrings, giving large, if not very lovely, occupation to husbands and wives alike, and filling the streets with busy industry and ancient and fish-like smells in the season, as it is now. But there was enough of leisurely traffic to keep life going in a way of homely comfort, nobody being very rich, nor any very poor. The old and feeble were supported by the little revenue supplied by the "Plate" at the church door, where every worshipper placed his offering as he entered, often no more than a penny, but not to be omitted save at peril of self-respect and good report —and by the neighbourly kindness of the well-to-do; while the old sailors had their little pensions from the Sea-Box, and the fisher-folk rejoiced in the summer harvest of the "drave" or shoal of herrings, which, I have heard an old Fife lady say, came by a special arrangement of Providence along with the new potatoes, and filled the cottages on the head of the cliffs with food and gladness. Now the drave furnishes herrings to be salted and packed in barrels, and the new potatoes are sent off by railway to Edinburgh and Dundee. For some things, certainly, the old times were better, more abundant and comfortable in their way, if money was scarcer and luxuries fewer.

Tom Chalmers went naturally with his big and little brothers—there were nine boys in all—to the parish school, which was not in very effective keeping at the time, and where he was remembered as "one of the idlest, strongest, merriest, and most generous-hearted boys in Anstruther school." That he fought as well as played there can be no doubt in such a vigorous atmosphere, but there is a pretty anecdote of the sturdy independence and sense of the little lad, who is said to have taken refuge in a cottage when a "bicker" was going on, in which sharp and cutting mussel-shells were the missiles. "I'm no for powder and shot," he said. A more remarkable, and indeed quite singular, little scene occurred, we are told, still earlier, at three years old, when he was found in his nursery, in the dark, pacing up and down and repeating to himself the cry of David, "Oh, my son Absalom: oh, Absalom, my son, my son!"—the wonderful story, and that wonderful outcry of passion and anguish, having somehow caught the child's ear at an age almost too early to be conceivable as touched by such profound emotion at all.

That he should have declared his determination to become a minister at a very early age was not wonderful, for the minister was at once the most influential person in it, and the head of the village hierarchy, occupying a position which naturally attracted the first stirrings of childish ambition. But it cannot even be considered certain that it was from any special aptitude or progress in his work at school—where there was apparently more flogging than teaching—that young Tom Chalmers was sent with his elder brother, William, to the University of St. Andrews, when he was eleven years and a half old. This wonderful proceeding was common in Scotland at the time, though excessive in his case, his brother having the advantage of thirteen years of age, and being therefore quite matured and fit for graver studies. John Campbell, afterwards Lord Campbell and Lord Chancellor, entered the University at a still earlier age. The urchin in his little red gown could not spell, and no doubt was "Fifish—a wee by the East-Neuk," and spoke the broadest dialect of his country, the accent of which was a thing he never overcame, even at the height of his fame. A grave chronicler describes him as "volatile and boyish and idle in his habits, ill-prepared by previous education (at eleven and a half!) for reaping the full benefit of a college course." The sturdy little fellow played golf and football for his first two sessions, which were of six months each, the whole academical year in Scotland, and this no doubt did him more good than the lectures on Latin of "that distinguished philosophical grammarian, Dr. John Brown." However, in his third year, when he was "rising" fourteen, the boy settled down to his work, and his biographer, Dr. Hanna, tells us St. Andrews was "his intellectual birthplace." Mathematics was the branch of study which chiefly attracted him, and in that he attained considerable distinction. But his rapidly-developing mind became soon the scene of those whirlwinds and tempests of thought which have been supposed to be the special characteristic of our own age, but which no doubt accompany the progress of every new and inexperienced thinker animated by that sense of new discovery and original impulse which is the inheritance of youth. It is in vain to assure the boy that others have trod that path before him; his own fresh impressions are always, to his mind, the first that have ever been received. Younger Chalmers doubted, and soon dropped, Calvinism, in which he had been brought up. His father's somewhat stern religion had always seemed to him severe, and now no doubt had the air of an old-fashioned system, a part of the old Toryism and unbinding character of the elder race. In the livelier University circles of St. Andrews, a religion more intellectual, more liberal, conforming to the standards of the Church as necessity required, but indifferent and superior to them, was at that time in vogue, and philosophy had much stronger claims upon the educated and progressive than religion. "We inhaled," Chalmers himself said in later years, "not a distaste only, but a positive contempt for all that is properly and peculiarly gospel, insomuch that our confidence was nearly as entire in the sufficiency of natural theology as in the sufficiency of natural science." The young student became deeply engaged with the study of Godwin's *Political Justice.* He began to doubt the sincerity of those who held the orthodox side, and cavalierly declared that he "had not been paying attention, but thinking of something else," during a brilliant lecture upon those contemned principles. In short, in his old-fashioned way, and by a technique somewhat different, he passed in the self-confidence of his young soul through the same phase of mingled questioning, scepticism as to others and immense faith in his own judgment, which we of the nineteenth century have been in the habit of claiming as specially our own.

It developed, however, into something very individual in the large and ardent spirit of the young philosopher. From Godwin's *Political Justice* he stepped by some turn of the mental balance into Jonathan Edwards' *Treatise on Free Will*, which he studied "with such ardour that he seemed to regard nothing else, and would scarcely talk of anything else." This tremendous system, which to many minds suggests nothing but an inexorable bondage, more strong than iron or steel, more terrible than the Fates, influenced the mind of Chalmers in a different and characteristic way. "He rose to the sublime conception of the Godhead as that eternal, all-pervading energy by which this vast and firmly-knit succession was originated and sustained, and into a very rapture of admiration and delight." He refers almost with awe, in his journal many years later, to this condition of mental ecstasy, which must seem a very strange thing to those who entertain the common, it may almost be called vulgar, conception of Calvinism as of a system in which nothing is thought of but reprobation and everlasting torture. This is, at least, a new view for the reader of the present day.

"I remember (Chalmers says) when a student of divinity, and long ere I could relish evangelical sentiment, I spent nearly a twelvemonth in a sort of mental elysium, and the one idea which ministered to my soul all its rapture was the magnificence of the Godhead, and the universal subordination of all things to the one great purpose for which He evolved and was supporting creation." Alluding (his biographer adds) to this singular period in his mental history, he has told a member of his family that not a single hour elapsed in which this overpoweringly impressive imagination did not stand out before the inward eye, and that his custom was to wander early in the morning into the country, that amid the quiet scenes of nature he might luxuriate in the glorious conception.

A young man capable of such a solemn rapture is no doubt a very rare figure among the crowds of young men at any university: and such feelings must have been kept sedulously within the privacy of his reticent Scotch nature, which would have "thought shame" to unfold its inner emotions to any eye, only to come forth when the long levels of time had made the early landscape fair, and opened his mouth in the desultory narrative of recollection to those most near and dear. His biographer remarks upon a journal kept in the summer of 1796, which is full of the most practical details of a journey, with many and accurate notes as to the locks in the Forth and Clyde canal, then the new and admired way from Edinburgh to Glasgow: "Left to his own unaided conjecture," says Dr. Hanna, "the reader of this journal might rather have imagined the writer to be some honest burgher's son, who, going to settle as a merchant in the south, was keeping his eyes quite open to all the new objects which met him by the way, and looking at them with a very shrewd and penetrating glance." This is, in fact, exactly what Thomas Chalmers was, as he pursued his leisurely journey by canal and smack to Liverpool, where his merchant-brother received the large-limbed student, whose mind was filled with the practical ideas of the home at Anster, where there were so many sons to put forth in the world: and who felt no natural need to give out the rumbling thunder of his half-developed mind, in which he dwelt apart, his thoughts communicable to "the quiet scenes of nature," but not in any book or to any human ear.

It was the habit of the time that the members of the University should "assemble daily in the public hall for morning and evening prayers, which were conducted by the theological students." Clerical education in Scotland is much more distinctively professional than on the other side of the Tweed, and the divinity students are made to prepare for their future occupation from the very beginning of their special studies. At the present time it is the practice that a sermon should be preached by each in the critical presence of his professor and classmates, periodically during the session, which must be a trying ordeal. Still more trying in a church, where every prayer was expected to be an individual composition, must have been this ordeal, to which in the present day we cannot help attaching a suspicion of irreverence, as if a prayer intended for the ear of the Almighty, with expressions of devotion and supplication representing the voice of the people, might be criticized and commented upon as if it were an oration in the ordinary sense of the word. This, however, is a drawback to the freedom of individual prayer so strongly insisted upon by the Scotch Church, which is inevitable. When Chalmers, in his turn, conducted these services, his prayers made, we are told, "a powerful impression." The people of St. Andrews flocked to the hall when it was known that he was to officiate. "The wonderful flow of eloquent, vivid, ardent description of the attributes and works of God, and still more perhaps the astonishingly harrowing delineation of the miseries, the horrid cruelties, immoralities, and abominations inseparable from war, which always came in more or less in connexion with the bloody warfare in which we were engaged with France, called forth the wonderment of the hearers," we are told by one of them, after fifty-two years. Chalmers was only sixteen when this strange trial of his power was made.

Dr. Hanna quotes from one of his college essays a striking passage which shows that the young man's style was not remarkable only in prayer : for the page which we shall here repeat represents already very fairly the measured and dignified diction, with a flavour of Johnson and the elder age still in it, which was capable of being expanded by natural fervour into that eloquence which made him in his day one of the greatest of preachers. It is on a subject congenial at all times to that perfervid disposition which has always been characteristic of the Scot—though how that quality, attributed to the ancient Celtic race, could have become so essential a part of the modern Anglo-Saxon Lowland character, wholly apart from and inimical to the Celt, is a problem which might task the best powers of the ethnographist. Are there warm embers in the very soil of Fife—that most modern, rational, and discreet of counties—which communicate the old fire of contending Picts and Scots, to what is called in modern phrase the canny Scotchman? At all events the appropriateness of the old description is very apparent still. Young Chalmers, somewhere between sixteen and eighteen, discoursing of enthusiasm in his old note-book for the ear of his professor, wrote as follows—

"How different the languor and degeneracy of the present age from that ardour which animated the exertions of the primitive Christians in the cause of their religion! That religion had then all the impressive effect of novelty. The evidences which supported its divine origin were still open to observation. The miracles of Christianity proclaimed it to be a religion that was supported by the arm of Omnipotence. The violence of a persecuting hostility only served to inflame their attachment to the truth and to arouse the intrepidity of their characters. Enthusiasm is a virtue rarely produced in a state of calm and unruffled repose. It flourishes in adversity. It kindles in the hour of danger and rises to deeds of renown. The terrors of persecution only serve to awaken the energy of its purposes. It swells in the pride of integrity, and great in the purity of its cause, it even scatters defiance among a host of enemies. The magnanimity of the primitive Christians is beyond example in history. It could withstand the ruin of interests, the desertion of friends, the triumphant joy of enemies, the storms of popular indignation, the fury of a vindictive priesthood, the torments of martyrdom. The faith of immortality emboldened their profession of the gospel, and armed them with the contempt of death. The torrent of opposition they had to encounter in asserting the religion of Jesus was far from repressing their activity in His service. They maintained His cause with sincerity, they propagated it with zeal, they devoted their time and their fortune to its diffusion. Amid all their discouragements they were sustained by the assurance of a heavenly crown. The love of their Redeemer consecrated their affections to His service, and enthroned in their hearts a pure and disinterested enthusiasm. Hence the rapid and successful extension of Christianity through the civilized world. The grace of God was with them. It blasted all the attempts of opposition.

It invigorated the constancy of their purposes. It armed them with fortitude amid the terrors of persecutions, and carried them triumphant through the proud career of victory and success."

Dr. Hanna tells us that a whole lifetime after, at the crowning point of his career, the old man eloquent took up these boyish words and poured them forth over the heads of the little army whom he was about to lead forth, if not to fight and triumph, at least to sacrifice and renunciation—with an effect impossible to describe.

When his education was nearly drawing towards its close, the last year of his theological studies requiring only a residence of three months at the University, it was thought well that the youth, then eighteen, should take a tutorship, and so begin to help himself. Up to this time the circumstances of his family had made it unnecessary that the boy should, as so many boys did, maintain himself in the long interval of his studies—the yearly vacation of six months or more. But there were fourteen children of his father's house, and it was more creditable, according to all the wholesome ideas of his time, that he should now begin to exert himself. The history of this tutorship is told with great gravity by Dr. Hanna, and it is certainly a powerful example of the woes and slights which extremely impatient merit refuses to take from the unworthy; yet the character of the youth, and his stand for himself, illuminated by his future fame, gives a humorous aspect to the story. He had ten children to teach, the eldest of whom, about fifteen, had already been two years at college, but set a very bad example to his juniors, none of whom had the least regard for the position of their boy-tutor. His hours were "from seven till nine in the morning, from ten till twelve in the forenoon, from two till three, and from four till six;" and he was treated with a contumely that stung his youthful pride and independence.

"The people of the house don't seem to know the place in which a tutor should stand: hence a cold, contemptuous reserve which I was never accustomed to, and which exposes me to the most disagreeable feelings. The vexation of mind that arises from this circumstance is much heightened by the difficulties of my employment. My predecessor, as I have reason to believe, in compliance with the wishes of the female part of the family, allowed his pupils several improper indulgences: hence they had contracted habits quite incompatible with the order and discipline which ought to be observed, and I was obliged to have recourse to strong measures in order to root them out. This gave offence, I thought, to the ladies of the house, and I ascribed to this in great part their high looks and sour, forbidding deportment. I have been a stranger to real enjoyment since I came here. I place my happiness in the reciprocal returns of friendship and goodwill; but this is to me a solitary desert, and I have nothing in it wherewith to call forth my affections."

In a letter to his father his grievances are repeated in the same serious and indignant tone. "In consequence of the low idea they have got of the respect due to a tutor, it is impossible for me to talk with freedom and confidence. I have observed more than once my attempts to participate in the conversation discountenanced by the frown of superior dignity.

Hence those who frequent the house—many of whom would bow full low in your dining-room—regard me as unworthy of their notice, and return my salutations with cold indifference." Wounded feelings of this description have rarely been expressed with so much lofty and serious indignation, and while wholly sympathizing with him, we find it difficult to suppress a smile at the solemnity of eighteen, which desires not to express any exaggerated sentiment, but to "endeavour to make propriety the standard of my conduct," and begs to be advised how best, while preserving a respectful demeanour, he can "act his part with dignity and effect." The last straw was added to his burden when he discovered that his employers were in the habit of having supper-parties in which he was not included. The idea that he is thought "unworthy of supping in the same room with the family" fires his blood. "My pupils often have this privilege when there is company, whilst I, regarded as inferior to them, have supper in my own room!" Flesh and blood could not stand this indignity, and the fiery youth took a characteristic way of vindicating himself. "Whenever he knew that there was to be a supper from which he would be excluded, he ordered one in a neighbouring inn, to which he invited one or more of his own friends."

"To make his purpose all the more manifest, he waited till the servant entered with his solitary repast, when he ordered it away, saying, 'I sup elsewhere to-night.' Such curiously-timed tutorship suppers were not very likely to be relished by Mr. ——, who charged him with unseemly and unseasonable pride. 'Sir,' said he, 'the very servants are complaining of your haughtiness. You have far too much pride.' 'There are two kinds of pride, sir,' was the reply. 'There is that pride which lords it over inferiors: and there is that pride which rejoices in repressing the insolence of superiors. The first I have none of, the second I glory in.'"

The large youth of eighteen, thrilling with so passionate a sense of injury, flinging his thunderbolt at the "insolent superior" with all the tragic gravity of his age, affords a whimsical picture. It was no laughing matter to young Tom Chalmers—with the sense of his substantial father, as good as any man, behind him, and of the contemptible guests who would "bow full low" in that father's dining-room, yet dared to insult the son: but the scene is full of unconscious humour. If the little rebels of that school-room were ever heard of in after life, it would probably be from the circumstance that Chalmers in his youth was once their tutor. And the scene altogether throws a curious light on the mental condition of another young Scotchman, a little later in the generations. Thomas Carlyle, petted and honoured by the Bullers, yet never quite able to make up his mind that these kind people really meant nothing but kindness, had the shadow of that other kind of tutorship so deeply impressed upon his mind, that he never got quite free from it, or escaped from the doubt that a profound scorn, more refined than in the case of the Scotch bourgeois yet equally derogatory, was at the bottom of their supposed condescension to himself. The one incident lends a subtle light of interpretation to the other.

Chalmers, however, soon withdrew from the position in which he was thus exposed to contumely, and at the age of nineteen entered upon the exercise of his legitimate profession, being licensed as a preacher, the first step in the Scotch Church, in 1799. It was not lawful to admit any probationer before the age of twenty-one "except" as was provided by law, "such as for rare and singular qualities shall be judged by the general and provincial assemblies to be meet and worthy thereof." Upon this condition the friends of young Chalmers took their stand, one Fife minister, whose name is not preserved, asserting his claim as "a lad o' pregnant pairts." The description is picturesque, and nothing could be more entirely justified. But the privilege thus accorded was not hastily entered upon. He was not possessed at this time of his life by strong religious feeling of any kind. The mind which had been rapt in intellectual ecstasy by the noble conception of one great, all-pervading Godhead, and

> "One divine far-off event
> To which the whole creation moves,"

had relapsed into calm, uninspired by anything more emotional than mathematics. He was no heaven-devoted priest or apostle. The life and energy of a robust young man, full of ambition, eager for achievement, was in all his veins. He settled in Edinburgh for the next two winters, hoping for pupils by whom to pay his expenses, and though not successful in that point, evidently maintaining himself, by the aid of "any little thing that may offer," and the hospitality of a relative "whose conduct is distinguished by all the regard of a parent," the young man announced in his solemn phraseology. Apparently, between the calm of this period and the year of enthusiasm above-described, there had intervened a period of great mental struggle, doubt, and uncertainty. He had been licensed to preach the gospel while in this condition of miserable questioning as to whether there was any gospel to preach. The books that undermined his faith, and the considerations which restored it, are both old-fashioned to this generation. We have gone on to other methods, but the result is the same. He changed his intense conception of God for an unwilling and horror-stricken adoption of the system of natural law which seemed to make God unnecessary: then recovered his faith by a gradually growing conviction that the adaptation of means to an end, visible through all the universe, could only be the work of a Supreme and All-understanding Being. One of his friends gives a brief account of the trouble of mind in which this internal tempest involved him. He was "in a state of great excitement and unhappiness." "One very common expression in public prayers, and which showed the state of his mind at the time, 'Oh, give us some steady object for our mind to rest upon,' was uttered with all his characteristic earnestness and emphasis." This ordeal, which so many of the finest minds go through, is not, however, dwelt upon in his biography. There is very little information on the subject. In later years he referred to it occasionally, but without detail. To a correspondent who consulted him on the subject, being at the time in a state of "philosophical scepticism," he recommended Beattie's *Essay on Truth*, a now forgotten work, as "the book to which I was most indebted for my deliverance," as well as the lectures of Professor Robison. And he added a strenuous recommendation to prayer even in the midst of this chaos. "Under all the difficulties and despondencies of such a state I would still encourage you to prayer," he says. "Cry as you can: with real moral earnestness and a perseverance in this habit, light will at length arise out of darkness." He himself acted in this same way, so inconsequent if any real inability to believe in God existed in the chaos. "He was exceedingly earnest in seeking the light of truth at that time in his private devotion, and was often on his knees at the bed-side after I had gone to bed," says the friend, who seems to have known most of this unhappy interval, in the close intimacy of a companion who shared his bed-chamber. There are many strange things in the minds of those who "say in their heart there is no God," all manner of indignations, accusations, resentful passion against the Being who they allege does not exist—but few, perhaps, more wonderful than this, the appeal to Him who is not, to prove and justify Himself!

It had all, however, come to an end, both the ecstasy and the misery: and this large, impetuous, awkward young soul, stumbling upon the brink of life, had secured to himself a standing-ground of more or less satisfactory religion or belief, enough to satisfy the requirements of his mind for the moment, putting aside the question out of the number of problems which there was an absolute necessity to solve. He did not want to be thrust into work which would require a more intimate consideration of these problems. "I find my time so profitably employed that I would be sorry for any interruption for the winter," he writes to his father; the interruption meaning a living which, as may be read between the lines, the Chalmerses confidently expected to come through the means of the landed family, supreme in the district, whose political ambitions Mr. John Chalmers had served in his capacity of Provost of

Anstruther. A glimpse at an entire world of ancient habits and hopes is given in a fierce letter written by the young man, apparently on the downfall of some of these hopes. These were the days before Reform, when the little town councils of the small burghs formed all the constituency, and an election was almost a personal transaction between the half-dozen men in a town, who were probably swayed by the strongest individual among them, and the neighbouring county potentate, who sought their suffrages for himself or his nominee. This is not in the least degree to say that the bailies and provosts were venal, and sold their trust. No doubt John Chalmers of Easter Anstruther thought like his laird and landlord, and was very probably the most sincere politician of the two; but as it was upon his constancy to his principles that Sir Robert's election depended, there was nothing more natural than that Sir Robert should remember the circumstance when a piece of patronage fell into his hands. It was a succession of events which seemed the most natural in the world. Did one of the Anstruther churches, Kilrenny or Sellardyke, fall vacant while young Tom Chalmers drove along his mathematical chariot in Edinburgh, deprecating any "interruption"? Something like this must have occurred, we imagine, from the fury of a letter in which he pours out his anathema upon the "family which politically had been deeply indebted to his father," the sting of being passed over having, it would seem, burnt out his dislike of the "interruption." It is thus that the young man writes to a friend of his own age, always in the grandiose diction on which our own slipshod familiarity of language throws an almost comic light—

"The country here bears with it every symptom of decay, a languishing trade, an oppressed tenantry, a rapacious gentry. Excuse my croaking. I love to unburden myself of those unpleasant feelings which weigh down my spirit. With what eagerness, with what patriotic ardour, would I take up arms in defence of my country—would I lend all my efforts to oppose a threatened invasion, were I conscious of defending a righteous order of things. With what reluctance and disgust must I concur in what are called the exertions of patriotism, when I observe none interested but a set of insolent oppressors, who display their loyalty, not by rewarding its friends, but by persecuting its enemies—not by encouraging the pure virtue of public spirit, but by crushing all attempts at even an innocent freedom of observation and thought! Ah, my dear sir, if you felt that burden of indignation which oppresses my feelings when I behold the triumph of successful villainy, the contempt which attends the simplicity of virtue, the base ingratitude of those who have availed themselves of the interest and exertions of unsuspicious friends! I swear at this moment I feel a sentiment of superiority which I would not forego for all the luxurious pleasures, all the flattering distinctions of wealth. I heave with a secret aspiration of contempt for the unprincipled deceit, the mean hypocrisy of our dignified superiors. But I go too far. The great whom I have had the misfortune to be connected with are not only a disgrace to rank, but a disgrace to humanity. They are by no means a fair specimen; and I must still consider it as my duty to resist the inroads of foreign enemies. It would be well, however, for the great to reflect on their critical and dependent position

—to abolish that putrid system of interest which threatens to extinguish all the ardours of a generous and patriotic sentiment, to adopt a more just and liberal conduct to inferiors."

All this fiery declamation presumably means only that the reigning lord of Balcaskie had given a vacant living or other appointment away to some other supporter, who probably had an equal right to the gift in the same way. We doubt whether a Socialist of the present day could speak more strongly. All the vehemence of disappointed youth is in the outburst—and the swaying round of the balance of disturbed reason enough to make the young man feel that it is still his duty to resist invasion, even though the Anstruther family has not redeemed its pledges, is almost too humorous to be real. Yet we remember to have heard language of a very similar kind from the lips of old people conscious of having served the ends of some county magnate, and of having been overlooked when a return was possible. Is the feeling extinct in the present day, despite of all the safeguards of household suffrage and the ballot, on one side, and universal examination on the other? We doubt if it will ever be extinct. In the absence of the expected preferment, young Chalmers entered upon the duties of his profession—having, as we have seen, no overwhelming desire to take them up—as assistant to the parish minister of Cavers, in Teviotdale, to which he was recommended by the friendly zeal of one of his college comrades, who had held the appointment before him. He remained there for about a year, acquiring a little experience in parish work, which he performed punctually, though without any deep sense of its importance. His heart was in the class-rooms at St. Andrews, and all his ambitions fixed upon a chair there, for the attainment of which he used every energy, especially when the appointment vacant was that of Mathematical Assistant—an appointment very different from that of parish minister, but one which roused the hopes of the young man much more warmly than any prospect of a mild country living. As it happened, he attained both at a stroke, having been appointed at once to the mathematical post for which he longed, and to the little rural parish of Kilmany.

Those were the days in which pluralities of a wealthier description abounded in the Church of England, and when it was still possible to hold two posts at a time, even in Scotland, the National Church being in a state of great quiescence—"Moderate" to its fingers' ends, and easily satisfied with the respectable fulfilment of necessary duties. Chalmers himself had as yet no strenuous religious feeling. He writes of himself, while at Cavers, that he had been "much resorted to of late" for assistance on "sacramental occasions." These were the infrequent but high ceremonials of the Scotch Church, the "Communion Seasons," celebrated once in the year or half-year, by which the whole population was moved as by one of the Jewish feasts, and scenes were sometimes beheld such as justified the tremendous satire of Burns's *Holy Fair*. They were still occasions by which the rural populations dated the course of events, times of almost convivial meeting, and of much hospitality and social enjoyment, even in the sober atmosphere of the Manse, when young Chalmers informed his father of the fact that he was "much resorted to." "This, in so thinly-peopled a country, necessarily subjects me to long journeys, which I find, however, to be a pleasant and healthy relief from the labours of study. I don't think," he adds, "I will ever allow myself to be so carried away with the attractions of science as not to intermingle a sufficient degree of exercise and amusement."

It is whimsical to hear of "exercise and amusement" in the midst of the hard labours of mathematical science, as being attained by those ministrations on "sacramental occasions," which were the most solemn moments of the Church. But no doubt the Jewish feasts too were not only the highest ceremonials of worship, but also the periods of completest social enjoyment, in that old economy from which we have borrowed so much.

The young man who expressed himself with such straightforward honesty as to the "ploys" peculiar to his clerical profession, was settled, in the year 1802, when he was exactly twenty-two years old, in the parish of Kilmany, and in his mathematical chair—with the short interval of a few winter months, in which he devoted himself exclusively to the latter, between. It was but a deputy professorship he held, the professor *de jure* being alive and watchful, though unable to fulfil the duties of his post; but the appearance of the young enthusiast, scattering fire and flame amid the high and dry teachings of the University, was too remarkable a disturbance of all routine to be taken very peaceably. He burst into the dry fields of geometry like a meteor lighting up those arid plains till they blossomed like the rose. Dr. Hanna gives us several quotations from those early lectures, which are astonishing in their dignified and somewhat elaborate style and fervent enthusiasm. "Mathematics," he says, "have been condemned as contracting the best affections of the heart, chilling the ardours of its benevolence, blasting its heavenward aspirations."

"Dr. Johnson, who possessed the powers of genius without its liberality, and who appears to have cherished an immovable contempt for mathematics, has directed all the powers of his ridicule against the ludicrous peculiarities which he is pleased to ascribe to mathematicians. He conceives a fire raging in a neighbourhood and spreading destruction among many families: while all the noise and consternation is unable to disturb the immovable composure of a mathematician, who sits engrossed with his diagrams, deaf to all the sounds of alarm and of distress. His servants rush into his room, and tell him that the fire is spreading all around the neighbourhood. He observes simply that it is very natural, for fire always acts in a circle—and resumes his speculations. You may be afraid to encounter a study which begets such insensibility. Let me tell you that your apprehensions are groundless, that it is not the effect of this study to divest you of all that is human, or to congeal the fervours of a benevolent or devoted heart. I appeal to the example of our illustrious countryman. Amid the splendour of his discoveries, and the proud elevation of his fame, Newton rejoiced in all the endearments of friendship. In the spirit of a mild and gentle benevolence he maintained an inviolable serenity. It is said of him that he had the modesty of a child. In the society of his friends, the consciousness of his superiority seemed to desert him. His eye beamed with inexpressible benignity—he indulged in all the luxury of affection, and could descend to the sportful effusions of familiar intercourse. His fame went abroad throughout all the world: but he would not confide his happiness to the treacherous breath of applause. He founded it on a more secure foundation. He felt it in the affectionate homage of those friends to whom his worth endeared him. He felt it in the consciousness of an unblemished life, in the overpowering impressions of adoring piety. Newton, we invoke thy genius! May it preside over our labours, and animate to the arduous ascent of philosophy. May it revive the drooping interests of science, and awaken the flame of enthusiasm in the hearts of a degenerate people. May it teach us that science without virtue is an empty parade, and that that philosophy deserves to be extinguished which glances contempt on the sacred majesty of religion!"

The young man who uttered these large sentences with all that force of parallelism which the eloquence of Scotland has taken from the Hebrew poets, and an enthusiasm which rose through every successive period—with his broad local utterance and the inspired awkwardness of his large gestures as he leant over his desk, himself carried away by the impulse which he longed to communicate—filled St. Andrews with wonder and dismay. There was plenty of humour and frolic in the old University. The professors, many of them witty men and jovial, the students a little "wild," playing many pranks which were not perhaps quite consistent with decorum, were all equally startled by this new voice which rang into all the echoes, proclaiming the most abstruse of studies as if it had been poetry, and claiming attention as if the youth still labouring for utterance had been a prophet and a sage. "God forbid," he said, on another occasion, when the winter had changed into spring, and the young men's fancies lightly turned towards the links and the sea-shore, and all manner of diversion instead of work—"God forbid that I should interrupt the harmless amusements, or blast the innocent gaiety of youth. Let the morning of life be consecrated to enjoyment. May cheerfulness gladden your early years, and may your lives retain the uncorrupted simplicity of virtue. I have too ardent and sincere an affection for youth to look with an eye of severity on their amusements, or to throw a damp over the sportive gaiety of their dispositions. Let me never interfere with their enjoyments, but to convince them that a life of unlimited indolence will entail upon them all the miseries of languor and disgust; to convince them of the necessity of exertion; that industry invigorates the faculties and preserves them from decay; that activity sustains the energy of character; that the preparations of youth decide the respectability of manhood, and enrich the mind with the fairest treasures of cultivation and science and morality."

The sage who thus spoke had just attained the venerable age of twenty-three: but that was maturity itself in the fervent development of his mind, and in contrast with the youths who crowded around him, many of them mere school-boys in age, some, let us hope, capable of being fired with the spirit of their instructor: but the older professors, who stirred up no enthusiasm and spoke no such burning words, did not like this strain, which was so unlike the ordinary prosings of academical discourse. Least of all did the special professor, whom young Chalmers "assisted," like it; and his manner of showing his dislike was in the highest degree insulting. He gave certificates, we are told, to the students whom he had not instructed, and of whose progress he was ignorant, without consulting their real teacher. That teacher was as hot of temper, and as determined to put up with no indignity, as he had been when a boy-tutor five years before. While the public examination was going on, which "it was the practice in St. Andrews to have at the end of each session in presence of the professors," the young Assistant in Mathematics stepped forward before he began his examination of his pupils, and "broke out into a severe invective against Professor Vilant." "It was amusing," says Hanna, "to see the academic board. Old Mr. Cook, irritated and vexed; Mr. Hill, puffing and fidgeting; Dr. Playfair, getting up twice or thrice and tugging the speaker by the arm; Dr. Hunter, with unvarying countenance, his eyes sedatively fixed on the floor; Dr. Rotheram, laughing and angry by turns." It is not to be wondered that the Assistant in Mathematics got his dismissal on the spot!

He was on the whole, and by every authority, at this period of his career an unmanageable youth. His ordination to the cure of souls at Kilmany was to take place in May, and his father, in Anster, a very grave and profoundly religious man, looking on at all this with very serious eyes, was anxious that his hot-headed Tom should spend the little interval between the breaking-up of the classes, in the end of April, and this solemn ceremony, at home. The old gentleman thought that rest and quiet, and the subdual of all such hot emotions in the calm of the paternal house, would be the best preparation for taking those vows upon him; but our young man was not of that mind. His own desire was to spend the interval in Edinburgh, which he did, asserting his intention with some petulance. "I confess I like not these views of religion which suppose that the business, or even the innocent amusements of the world, have a dangerous tendency to unsettle the mind for serious and elevating exercises. I feel that the solitude of a few days would be to me a painful and unmeaning solemnity," he says. He felt no desire to watch his arms ere he should receive the spiritual knighthood. All that was plain sailing enough to his impatient spirit. What he wanted was to explain his position to his friends in Edinburgh, and to taste the sweets of intellectual intercourse before he bound himself down to his country parish. It may be supposed with what grave looks and shaken heads this letter would be received in Anster, and how many prayers would rise for the rebellious young man, who probably did not pray for himself.

He seems, however, to have made a very hearty and genial young minister, taking a lively, natural interest in the setting up of his new house—the first house he had possessed of his own—and careering through his little landward parish of a hundred and fifty families with, to use his own phrase, "his affections flying before him," and winning all hearts. Such a man, large in movement, hearty in speech, full of local interest and accent, both in language and atmosphere, is always popular in a Scotch parish. But while he roamed about the soft uplands of Kilmany, between Forth and Tay, his mind was full of warlike thoughts. "Acquainted with every family, and familiar at every fireside," he already was making friends wherever he moved; but it was not wonderful that having done so much he should feel that there was little to do for his abounding energies in that mild parish, while so much lay outside. And he would not be beaten: that was the one thing impossible. His head was full of ambition, and his heart of a natural desire for companionship and intellectual sympathy, not to say that the wrongs, or what seemed to him the wrongs, of his dismissal from St. Andrews were hot within him. His rapidly-formed resolution to return to the scene of his humiliation, and re-assert and vindicate himself by opening private mathematical classes there, roused St. Andrews again as by the sound of a trumpet. He was coming back, the young rebel, to beard the lions in their den, and pluck the beards of the professors; and fury and dismay rose in the bosom of the United Colleges. It was such a thing as never had been done before, and every tradition was outraged by it. But for this he cared nothing, in his determination to show himself a better man than any of them. He had to beard more than the professors—the distinct opposition of his good father, who cared little for St. Andrews or its lecture-rooms, but much for Kilmany and the claims which his parish had upon its minister. The young man's special pleading on this point is remarkable. He assures his father in his letters that "no minister finds it necessary" to devote his whole time to his parish. He himself has quite as much time on his hands unemployed as will be taken up by his mathematical classes. "With regard to non-residence, it will only be for six months," during which time his two neighbours will attend to any incidental duty. In short, his heart was set on his scheme of returning to St. Andrews and proving his superiority to all censure, and neither the opposition of the University, nor the grieved disapproval at home, had any effect upon him. He drove, like Jehu, furiously over every obstacle. One of the professors, supposed to have said that Mr. Chalmers had promised not to return as a teacher to St. Andrews as a condition of his appointment to Kilmany, was required at once to contradict the report. Not doing so, he was attacked in the street by the young rebel. "I said to him I was sorry, from the proceedings of last night, to be under the necessity of pronouncing him the author of a false and impudent calumny." Strong words, and no doubt uttered with all the heat and vehemence of his nature; but strong language of this kind, especially in self-defence, is a thing which has never been objected to in Scotland. Notwithstanding the boldness of the attempt against the whole University and its power and influence—or perhaps in consequence of that boldness—the young man's rebellion was very soon accepted and supported more or less by the community. Before long he set up a class of chemistry, which was quite a new thing, and mitigated the disapproval of the authorities.

"He had three classes of mathematics as well as this class of chemistry to prepare for and conduct. He had, besides, the pulpit of Kilmany to supply, going out generally to the manse every Saturday, and returning early every Monday; yet he wrote to his father as if he had now got into and was breathing the proper element of his being. 'My hands are full of business. I am living just now the life I seem to be formed for—a life of constant and unremitting activity. Deprive me of employment, and you condemn me to a life of misery and disgust.'"

This strong, laborious force to which inaction was despair, and which rejoiced as a bridegroom to run its race, ended finally by overcoming all opposition. The lectures thus established in despite of every authority carried away all who listened to them. The natural fire of his high spirit, and the swelling of heart and style, amounting almost to passion, with which his sentences rolled on, in themselves a little formal yet instinct with this rising tide of vigour and life, at once excited and held fast all hearers. He was unconscious as yet, if we may so speak, of the higher mysteries as well as of the discouragements of life. He felt himself able to do whatever might become a man, and he had not a doubt of the power of others to do so also, if the matter were but set before them, and all the great inducements and high impulses towards virtue, nobleness, independence, and the splendid paths of philosophy set before them. "What enterprise," he cries, "is too daring for the intrepidity of philosophical speculation? Who can presume to restrain the flights of human curiosity? Who can control the proud and aspiring energies of the mind? Who can stop the ambitious excursions of philosophy?" Then the orator changes his tone with all the native instinct of art, and sets forth with a skilful subdual yet exaltation the contrast between human weakness and greatness, the one so profound and pitiful, the other so illimitable and great.

"I know nothing more calculated to illustrate the triumphs of the human mind than to contrast its gigantic efforts in the walks of speculation with the extreme helplessness and infirmity of our physical constitution. Man is the being of yesterday: he is a flower which every blast of heaven can wither into decay: the breath of his life is a thin vapour which every wind can dissipate into nothing: his inheritance is the gloom of a silent grave, where he will sleep with the dust of his fathers. He is the poor victim of passion and of infirmity: from the feeble cry of infancy to the strength and independence of manhood a thousand ills pursue him—a thousand anxieties torment his repose. He at one time labours under the hardness of poverty: at another pines away in the infirmity of disease: at another weeps the treachery of violated friendship: and at another mourns the awful desolation which death makes among friends and among families. Yet amid this wild war of accident and misfortune he has displayed the triumph of his energies: he has given his few peaceful moments to the study of philosophy: he has sent abroad his penetrating eye, and caught the finest tokens of magnificence, simplicity, and order: he has enriched science with a thousand truths, and adorned the walks of literature with a thousand delicacies."

"What to me is this quintessence of dust?" says the musing poet; but to young Chalmers it was much, it was everything, the mightiest engine, the most powerful agent, the conqueror and the governor of the world.

This ornate speech, of which he had so soon attained the secret, was no doubt more then, than even in his later years, marred to the fastidious by the broad accent and cadenced chant of Fife, and by various peculiarities of manner, the rude and simple gestures of natural eloquence, the impetuous force of delivery, which made the veins stand out on his forehead, and the foam fly from his lips. But in his native county, the tone, the movement, the overpowering vehemence and earnestness were no drawbacks, but rather the reverse. They showed the sincerity, the profound conviction of the speaker, to whom his philosophy had all the excitement and charm of poetry and music, transporting his spirit, making his heart beat and his bosom swell. "And although," says Dr. Hanna, "strong personal feeling was at times expressed (as when he accused an astonished Don of a false and impudent calumny), such a genial humanity breathed about him who uttered it, that the very professor upon whom his stroke at first seemed to fall the heaviest, was one of the first to extend to him the forgiving hand of friendship." This was exceedingly creditable to the professor, more so, we think, than to the "genial humanity" which was so bent upon self-vindication. Perhaps, however, quiet St. Andrews, not an exciting place at any time, was grateful for the sensation which stirred up everybody, and gave all the freshness of a standing controversy to be discussed in every corner, and which moved small and great, in the little stagnant town. An attempt to bring the young minister to book for his neglect of his parish, on the other hand, came to nothing; and the young man, with the wind in his sails, rushed successfully and impetuously on.

We may instance one or two examples of that old-fashioned fervour of style at which we smile nowadays, in occasional utterances in the pulpit and out of it, of this youthful minister and "canny Scotsman." The reader will be glad to hear that his patriotism had quite recovered the shock given it by the misbehaviour of the gentry referred to on our earlier pages. Those were the days when invasion was a possibility which fired the British blood, when scenes were enacting such as those which are described by Sir Walter Scott in the *Antiquary*, and the three kingdoms (or at least the two kingdoms) were ringing with expressions of defiance.

> "We'll boldly fight, like heroes bright,
> For honour and applause ;
> And defy the French, with all their art,
> To alter our laws,"

was the outcry of popular song. And a still more martial utterance came from the pulpit of Kilmany, where the young minister stood like a battalion, shouting forth the voice of battle. He ended his sermon, no doubt, in the midst of that half-sob of labouring breath with which the crowd follows the solemnity of such a climax.

"May that day when Buonaparte ascends the throne of Britain be the last of my existence; may I be the first to ascend the scaffold he erects to extinguish the worth and spirit of the country; may my blood mingle with the blood of patriots, and may I die at the foot of that altar on which British independence is to be the victim!"

These words have an almost ludicrous aspect to the reader now in their tragic sincerity; but it must be remembered that "Buonaparte" had ascended many thrones in the sight of a terrified world, and that the most sober lookers-on anticipated nothing less than a desperate struggle for freedom. Chalmers joined the volunteers, not only as their chaplain, but enrolled on the fighting force as a lieutenant, and no doubt would have scented the battle from afar with all the passion of the war-horse. The only incident, however, of his military service is one which breathes the soul of kindness. He met, we are told, an old acquaintance in Kirkcaldy, where the volunteers assembled, in great poverty and distress; and turning over in his mind how to help the poor man and his family, organized at once, in his panoply of war, a course of chemical lectures—chemistry being then, we may appropriately say, his *cheval de bataille* and favourite subject—the proceeds of which gave to the sufferers a new start in life. Thus was Chalmers' campaign conducted, if not against Buonaparte—whom he would no doubt have assailed single-handed had the necessity arisen—but against other perennial usurpers against whom the true patriot can always do battle.

Another instance of the young man's grandiloquence is also one that touches the heart, and may remind the reader of that other great Scotsman, who, amid all the imperial subjects he treated in his life, never found more splendid tones of almost lyrical, impassioned laudation and lamentation than those he poured forth over his own old peasant father, a humbler personage still than good John Chalmers of Anster. Thomas had received from his elder brother in England a communication of some importance, desiring him to inform their father that James had joined the Church of England. This Thomas declined to do, declaring that "your apostasy from the Kirk would have horrified him."

"But whatever I say," exclaims the young minister, "may the vengeance of heaven pursue me if I feel contempt for that man who has passed through the world unstained by its corruptions, who has walked the manly career of independence and honour, who has escaped the infection of a degenerate age, and can boast a mind that has retained its integrity amidst all the seductions of policy and interest. Such is the character of our good father. May the Great Spirit bear up the weight of his old age, and blunt the arrow that gives it rest!"

There could not be a better expression of a son's admiration and respect, and no doubt it was most fully deserved; which does not diminish an absurd recollection penetrating our mind of the voice of the songster—

> "May I perish if ever
> I plant in that bosom a thorn."

After all these solemnities, however, we may quote as a relief the following pleasant account of the wandering of two young ministers about the pleasant country from one genial manse to another, two light-hearted young men, in the height of June, and amid the unquestioning hospitality and open hearts, which all who are familiar with rural Scotland know to exist there still. Chalmers had been paying his first visit to London, and on his return stopped to see Mr. Shaw of Roberton, his early friend and first patron, who had procured for him his earliest clerical employment. It is the latter who tells the tale—

"I proposed when he left to accompany him to Dr. Hardie's, about six miles distant, whence he intended to get to Pennycuik next day. We set out accordingly on a Monday after breakfast. The next morning I expressed a wish that we should go as far as Galashiels, and call on Dr. Douglas, to which he consented on condition that it should be only a short call. There, however, we were induced to spend the day. Next morning we took our departure on the way to Peebles; but in passing the hospitable residence of a family with whom I was intimately connected, I prevailed on him to call, and being much delighted with our kind reception, we remained till next morning. On our way up the Tweed I suggested calling on my friend Nicol, of Traquair, whose manse was situated only about half a mile off the road. 'Well, sir,' was the reply, 'but it must be only for a minute or two, as I must get to Pennycuik this night.' There, however, we spent the day most comfortably; and in the evening were so delighted with the music of the piano, that we could not refrain from dancing a few merry reels. At last Chalmers took hold of my arm and exclaimed, 'It's out of the question my getting home this week. You have a good horse, so you must just proceed to-morrow to Kilmany, and I will go back to Roberton."'

In all this Chalmers has appeared in the first flush of natural strength and impetuosity, a man of extraordinary talents, energy, and force of character, impressing himself with a sense of greatness upon all who came in contact with him, but with great impatience of any restraint, a high temper, a readiness to resent and avenge every real or supposed affront, and a determination to carry his point and have his own way, which had as yet yielded to none of the subduing influences of life. As minister of the little rural parish of Kilmany, he had in fact not occupation enough for his fervent spirit, and his comprehension of his office was a very small and circumscribed one, requiring little beyond the letter of his prescribed functions. His proud assertions, over and over again repeated, that nobody suffered from his absence, and that all the duties of his parish were performed, though he was there, during one winter at least, only from Saturday evening to Monday morning, are actually the indictment against him, not so much as an offender against ecclesiastical law as against every ideal of a clergyman's work. "There is almost no consumption of individual effort in the peculiar employment of a minister," he says in those days when philosophy was the inspiration of his existence, and the quiet of the rustic manse and church unendurable to a mind eager for work, for applause, and for the exercise of those fiery faculties which he felt to be burning away in utter waste, but capable of lighting up the world. That a young man of genius should feel in this way will be surprising to no one, or that he should turn against the bondage which held him fast and confined him to the composition of a few sermons and the society of a few country folk. After the first winter, however, he does not seem to have attempted to keep up the mathematical classes at St. Andrews, which were intended as a vindication of his powers against the censure of the authorities, though he continued, and poured out his fervent spirit in a course of lectures on Chemistry, by which, without exhibiting himself any longer as in violent opposition to his University, he could yet keep up his intellectual interests and occupy himself with congenial work. Even in quiet Kilmany the young minister in his zeal pursued the same subject, showing the astonished cottagers all manner of wonderful things. "Our minister," said one woman to another, "is naething short o' a warlock: he was teaching the folk to clean claes butt (without) soap." "Eh, woman!"

said another, with true practical humour, "I wish he would learn me to mak' parritch butt meal!"

When these occupations failed him, or rather when he had exhausted the moderate interest which could be aroused on such subjects, he took to literature, and flung himself into an "Inquiry into the extent and stability of national resources," a subject which at that time was calling forth much interest. It was in the middle of the great war, when the resources of Great Britain were tried to their utmost, and Chalmers' object, a most singular one to our present modes of thinking, was to show that the country might maintain its greatness altogether independently of trade and manufacture. *Britain Independent of Commerce* was the title of a pamphlet published just before the treatise of the minister of Kilmany, in which he set himself to consider "the case of a country secluded from all foreign intercourse." The chief point of interest in this work is the curious side glimpse it gives us into the constitution of the time. It is a position in which we can hardly by any effort of imagination place ourselves. The argument is confusing from this very incapacity of the mind to enter into such an impossible supposition. These little islands, not then described as separated from an open continent only by the "silver streak" of natural defence, but with a fierce and stormy sea enveloping all their borders, and alone preserving them from an invader who had ranged over almost every other country in Christendom—standing fiercely on their defence, and endeavouring to demonstrate to themselves the sufficiency of their insulated position, alone and self-supporting in face of the world—afford us a picture so strange that it is almost impossible to realize it. Yet the argument was lofty and patriotic, and it can never be left altogether out of the question that such a position might recur again, unlikely though it seems. Some practical suggestions, one in respect to the levying of an income-tax, another as to the treatment of soldiers ("Let Government go to market and enlist for a term of years: let it no longer be a slavery for life"), show how statesmanlike was the mind then casting about in the silence and solitude of the little country parish for something to occupy it. Had Chalmers been born in another class, had Parliament and the Councils of State been his natural sphere instead of the more confined circles of the parish and presbytery, we might have seen a patriot Prime Minister as powerful as Pitt, endowed with a weighty and impressive eloquence to carry forward the large schemes of his ever-working intelligence, and the power of sweeping an entire country with him in the force of his mighty enthusiasm. It has always seemed to us that this was his natural sphere. We cannot agree in the view that a man of genius, in whatever form his genius shows itself, should be accepted as the natural leader of his time. Burns, notwithstanding all that his illustrious countryman may say, would have excited little confidence in us as a king of men; but Chalmers has every indication of having been born to that office. He exercised it royally for a time in a lesser sphere, but he was fitted for its exercise on the highest scale had the opportunity ever fallen into his hands.

His larger aspects were not without recognition in this first stage of his life. His first appearance in the General Assembly, the parliament of Scotch Churchmen, was made in 1809, when he made a speech on one of the least attractive of subjects, on the Augmentation of Stipends, a matter not only interesting to him as a Social Economist, but coming home with special warmth to his business and bosom from the fact that he was himself in the agonies of an application for augmentation. It was no doubt also a subject of great moment to the body of ministers whose practical well-being was affected by the regulations on that point. The speech of Chalmers had a great effect. He was unknown to the Church save in his own district, and burst upon the Assembly, which he was afterwards to sway with so much force, as a revelation. "Do you know anything of this man?" asked one of the fathers of the Church. "He is surely a most extraordinary person;" and such was the general opinion. "Beseech Chalmers of Kilmany to publish his speech," said the well-known Dr. Andrew Thomson. A breath of sudden fame rose about the young man. At the same time he was asked to become a contributor to the *Edinburgh Encyclopædia*, and undertook, in addition to an article on "Trigonometry," the "Christianity," a curiously differing subject; which, so strong was the impression he had already made, was given up to him by much older and more experienced, as well as more orthodox, men. Thus far had his reputation risen in the course of six or seven years. He was now twenty-nine (1809), approaching maturity, full of ambition, energy, and strength.

But this beginning, so full of expectation and promise, was also in one way an ending. It was the conclusion of the first chapter of his life. Amid all his studies and works the young minister had scarcely claimed, even to himself, to be a religious man, or one to whom the spiritual life was of high importance. He did his duty so far as he understood it, preached his best, held visitations and examinations according to the practice of the Church and time, was always kind, ready to help, with an open house and a friendly word for all who did not palpably cross his path or thwart his will. But there now came a time when clouds gathered over the prosperous firmament. Death appeared in the family at Anster. One after another of his brothers and sisters died, some in the family home, one at sea. He was brought to the verge of that passage which leads either in light or in darkness to that which eye hath not seen nor ear heard, and saw those whom he loved pass beyond with that aching incapacity to follow them even in imagination, which only those who have watched at death-beds know; and he had himself a severe and lingering illness, which looked as if it might have had the same termination. All these things shook the confident young soul which had hitherto thought of nothing but the questions of science, and the onward sweep and rush of a high career. He was brought to a sudden stand before these mysteries. He could no longer impose his vehement will upon the world, and carry everything before him. Something more was in the tragedy of life than had been dreamt of in his philosophy. What was it? He had come to that crisis which occurs to most men one time or other in their lives. What was before him was no longer plain sailing. What was behind did not give him the satisfaction he had felt in it before. The incompleteness, the dissatisfaction of existence, its jarring tone among the calm accords of nature, came suddenly upon him like a lion in the path. He could not pass it by, or turn aside, or flee. The difficulty had to be met and solved somehow, or he must cease to live.

Sometimes such a crisis is stumbled through and passes without anything happening in particular, and the stream flows on again; but the minister of Kilmany was not of the common clay to which this is possible. He had to sound to the depths of his own mental and moral uneasiness by stress of nature. The first result was an anxious, even pathetic, struggle to make a better man of himself. Every little impatience, every hasty word, and it was his nature to say many, became a subject of penitence and of prayer. Instead of his old confident sweep of life, he began to pause at every step, to take himself to task, to wrestle with the defects of his impetuous character, which would be always pressing to the front. Indeed, that hasty, spontaneous, exuberant nature would seem to have had much to correct. One of his constantly-recurring subjects of regret and humiliation was his behaviour in the home circle at Anster, where now the parents were old and worn-out and slow to comprehend. "I have little or no indulgence for the infirmities of the aged: and nothing galls me more than to be obliged to repeat the same thing to the deaf and careless," he cries with a moan to himself over his irritability, which is half-tempered by a sense that his impatience is not without excuse. But the spectacle of a man thus fighting down his faults, living in a perpetual struggle against them, is a curious and scarcely an inspiriting one. The light turned inward reveals often much that is not actually there, if we may use such a phrase—the shadows that are momentary and fleeting standing out under its illumination like solid masses of gloom.

The result of this struggle, continued through more than a year, was that Chalmers at last found the secret which solves all these mysteries, the redemption and the Saviour, which he had preached in conventional words for years without ever realizing the force of what he himself said. The records of conversion are many and various, and it is a little difficult through his journals and self-communions to come to the point at which the path turns, and the troubled wayfarer, painfully stumbling out his own darkling road, at last reached that strait and narrow way in which he found life and freedom. His own account of the final crisis is the best that can be given. It is contained in a letter to his brother—

"I stated to you that the effect of a very long confinement, about ten years ago, upon myself was to inspire me with a set of very strenuous resolutions, under which I wrote a journal, and made many a laborious effort to elevate my practice to the standard of the Divine requirements. During this course, however, I got little satisfaction and felt no repose. I remember that somewhere about the year 1811 I had Wilberforce's *View* put into my hands, and as I got on in reading it, felt myself on the eve of a great revolution in all my opinions about Christianity. I am now most thoroughly of opinion, and it is an opinion founded on experience, that on the system of 'Do this and live,' no peace, and even no true and worthy obedience, can ever be attained. It is 'Believe in the Lord Jesus Christ, and thou shalt be saved.' When this belief enters the heart, joy and confidence enter along with it. The righteousness which we try to work out for ourselves eludes our impotent grasp, and never can a soul arrive at true or permanent rest in the pursuit of this object. The righteousness which by faith we put on secures our acceptance with God, and secures our interest in His promises, and gives us a part in those sanctifying influences by which we are enabled to do, with aid from on high, what we never can do without it. We look to God in a new light—we see Him as a reconciled Father: that love to Him which terror scares away re-enters the heart, and with a new principle and a new power, we become new creatures in Jesus Christ our Lord."

This sudden apprehension and warm adoption into his life of principles so well known, upon which he had been nursed from his cradle, and which he had vaguely preached for years, was the turning-point in Chalmers' career. The ambitious young mathematician, eager for work, finding nothing that occupied his exuberant energies in the career of a minister, and continually dreaming of fresh woods and pastures new, turned from all that tumultuous though innocent past with disgust, and flung himself with impetuosity unsubdued, though the current of its outflow was changed, into the occupations of a fisher of men, a devoted pastor and priest, having no thought but the saving of souls. It was in all the emotion of this new enthusiasm, transformed by the love of Christ which had taken possession of his soul, that the remaining part of his life at Kilmany was passed. He formed soon after what can be called nothing but a romantic friendship with a young man across the Tay, in Dundee, with whom he maintained a close religious correspondence:

and the rebound of his overwhelming spiritual impulse made many other such links around him, in the fervour of the new life. Two youths of his parish, with the inspiration of his ardent addresses in their minds, walking and talking together upon the Gospel message, found for themselves a little oratory in a wood, "under the shade of a branching fir-tree," to which, by the practice of years, they made a little private pathway of their own, through the copse and undergrowth, and where they prayed together in a mutual ecstasy of faith and adoration. Thus the new leaven worked, and the soft and homely natural scenes of the rural parish became identified to many with the highest devotion of Christian thought.

During his stay at Kilmany, Chalmers, after many resolutions against it—chiefly as would seem on account of his own conscious impatience of character and fear of finding any close companionship become irksome to him—married, his scruples being vanquished in the ordinary happy way by that love which scorns all foregone conclusions. He spent a little more than ten years in this first charge, which thus witnessed the complete equipment of his life. He left it at the age of thirty-four, in full manhood and development, and plunged at once into the wars and tumults of a very different and much-widened sphere.

CHAPTER II.

CHALMERS had no gradual ascent to the highest place which was possible to any member of a clergy in which the degrees of an ecclesiastical hierarchy are unknown. From the rural seclusion of Kilmany he made but one step into a position of the highest influence and importance in Scotland. "Presbyterian parity," the equality which is supposed to reign among all the ministers of the Scotch Church, is of course neutralized, as every rule of equality always is, by the unfailing laws of nature: and no archbishop could have a more elevated place in the estimation of the province over which he reigns than had the young Fife minister who came from his native county with its accent strong upon his lips, and its homely rural customs in his life, to rule as with a flaming sceptre the crowds, both rich and poor, of the opulent and energetic city, which is in its way a metropolis too, supreme in the wealth, the industry, and the energy of Scotland as Edinburgh has always been in law and literature. The Glasgow of those days was not much more than half as populous or as rich as now, when it is beyond dispute the second city in the empire. But it was as great according to the standard of the day, and full of all the warring elements of national life—

the exceedingly rich, capitalists and merchant-princes who had brought their wealth from afar, who had woven it out of Indian cotton, and forged it out of iron and steel, if not with the actual sweat of their brows, at least with labour as incessant and much more anxious than that of the artisans who were their coadjutors in the work: and of these coadjutors themselves, the so-called poor, always a little embittered by the contrast between their poverty and the wealth of their employers, always at the mercy of any demagogue who assured them that it was they who made the money which the others enjoyed—a dogma so false, yet so true and bewildering to the half-educated mind which has no power of grasping so large and difficult a subject, and does not possess that highest reason which can understand and bow to inevitable law. This rich and solid city, one of the most luxurious on the face of the earth, held thus continually in its bosom the embers of a fire which might blaze up at any provocation and for a moment overturn all the bulwarks of peaceful life—a danger which was then so much the greater since reform had not yet begun to operate among them, and the masses had no way, save by the useless roar of attempted revolution, to make themselves heard at all. It is still too much the case that these masses settle in crowded lairs, crammed together as cattle are no longer allowed in the interests of their masters to be crammed; while the other part of the community "expatiate," as Chalmers himself would have said, in the surrounding paradise of western woods and waters. But yet attempts have been made since then in a hundred different ways to liberate and elevate them, which nobody had thought of when Chalmers went to Glasgow. He went there with his head full of this great social question, and of an immense and ardent desire to go forth among the poor, and seize by sheer force of affection and brotherhood these often rebellious, almost always discontented, roughly-resistant, and suffering throngs. His advent altogether upon that crowded scene was an extraordinary one. Glasgow is nothing if not hospitable, and the new minister of the historic "Tron" might have dined out at the most luxurious of civic feasts every day. He might almost have dispensed with a table of his own. He might, as he would himself have said, have "eaten of the fat and drank of the sweet," to the gratitude and enthusiasm of the Glasgow citizens, to whom "the doctor's" presence at their board was an honour and delight. But this he vehemently defended himself from, before he would consider the question of their "call" at all. He would not have his time encroached upon by invitations, by calls, by what is called social intercourse on a large scale. This was the first of his stipulations. Turtle and champagne were no part of his programme. If his old violence of temper ever broke forth, it was when he was wooed and besought and pressed beyond patience to the tables of his rich parishioners. Patience was not at any time his leading virtue, and his resistance to these civilities was almost fierce; but he "drank tea" with pleasure in a poor house in the interval between his afternoon visitation through the crowded "Lands" of the Gallowgate, and the evening address which he, whom thousands crowded to hear, gave to the unkempt folk he had gathered together on almost every day of the week. This was the spirit in which he went from the little country parish, where he knew every individual soul, to the great bustling, noisy metropolis of Western Scotland, where the wealthy Glasgow citizens pounced upon him, delighted with the glory and joy of having the famous orator of the time in the midst of them. Their disappointment in this respect must have been extraordinary, for it was with nothing less than a gesture of disgust that he turned from their endless feasts.

This is perhaps the best place in which to quote the following portrait of Chalmers, at the height of young manhood, aged thirty-five, which is painted for us by no less admirable a hand than that of John Gibson Lockhart, then himself a very young man at the outset of his brilliant career.

"At first sight his face is a coarse one, but a mysterious kind of meaning breathes from every part of it that such as have eyes to see cannot be long in discovering. It is very pale, and the large, half-closed eyelids have a certain drooping, melancholy weight about them, which interested me very much, I understood not why. The lips, too, are singularly pensive in their mode of falling down at the sides, although there is no want of richness and vigour in their central fulness of curve. The upper lip, from the nose downwards, is separated by a very deep line, which gives a sort of leonine expression of firmness to all the lower part of the face. The cheeks are square and strong in texture, like pieces of marble, with the cheek-bones very broad and prominent. The eyes themselves are light in colour, and have a strange, dreamy heaviness that conveys any idea rather than that of dulness, but which contrasts in a wonderful manner with the dazzling watery glare they exhibit when expanded in their sockets, and illuminated into all their flame and fervour in some moment of high entranced enthusiasm. But the shape of the forehead is perhaps the most singular part of the whole visage; and indeed it presents a mixture so very singular of forms commonly exhibited only in the widest separation, that it is no wonder I should have required some little time to comprehend the meaning of it. In the first place it is, without exception, the most marked mathematical forehead I have ever met with, being far wider across the eyebrows than either Mr. Playfair's or Mr. Leslie's, and having the eyebrows themselves lifted up at their exterior ends quite out of the usual line, a peculiarity which Spurzheim had remarked in the countenances of almost all the great mathematical or calculating geniuses, such for example, if I rightly remember, as Sir Isaac Newton himself. Immediately above the extraordinary breadth of this region, which in the heads of most mathematical persons is surmounted by no fine points of organization whatever, immediately above this in the forehead there is an arch of imagination carrying out the summit boldly and roundly in a style to which the heads of very few poets present anything comparable; while over this again there is a grand apex of high and solemn veneration and love such as might have graced the bust of Plato himself, and such as in living man I have never beheld equalled in any but the majestic head of Canova. . . .

"Neither, perhaps, did the world ever possess any orator whose minutest peculiarities of gesture and voice have more power in increasing the effect of what he says—whose delivery, in other words, is the first and the second and the third excellence of his oratory, more truly than is that of Dr. Chalmers. And yet, were the spirit of the man less gifted than it is, there is no question these, his lesser peculiarities, would never have been numbered among his points of excellence. His voice is neither strong nor melodious; his gestures are neither easy nor graceful, but, on the contrary, extremely rude and awkward; his pronunciation is not only broadly national, but broadly provincial, distorting almost every word he utters into some barbarous novelty which, had his hearers leisure to think of such things, might be productive of an effect at once ludicrous and offensive in the highest degree. . . I have heard many men deliver sermons far better arranged in regard to argument, and have heard very many deliver sermons far more uniform in eloquence, both of conception and of style; but most unquestionably I have never heard, either in England or Scotland, or in any other country, any preacher whose eloquence is capable of producing an effect so strong and so irresistible as his."

It was on a very striking and interesting occasion that the little group of notables from Glasgow made their way to the northern corner of Fife to hear the minister with whose voice all that portion of the country was beginning to ring. It was on a Sunday in October —"a brilliant autumn day"—and the whole countryside had gathered to hear the minister of Kilmany preach the funeral sermon of another young minister, his own contemporary and class-fellow, John Henry of Bendochy, whose health had been ruined by his most heroic exertions to save the crew of a vessel wrecked on the gloomy reefs of St. Andrew's Bay. This young man, while still a divinity student, had brought ashore man by man, through a tempest which the most experienced seaman did not dare to face, the entire crew, seven sailors, of the wrecked boat; and though he lived long enough to complete his studies and enter upon the work of his profession, he died shortly after his appointment. These circumstances no doubt increased the usual crowd which streamed after Chalmers wherever he preached, and which was so great on this occasion that the Glasgow visitors lighted upon a very curious scene. The little parish church of Bendochy could not hold half the multitude, and a window of the church was accordingly taken out and a temporary platform made with boards placed across the sill, from which the preacher could be heard, not only by the crowded assembly within the church, but by the throngs who could get no further than the churchyard. The scene was so solemn as well as picturesque, that it is half profane to allow such a ludicrous suggestion to steal into our minds, but it is difficult not to think of a London manager coming down by stealth to judge of the qualities of a provincial performer, when we think of those grave men from the West mingling among the crowd, with their minds full of the "Tron," and the desire to secure for their great city the best preacher in Scotland. What contrast could be greater than the glow of the ruddy October sunshine, the peaceful security of the rural landscape, and the grave of the young hero at their feet, whose valour had brought him to that speedy termination of human work and effort? The effect of the great oration which followed, and which held that throng spell-bound, is said to have been indescribable. "I have heard many eloquent men," says a spectator, "but this I have never seen equalled or even imitated." The Glasgow inquirers stole away awe-stricken like the rest, and overwhelmed by excitement and emotion, but afterwards spared no pains till they succeeded in transferring the minister of Kilmany to their own much greater and more influential sphere.

The Tron Church of Glasgow, filled with the wealthiest men in Scotland and surrounded by the most interesting and the most dangerous crowd, was something more than a bishopric to the aspiring and energetic soul of the young parish minister. Of ambition, in the vulgar sense of the word, Chalmers would seem to have been wonderfully free—even of that loftier kind which finds animation and inspiration in the prodigious influence of leadership and the enthusiasm of a crowd. That such a man having attained such a position should have flung it by again in a few years for the retirement of St. Andrews, would be incredible if his impatient and somewhat arbitrary character had been mingled with vanity or any love for the intoxicating atmosphere of the multitude. And he hesitated at first whether it was or was not his duty to leave his little rural sphere, even for a place in which his opportunities of work would be so much greater. We are not told what the homely, anxious parents in Anster, ever afraid lest Thomas should be uplifted by the applauses of men, thought of the matter; but there was one of his many brothers and sisters who had a distinct opinion of his own on the subject. James Chalmers, the eldest of the family, who occupied the position of head clerk in a merchant's office in London, and was evidently as strong in his character and definite in his views as the younger brother, whom at the height of his fame he would never go to hear, declaring cynically that he had heard, "and did not think much of him—half-an-hour after he was born!" James did not like the idea of Glasgow, and gave Thomas the benefit of his opinion roundly, as follows—

"I am much concerned to learn that the allurements of the perishable mammon are likely soon to have an effect upon you, and make you resign all your earthly comforts and domestic quiet; but I still hope that you will look before you leap, and think better of the business before you accept of any nonsense that may be offered. A situation of an additional £100 a year may perhaps be held out to you, but you should take into the account how far that situation may expose you to expenses exceeding the addition of income which it renders, what company and connexions it may lead you into, how far it may incroach upon the time which you have hitherto allotted for study, or devoted to the pleasures and endearments of domestic life, what effect the sudden change from a quiet country life to the din and bustle of the great city is likely to have upon you, and how far you think you can relish the formal and empty *fal-lal* of refinement when compared to the honest but humble society to which you have been accustomed at Kilmany. Besides, Kilmany is the place where you began your career. The Rev. Mr. Chalmers of Kilmany is known: his fame is far spread, his character is respected, his reputation established, and his abilities acknowledged and admired. But the Rev. Mr. Chalmers of Glasgow is another person: he has to begin the world afresh: and there is no doubt but he will be considered in the literary as well as the religious world as a very different person from his Reverence of Kilmany. Shining abilities are naturally looked for and expected to be met with at the seat of learning, and of course are not estimated so highly as when they proceed from humble life. Think of all these things, and consider also how greatly it will add to your character, that instance of self-denial which your refusal of the offer will not fail to impress upon the minds of all who know you and have heard of you. Keep fast by what you have got, and be contented still to remain the minister of Kilmany, and leave Glasgow to those hunters after the world and vain glory who may be disposed to throw themselves in its way. Never you mind the call of the Lord, as it is called. I have no other view than your own happiness: for I am convinced that if you do accept this offer, you sacrifice your comfort and happiness for ever. You will have no time for study: you will be deprived of all the comforts of a home, for you will be continually carried down a current of formal visits and complimentary calls and invitations and botherations of all kinds."

This ingenious but perverse argument is one which used to be almost universal in Scotland; the idea that a man might honestly see it to be his duty to leave a humbler sphere for a greater one—when he was a clergyman—being, in the opinion of the common people, sheer hypocrisy and falsehood. "Would he feel it to be the call of the Lord if it was to a smaller stipend?" the satirist used to say with conscious superiority: we do not know if he does so still. It was a curious evidence of the high ideal which, in lack of any special devotion to it in their own persons, these critics fixed upon the minister as a necessary consequence of his profession. It gives us, too, a wonderful view of the elevated conception then formed of a section of society which we are not in the habit of considering as at the height of refinement, by the unmoneyed classes. Chalmers himself, in his answer to this letter, hopes that his wife will be wiser than to allow herself to be "seduced by the example of female acquaintances," and to "step down from the dignified simplicity of a minister's fireside and mingle in all the extravagances of parties and *second courses,* and splendid drawing-rooms, and the whole tribe of similar abominations." Few Scotch ministers nowadays are likely to consider an additional dish or a highly-decorated drawing-room as abominations, or as inimical to the dignified simplicity of the manse. There are some things in which social habits have certainly changed very much. The alarm which Chalmers felt for the vortex of gaiety and pleasure into which he felt that nothing but a determined resolution would prevent him from plunging, and the extreme fascination of Glasgow elegance and luxury, was indeed his only difficulty in accepting the new appointment. The thought of the dinner-parties filled his soul with panic, while the prodigious work upon which he was about to enter conveyed nothing but exhilaration to his mind.

When he finally took up his residence in Glasgow he describes himself as "teased with invitations," "beset with polite attentions"; but these proved to be by no means the only troubles with which he had to contend.

The extreme amount of secular business thrown upon his shoulders was still more galling and persistent than the attentions of society. "What think you of my putting my name to two applications for licences to sell spirits, and two certificates of being qualified to follow out the calling of a pedlar in the course of yesterday?" he asks one of his correspondents.

"This, sir, is a wonderful place; and I am half entertained and half provoked by some of the peculiarities of its people. The peculiarity which bears hardest upon me is the incessant demand they have on all occasions for the personal attendance of the ministers. They must have four to every funeral, or they do not think it has been genteelly enough gone through. They must have one or more to all the committees of all the societies. They must fall in at every procession. They must attend examinations innumerable, and eat of the dinners consequent upon these examinations. They have a niche assigned them in almost every public doing, and that niche must be filled by them, or the doing loses all its solemnity in the eyes of the public. There seems to be a superstitious charm in the very sight of them. I gave in to all this at first, but I am beginning to keep a suspicious eye upon these repeated demands ever since I sat nearly an hour in grave deliberation with a number of others upon a subject connected with the property of a corporation, and that subject was a *gutter*, and the question was whether it should be bought and covered up, or let alone and left to lie open."

His first impression of Glasgow as a whole was not

indeed at all favourable. He began his residence alone, without the society of his wife, in the height of summer, when all who can do so leave a town which never has been particularly attractive in itself. "I can give you no satisfaction," he wrote to a correspondent in Fife, "as to my liking or not liking Glasgow. Were I to judge by my present feelings, I would say that I dislike it most violently. What is to come out of it I know not, but I may at least say that all around me yet carries the aspect of desolation." No doubt he was surrounded by the smaller officials, eager to secure, in the absence of more considerable personages, his first favour and notice: and all the disagreeables of change, and the pangs of regret, and the doubts as to whether he had done wisely, overwhelmed him in the lodging which had neither the appearance nor the society of home. But the circumstances ameliorated, and so did his feelings, and perhaps the first evidence and proof that he had taken kindly to his new position was in the touching little episode of another romantic friendship, the account of which comes in strangely with one of the most effective of literary expedients—

> "The sound as of a hidden brook,
> In the leafy month of June";

in the midst of the hurry of public business, the excitement of oratory, and the atmosphere of crowded churches with which this period of his life was full. The object of this friendship was a young man bearing the unremarkable name of Thomas Smith, who was, "so far as was known to Dr. Chalmers, the first-fruits spiritually of his ministry in Glasgow"—a mild, well-educated youth, in all the beautiful fervour of youthful piety, no doubt enthusiastically attached to the already great man in the fervour of strength and manhood and genius, who took his pupil and friend into his big heart. This young man became so dear to Chalmers that he records a prayer in his journal, "Oh, my God, save me from all that is idolatrous in my regard for him!" They met daily, and took their walks together, discoursing between themselves of the love of God and the life of Christ, like the two who once upon a memorable morning walked over the hills of Judea to Emmaus; and again in the evening, when the hard-worked minister, whose days had been full of incessant labour, looked for the coming of the young disciple as for one of the chief refreshments of his life, and when the hour of intercourse was spent chiefly in mutual prayer. Nothing could be in greater contrast with a daily existence full of the labour and cares of a large parish, where already questions not only of religion but of Christian economics and a statesman's large views and plans for the advantage of a troubled and suffering world were in the mind of the elder, than this ideal yet enthusiastic intercourse with the young soul, irradiated already by visionary gleams of heaven and the shadows that foretell an early grave. When these constant meetings were interrupted by more pressing duties on the one hand, and increasing ill-health on the other, letters full of anxious human affection as well as spiritual communion went daily from the minister's study, in the intervals of business and parish visitors and composition, to cheer the young saint on his death-bed. Chalmers had not been quite a year in Glasgow when this touching little episode came to an end. The young man died in that ethereal sanctity and perfection which is so beautiful in youth, when the beloved of God and man are taken away into the brighter sphere to which all their thoughts have tended. The minister came back from a visit to Fife to find that his spiritual child, his young squire and retainer, had gone suddenly from all his surroundings of anxiety and suffering. "Floods of tenderness" filled his soul. He was not a man whom we should have supposed open to such absorbing friendship, and there is a quaint stiffness in the "My dear sir," which is the warmest address in these singular letters. This was the custom of the self-restrained Scotch nature, which other nations find it so difficult to understand, though the correspondence is glowing with affection and feeling. Even in writing to his wife, and especially when telling her how necessary her society is to him, and how desolate he is without her, Chalmers has no other expression of devotion to give than the "Yours most truly," which we use in the most formal letters. And yet, if the phrase is taken in its real sense, what more could any husband say to any wife?

Nobody who has been in Glasgow will have forgotten the long crowded street, full of every imaginable variety of squalid crowd, sometimes hazy with sunshine, oftener gleaming with dark wetness from pavements and roofs, with a tall steeple standing out from the mists and throngs at the end—the Trongate and the Tron Steeple, as familiar to local regard as the Salt-market, which Bailie Nicol Jarvie has made immortal. The "comforts o' the Sautmarket" are very problematical now, and already, in Chalmers' day, the well-to-do classes had surged away from the old city centre, notwithstanding that the old college was still in the grimy depths of the town, keeping a certain hold upon a locality now given over to the swarming tenements of the poor. It was in the Tron Church, a building of the usual Scotch fashion, closely seated with pews and surrounded with galleries, that Chalmers began his work in Glasgow. It is a church-going town, and the crowd of worshippers that streams along the streets of a Sunday morning is as remarkable as any civic procession—a steady, largely-flowing flood pouring on in certain well-indicated directions to church and chapel, with a breadth of respectability and well-doing which is imposing. There, alas! as elsewhere, the dark depths of population behind, the streets and "lands" where men yawn in their shirt-sleeves, and women bustle among their children, in a Sunday idleness more productive of brawls than of comfort, contributes little at any time to the stream of church-goers which skirts, without ever being able to carry along with it, that inert mass, often apathetic, and sometimes resistant to all such influences. The appearance of Chalmers in the pulpit of the Tron Church moved all that was accessible in Glasgow with a thrill and new impulse of curiosity and interest. The fame which he had brought with him, the great impression which he had already produced wherever he had been heard, excited the population more than any great actor would have done, but perhaps with a not much differing sensation. There is, or at least at that period was, nothing which stimulated and roused the mind of Scotland like a sermon; it has been, from the time of Knox at least, the chief intellectual enjoyment of a keenly critical community, which has found in that weekly occurrence not only the exhibition of power and skill which all men love to watch, but the additional and still warmer interest of a personal share in the event, an awakening of all the critical faculties, an extended and universal discussion in which iron sharpeneth iron throughout a whole population. Even the dullest of preachers affords more or less this constantly-recurring diversion and occupation to his hearers: and it is needless to say that Glasgow streamed towards the Tron Kirk till every opening to it became almost inaccessible, and not only the seats but standing ground within frequently contained almost twice the number for which they were intended. Sometimes the closed doors were burst in by force by the pressure of the multitude assembled outside, and possession seized as by an invading army. Sometimes the entrance of the preacher himself, whose name had drawn this multitude together, had to be made as over a breach riven in the mass by the bodyguard around. In London, when the great orator from the North made his appearance there for the first time, this happened on several occasions; but even in Glasgow, which owned him, and had frequent opportunities of hearing him, the same thing occurred again and again.

He was now at the very summit and climax of life and genius—the *mezzo di cammin*—able for all things, shrinking from no work except those secular encumbrances of his position, sitting on committees and signing certificates, which as a waste of time raised in him characteristic tempests of indignation and resistance. The enthusiasm which filled the community passes description, or rather we should say, it is described again and again by spectators of each different scene with a confused use of superlatives, which produce in words something like the "great stour" with here and there a sword gleaming through, which Sir Walter considered the best manner of representing a battle. Nor was this confined to the Sunday services alone. The Glasgow merchants, waiting in the Tontine reading-rooms not far from the Tron that they might rush out at the first tinkle of the kirk-bell, and secure a place for the great weekly sermon at the height of the working-day; the students, who claimed remission of the fine for non-attendance at their classes, on the ground that they had gone to hear Dr. Chalmers; the busy people of every condition who snatched an hour at noon from the midst of their labours to hear the great voice in their midst—all these details are as picturesque as remarkable. The Tron Kirk was for the time being the centre of the city, as the old cathedral of St. Giles had once been in Edinburgh, giving forth not only Christian doctrine, but the highest criticism of life. The Astronomical Discourses, in which the glories of the amazing universe were shown to "utter forth a glorious voice," and proclaim not that man is too petty for the regard of God, but that the Divine Guardian of the world cares also for countless infinitesimal multitudes as well, and that the exclamation, "What is man that Thou art mindful of him?" is the adoring voice of faith, and not the scepticism of the philosopher: the Commercial Discourses, treating of homelier yet all-important subjects, of good faith, honesty, and honour in trade, as well as of mercy and temperance and judgment to come: and many great occasional addresses called forth by events of the moment, pealed out amid the silence of that crowd, with every man's breathing suspended as the great sentences rolled forth, not in the necessary service of Sunday—the Sabbath sermon, an inherent part of life—but in the middle of the week, in the voluntary Thursday morning assembly, in an hour which was worth money, the severest of all tests, to that energetic and money-making community. "Every breath is held, every cough suppressed," says one witness, "every one, riveted himself by the spell of the impassioned and entrancing eloquence, knows how sensitively his neighbour will resent the very slightest disturbance. Then by and by there is a pause; the speaker stops to gather breath, the moment is embraced, there is free breathing, suppressed coughs get vent, postures are changed, there is a universal stir as of persons who could not have endured the constraint much longer." The unconscious sound as of a great sigh bursting from the overcharged bosom of the multitude when the great oration came to an end, is described by many, the stir of recovered identity when the spell is broken which had welded the mass into one.

We may quote here, not as a specimen of his eloquence, but as a proof of the boldness and vehemence with which Chalmers denounced a positive evil, the following passage from his great sermon on the "Dissipation of large cities." Spectators speak of "the breathless, the appalling silence" with which this sermon was listened to: but there is in the following passage a certain unconscious touch of humour, something at least which conveys to us such a sense of the perturbation of some of the audience thus struck in the full centre of their shields—as to excite that faculty which in the midst of the most solemn circumstances is often capable of calling forth an involuntary smile.

"We have our eyes perfectly open to that great external improvement which has taken place of late years in the manners of society. There is not the same grossness of conversation. There is not the same impatience for the withdrawment of him who, asked to grace the outset of an assembled party, is compelled at a certain point in the progress of conviviality, by the obligations of professional decency, to retire from it. There is not so frequent an exaction of this as one of the established proprieties of social life. And if such an exaction was ever laid by the omnipotence of custom on a minister of Christianity, it is such an exaction as ought never, never to be complied with. It is not for him to lend the sanction of his presence to a meeting with which he could not sit to its final termination. It is not for him to stand associated for a single hour with an assemblage of men who begin with hypocrisy and end with downright blackguardism. It is not for him to watch the progress of the coming ribaldry, and to hit the well-selected moment when talk and turbulence and boisterous merriment are on the eve of bursting forth upon the company and carrying them forward to the full acme and uproar of their enjoyment. It is quite in vain to say that he has only sanctioned one part of such an entertainment. He has as good as given his connivance to the whole of it, and left behind him a discharge in full of all its obligations; and therefore, be they who they may, whether they rank among the proudest aristocracy of our land, or are charioted in splendour along as the wealthiest of our citizens, or flounce in the robes of magistracy, it is his part to keep as purely and indignantly aloof from such society as this as he would from the vilest and most debasing associations of profligacy."

"While uttering these words," said the reporter, "which he did with peculiar emphasis, accompanying them with a flash from his eye and a stamp of his foot, he threw his right arm with clenched hand right across the book-board, and brandished it full in the face of the Town Council, sitting in array and in state before him. Many eyes were in a moment directed towards the magistrates. The words evidently fell upon them like a thunderbolt, and seemed to startle like an electric shock the whole audience."

Perhaps it was on a similar occasion that he penitently records in his journal, "Preached in the Gorbals in the afternoon, *and exceeded.* Oh, for self-command in the pulpit!" With such a man, so unsubdued by any fear of men, in the pulpit, in the exercise of that boundless freedom of the preacher, whom nobody can without scandal interrupt or contradict, it may be imagined what were the feelings of the public authorities of Glasgow, when the minister of the Tron Church, a year after his appointment, gave forth as his text the words of the Apostles: "It is not reason that we should leave the Word of God and serve tables." In this sermon he entered into a detailed account of all the extraneous public duty with which the time of a clergyman was occupied and his mind distracted, the candidates for places, each surrounded by a crowd of backers up, the "printed forms with long blank spaces which the minister would have the goodness to fill up," and "how of all his doings in this department the simple achievement of seventy signatures in a day was all that his dizzy recollection had been able to retain." How fa he succeeded in getting free of this constant interruption there is no information to show, but as h possessed in a very special degree the talent of an administrator, and speedily filled his parish with what he himself called a lay agency, men inspired and guided by him, it is to be supposed that he managed to place some of his secular work on their willing shoulders. He was the master of the situation in every way, having in the first place that strong bulwark of a clergyman's independence, his position as a member of an Established Church, which no local opposition or displeasure could affect, and also the individual command which was given him by his indifference, so far as his own feelings were concerned, to the great sphere in which he was placed, and the longing of his heart for a quieter and less laborious position. He compares in his journal on many occasions the temptations of what he calls vanity, the desire of personal distinction which he could not by all his efforts shut out of his heart; but the man who could estimate popularity as he does in the following paragraph, which evidently gives a very true account of his feelings, must always have retained an almost fierce independence. He would seem to have had something like a personal disgust—what we call in Scotland a *scunner*—for the sensation of a crowd. He had been representing to his Sunday-school teachers and other agents the noble popularity, "the popularity of the heart, the only popularity that is worth aspiring after," when he is led into this outburst—

"There is another, a high and far-sounding popularity which is indeed a most worthless article, felt by all who have it to be greatly more oppressive than gratifying, a popularity of stare and pressure and animal heat, and a whole tribe of other annoyances which it brings around the person of its unfortunate victim—a popularity which rifles home of its sweets, and by elevating a man above his fellows, places him in a region of desolation, where the intimacies of human friendship are unfelt, and where he stands a conspicuous mark for the shafts of envy, malice, and detraction—a popularity which, with its head among storms and its feet on the dangerous quicksands, has nothing to lull the agonies of its tottering existence but the hosannahs of a drivelling generation."

There are perhaps few "victims" of this kind of reputation who are more sensible of its disadvantages than the popular preacher—which is not to say that he may not be very sensible to its flattery: but the "stare and pressure and animal heat" always seem to have stirred up the natural impatience of Chalmers' ever vehement character in an unusual degree. It was not only in Glasgow that he was exposed to these complimentary miseries. His reputation was now so universal that his appearance in Edinburgh, at the General Assembly, called forth an equal interest. That Scottish parliament is little understood out of its native realm, nor the importance and dignity in many cases of its deliberations, nor the attention it calls forth from all classes of the community, during its brief sitting of about ten days in the month of May. That interest, or at least that dignity, has no doubt sadly suffered since there have been two General Assemblies, dividing not only the Church, but the entire ideal of a Church; but in Chalmers' early days the Church was unbroken, and the Assembly was in a very true sense the Scotch parliament, with a sway over many things of the utmost importance and necessity. In the Assembly of 1816 there occurred a great debate on the subject of pluralities—in which Chalmers' was specially interested, and in which he took a remarkable part. It began "at eleven o'clock in the forenoon, and did not close till half-an-hour after midnight," one spectator describing how he "stood an entire round of the clock," from eleven a.m. till eleven p.m., to listen. In anticipation of this debate the strangers' gallery was occupied by an anxious audience at eight in the morning, and the crowd was so great that even the accommodation provided for members of the house was invaded. The speech of Chalmers was the central point of the discussion, which, we are told, was "conducted by both parties with great spirit and ability;" and he concluded his address by an appeal full of eloquence, that nothing should be permitted to draw a parish clergyman from his first duty to his people and district. "Who would view without alarm," he cried, "that neglected population which scowled upon you as you passed with an outlandish stare, who had never spoken to a clergyman in their life, and who were perfectly amazed when he began to put a few plain questions to them?" This subject filled the mind of the minister of the Tron, who carried with him night and day the thought of his own duties in that respect, with constant ponderings how to accomplish them, now the first problem in the world to his anxious consciousness. Among his audience on this occasion was the man in Scotland of whom the literature of the age stood in most fear—the famous writer, Francis Jeffrey, then editor of the *Edinburgh Review*, a critic accused of slaying poets right and left wherever he turned. "I know not what it is," said this high authority, "but there is something altogether remarkable about this man. It reminds me more of what one reads of as the effect of the eloquence of Demosthenes than anything I ever heard."

A day or two after Chalmers preached "before the Lord High Commissioner" in the High Church, the then sadly encumbered and gloomy St. Giles, which has now been restored to its original proportions. The Lord High Commissioner is a functionary generally chosen from among the highest nobility in Scotland, whose duties are to represent the Queen by occupying a sort of throne in the Assembly meetings, where, however, only the most formal recognition is accorded to him, and with the deliberations of which he has nothing to do. It is one of the compromises which abound in British law, an acknowledgment on the one side of respectful loyalty, and a token on the other of sanction and privilege, but totally without any other meaning and effect. The Scotch reader is impatient that such explanations should be given; but we think it is necessary for the English, and still more the American looker-on, who might easily suppose that some sort of influence or active share in the deliberations or conclusions of the Assembly were involved in the position of her Majesty's representative, whose office is purely formal and ornamental—picturesque, indeed, in a high degree, for he not only goes to the Assembly "in state," with a procession, in a place not much given to such celebrations, but he holds *levées* and entertainments in old Holyrood, to the great advantage of the pictorial side of life. This is, however, a digression. The High Church was surrounded as by a besieging army hours before the time of service on the occasion of Chalmers' sermon there; and was taken possession of in the same way by the charge of the crowd, and at the risk of life and limb. An almost forcible entrance had to be made for the Commissioner himself, the judges, magistrates, and other persons in authority; and again we hear of the hush of almost unearthly silence when the preacher began his discourse, the "suspiration of forced breath" when he paused for a moment, the stir and rustle of movement, speedily hushed again to that stillness in which the jar of a door or the slip of a book sounded like thunder and seemed like a crime—with, at the end—an addition still more remarkable—"a suppressed but perfectly audible murmur of applause, an occurrence unprecedented in the course of the delivery of a sermon, but irresistible in order to relieve our highly excited feelings." The sermon was one of those called Astronomical, and from the text, "What is man, that Thou art mindful of him?"

An effect still greater was produced next year in London, where he went in May 1817, with the purpose of preaching the anniversary sermon for the London Missionary Society—the same anniversary sermon in which, some years after, Edward Irving broke forth from all conventional bonds, scorning instead of exalting the machinery of missionary societies, and holding up the very different model of an apostolical missionary without house or wife or remittances, before the astonished gaze of all the committees. Irving was not as yet visible within this horizon of the religious world; but he is singularly brought to the mind of the reader by the text used by Dr. Chalmers on this occasion, which was from the fourteenth chapter of 1st Corinthians: "Wherefore tongues are for a sign, not to them that believe, but to them that believe not: but prophesying serveth not for them that believe not, but for them which believe. . . . But if all prophesy, and there come in one that believeth not, or one unlearned, he is convinced of all, he is judged of all: And thus are the secrets of his heart made manifest; and so falling down on his face he will worship God, and report that God is in you of a truth." The words seem like a sort of unconscious prophecy of the excitement which was shortly about to rise over what was to some an extraordinary revelation from on high, and with others prompted the bewildered inquiry of the text, "Will they not say that ye are mad?" The Surrey Chapel was crowded "from seven in the morning," four hours before the service began, and as usual the throng was swept into absorbed attention for an hour and a half, breathing but as the preacher breathed, and stirring only when he paused to rest. "Old Rowland Hill stood the whole time at the foot of the pulpit, gazing on the preacher with great earnestness, and whenever any sentiment was uttered which met his approval, signifying his assent by a gentle nod of his head and an expressive smile." One of the Glasgow friends who had accompanied Dr. Chalmers to London, his publisher, Mr. Smith, the father of the youth whom he had loved and mourned, sent home an account full of enthusiasm and excitement. "I write," he says, "under the nervousness of having heard and witnessed the most astonishing display of human talents that perhaps ever commanded sight or hearing. Dr. Chalmers has just finished the discourse before the Missionary Society. All my expectations were overwhelmed in the triumph of it. Nothing from the Tron pulpit ever exceeded it; nor did he ever more arrest and wonder-work his audience. I had a full view of the whole place. The carrying forward of minds never was so visible to me: a constant assent of the head from the whole people accompanied all his paragraphs, and the breathlessness of expectation permitted not the beating of a heart to agitate the stillness." It would be hard not to sympathize with the elated disciple, companion, and satellite, to whom the success of "the doctor" in this vast new sphere conveyed something of that delight of the showman which we all feel when either scenery or personage connected with ourselves does its duty and overwhelms the rest of the world with admiration. Mr. Smith was a highly-favoured showman indeed, and describes how "we were introduced at the meeting of the Royal Society, where we saw all the most distinguished philosophers of the nation, and were also in the House of Peers during the debate on the Catholic question. . . . In every particular we were highly gratified." "The doctor came off with great *éclat*," he says on another occasion. Meanwhile the doctor's brother James, with a force of characteristic obstinacy more common in fiction than in real life, pursued his dogged way from his office in the city, and the Jerusalem coffee-house, where he took his relaxation, to his sober home at Walworth, and never once diverged from his daily path to hear Thomas preach, his dour Scotch pride and contempt of the applauses of the crowd embodying a higher family faith and estimation than any amount of enthusiasm.

When Chalmers preached again, it was no longer the Dissenting bodies alone which were stirred to their depths, but Society, always susceptible and eager for a new sensation, which rushed to the Surrey side and to the distant wilderness of London Wall to hear the new wonder. "All the world wild about Dr. Chalmers," says the great Wilberforce, who himself made a party with Canning and Huskisson to hear the great Scotch preacher, and records the emotion of the former, as does also another spectator, Lady Elgin: "I saw it myself." "I was surprised," Mr. Wilberforce says, "to see how greatly Canning was affected; at times he was quite melted into tears." "The tartan," he is reported to have said, "beats us all." On another occasion Wilberforce and various great ladies had to get into the church where Chalmers officiated, through a window, treading a plank which the fine people dared with almost more than manly courage, while the preacher himself had the greatest difficulty in getting in at all.

It is curious, amid all the inflation of these reports, and in sight of the shining faces of his attendants, to read what Chalmers himself said, impatient and disgusted as he had always been by the pressure of the crowd: "I pronounce London to be intolerable," he writes to the brother James, who contemplated these proceedings with grim humour from the calm of Walworth, delighted to feel himself out of it. "I have had to issue a whole swarm of refusals to your London applications, and I believe that the insufferable urgency to the place will drive me away from it as soon as I have liquidated my engagements to two societies." This impatience is highly characteristic of the man, but much unlike the usual temper of the popular preacher. His impetuous intolerance indeed on these points must have often conveyed the idea of high temper and egotism to the crowds of disappointed Church functionaries, for whose benefit he would not consent to make himself wretched. "Stare, pressure, and animal heat" revolted him throughout his life, and he turns his back upon his triumphs with an angry loathing, which half irritates the reader—for should not any man be grateful for human admiration and applause?—but with a long-drawn breath of relief on getting free, which at once changes his aspect. He arrived in London on May 12th, the day before his first appointment to preach, and he left it on the 26th, the day after the last. A fortnight of adulation and "urgency" was more than enough, and society had no charm to hold the impatient Scot, longing, if not for quiet, which was unattainable, at least for his own work done in his own imperious way.

On their rambling and devious way homewards—there were of course no railways in those days, and the pleasant, tedious journey was accomplished in a post-chaise, and capable of every kind of prolongation and detour—the little party, consisting of "the doctor," his wife, and Mr. Smith, traversed a great part of the west of England, and penetrated into Wales. The remarkable points in the journey, according to Mr. Smith, were Bristol, where Hannah Moore was visited, and John Foster the essayist, we fear a much-forgotten name, was "beyond all our expectations marvellous;" and Liverpool, where "kindnesses were almost overwhelming," and where they were much with Mr. Gladstone, a rich and liberal merchant there, in whose household apparently neither the doctor nor his companions noted a small boy of eight, who was destined one day to rule his country, and make much commotion in the world. It is needless to repeat here any further echoes of the applauses that followed the great preacher in his flight from town and its urgencies. The voice, however, of the well-known Robert Hall, himself so great in the same way, is worth hearing. He speaks of "the unrivalled and unbounded popularity which attended you in the metropolis," with a perception that there were drawbacks to this popularity which diminished its acceptability. "When you consider, however," he adds, "the thousands who have probably benefited by the unparalleled energy of your pulpit ministrations, you will be the more easily reconciled to the inconvenience inseparable from high celebrity. The attention which your sermons have excited is probably unequalled in modern literature, and it must be a delightful reflection that you are advancing the cause of religion in innumerable multitudes of your fellow-creatures, whose faces you will never behold till the last day." This testimony to an "unparalleled, unequalled, unrivalled, and unbounded" popularity came from no ignorant observer; and even if we allow a little for the fervour of mutual admiration and the habit of panegyric, it is still of the greatest weight. It was well for Chalmers that he found the greatest comfort in his impatient spirit in being well rid of all these superlatives.

All this, however, was not the chief occupation of his life at the climax of his career, which we fix as the time of his residence and work in Glasgow, from his thirty-fifth to his forty-third year. These popular triumphs were but the surface, a brilliant and dazzling one indeed of his great existence, but yet always to his own consciousness inferior to the real and strenuous object of it. He would not have been human had he not felt a certain enjoyment in the triumphs of his own eloquence and the consciousness of being able to sway at once the greatest and the simplest audience, whatever assemblage of his fellow-men he was brought face to face with, and could address with that voice and accent so full of imperfections, so unattractive to the cultured ear, yet which moved to enthusiasm, to rapture, to tears, the highest minds in England as well as the denizens of the Gorbals and Gallowgate; but yet, as we have seen, Chalmers, if not indifferent to his own power, was more impatient of its immediate results, less tolerant of the roar of popularity and the acclamations of the crowd than any orator that has ever been known. When he fled from the brazen trumpets and bellowing shouts of fame with the puckers of revolt upon his brow, and a fastidious disgust of all the noise and flurry depicted on a countenance which had no claim to extreme refinement, it was not the more congenial applauses of his rich and devoted adherents in Glasgow that he was thinking of, nor the sway of the ecclesiastical parliament, nor even the kindly crowds of the Tron Kirk. His whole soul was set upon a problem to which nobody as yet had found the solution—how to reach those darker crowds behind who knew nothing of the Tron Kirk or any other, where the labouring man, little known to his neighbours of the more comfortable classes, and eluding every evangelical effort, lay open to the foolish teaching of any demagogue, and all the impossible schemes of revolution: and the labouring woman toiled her life out in dirt and sorrow, without even that noisy alleviation of existence: and their children grew up untaught to an ever-worsening instead of bettering fate. These were the scenes to which he hurried home, and these the possible hearers of whom he was thinking when the London mob pressed about him with that stare and bustle which he loathed. The Surrey Chapel and the Scotch Church in Swallow Street were not fashionable resorts, but still less paradisical were the Gallowgate and the Saltmarket, upon which unsavoury, unmanageable regions the great preacher's heart was set.

We may add, before entering upon the narrative of his great raid upon that darkest Glasgow, and the wonderful if temporary result of his labours, some brief account of the literary work which he produced during his incumbency of the Tron Kirk. Sermons in general are perhaps scarcely to be called literary work: but the astronomical discourses are very little like ordinary sermons. There is all the glow and expansion about them which was natural to a mind full of the loftiest conception of his subject, and to a style in which some lingering trace of Dr. Johnson is combined with that large use of parallelism which constant occupation with the Bible in the noble diction of our Authorized Version does much to produce. Something, too, quite peculiar to himself, is in that effect, as of a swelling bosom and a long-drawn breath, with which these parallels fill and sweep along, rising to a climax which makes the reader too hold his breath, and half realize what must have been the excitement of the hearer to whom they came in all their first warmth and fervour. The effect is so strong, the swelling and inflation (in the better sense of the word)—or since that is suspect it may be more suitable to say dilation—of feeling and style alike so overwhelming—that even in the quiet and critical calm of a library, the reader feels himself carried along by it as by a great personal influence.

No better or more popular instance can perhaps be selected to give an example of his style and its remarkable and growing expansion, the high *crescendo* of an instrument more great than any resounding brass or tinkling string, than the comparison between the revelations of the telescope and microscope which occurs in the second of these discourses, that upon the "Condescension of God." His first sermon had been upon the wonderful words of the Psalmist, words perhaps first uttered in the vale of Bethlehem by the young shepherd who kept his flock under all the glories of an Eastern sky—and we know no evidence save those of arrogant conjecture against this authorship: but repeated consciously or unconsciously by every serious soul penetrated by the splendour of creation, in sight of the same wonderful spectacle, of which the furthest north does not diminish the beauty. "When I consider Thy heavens, the work of Thy fingers, the moon and the stars, which Thou hast ordained; what is man, that Thou art mindful of him? or the son of man, that Thou visitest him?" This is the subject of the entire series. It was intended to meet the argument of the sceptic, that in this vast universe the idea that God should have fixed so extraordinary an attention as is involved in the gospel scheme upon one insignificant atom in His creation, was untenable.

"It was the telescope that, by piercing the obscurity which lies between us and distant worlds, put Infidelity in possession of the argument against which we are now contending. But about the time of its invention another instrument was formed which laid open a scene no less wonderful, and rewarded the inquisitive spirit of man with a discovery which serves to neutralize the whole of this argument. This was the microscope. The one led me to see a system in every star; the other leads me to see a world in every atom. The one taught me that this mighty globe, with the whole burden of its peoples and its countries, is but a grain of sand on the high field of immensity; the other teaches me that every grain of sand may harbour within it the tribes and the families of a busy population. The one told me of the insignificance of the world I tread upon; the other redeems it from all its insignificance: for it tells me that in the leaves of every forest, and in the flowers of every garden, and in the waters of every rivulet, there are worlds teeming with life and numberless as are the glories of the firmament. The one has suggested to me that beyond and above all that is visible to man there may lie fields of creation which sweep immeasurably along, and carry the impress of the Almighty's hand to the remotest scenes of the universe; the other suggests to me that within and beneath all that minuteness which the aided eye of man has been able to explore, there may lie a region of invisibles; and that, could we draw aside the mysterious curtain which shrouds it from our senses, we might then see a theatre of as many wonders as astronomy has unfolded—a universe within the compass of a point so small as to elude all the powers of the microscope, but where the wonder-working God finds room for the exercise of all His attributes, where He can raise another mechanism of worlds, and fill and animate them all with the evidences of His glory. By the telescope they have discovered that no magnitude, however vast, is beyond the grasp of the Divinity; but by the microscope we have also discovered that no minuteness, however shrunk from the notice of the human eye, is beneath the condescension of His regard. The one is constantly widening the circle of His territory; the other is as constantly filling up its separate portions with all that is rich and various and exquisite. In a word, by the one I am told that the Almighty is now at work in regions more distant than geometry has ever measured, and among worlds more manifold than numbers have ever reached; but by the other I am also told that, with a mind to comprehend the whole, in the vast compass of its generality, He has also a mind to concentrate a close and a separate attention on each and all of its particulars: and that the same God who sends forth an upholding influence among the orbs and the movements of astronomy, can fill the recesses of every single atom with the intimacy of His presence, and travel in all the greatness of His unimpaired attributes upon every one spot and corner of the universe He has formed.

"They, therefore, who think that God will not put forth such a power, and such a goodness, and such a condescension on behalf of this world as are ascribed to Him in the New Testament, because He has so many other worlds to attend to, think of Him as a man. They only find room in their minds for His one attribute of a large and general superintendence, and keep out of their remembrance the equally impressive proofs we have for His other attribute of a minute and multiplied attention to all that diversity of operations where it is He that worketh all in all. And when I think that, as one of the instruments of philosophy has heightened our every impression of the first of these attributes, so another instrument has no less heightened our impression of the second of these, then I can no longer resist the conclusion that it would be a transgression of sound argument, as well as a daring of impiety, to draw a limit around the doings of this unsearchable God; and should a professed revelation from heaven tell me of an act of condescension in behalf of some separate world so wonderful that angels desire to look into it, and the Eternal Son had to move from His seat of glory to carry it into accomplishment, all I ask is the evidence of such a revelation; for, let it tell me as much as it may of God letting Himself down for the benefit of one single province of His dominions, this is no more than what I see scattered in numberless examples before me, and running through the whole line of my recollections, and meeting me in every walk of observation to which I can betake myself; and now that the microscope has unveiled the wonders of another region, I see strewed around me, with a profusion which baffles my every attempt to comprehend it, the evidence that there is no one portion of the universe of God too minute for His notice, nor too humble for the visitations of His care."

In another discourse he sets before us, with the same expansion of word and thought, the position of man, the spectator in this great universe. He describes the amazing width of prospect which is opened up by the "little organ of the eye"—

"It is this which enables him, by the act of a single moment, to send an exploring look over the surface of an ample territory, to crowd his mind with the whole assembly of its objects, and to fill his vision with those countless hues which diversify and adorn it. It is this which carries him abroad over all that is sublime in the immensity of distance; which sets him, as it were, on an elevated platform, from whence he may cast a surveying glance over the arena of innumerable worlds; which spreads before him so mighty a province of contemplation that the earth he inhabits only appears to furnish him with the pedestal on which he may stand, and from which he may descry the wonders of all that magnificence which the Divinity has poured so abundantly around him. It is by the narrow outlet of the eye that the mind of man takes its discursive flight over those golden tracks where, in all the exhaustlessness of creative wealth, lie scattered the suns and systems of astronomy.

"But how good a thing it is for the philosopher to be humble even amid the proudest march of human discovery, and the sublimest triumphs of the human understanding, when he thinks of that unscaled barrier beyond which no power, either of eye or telescope, shall ever carry him; when he thinks that on the other side of it there is a height and a depth and a length and a breadth to which the whole of this concave and visible firmament dwindles into the insignificancy of an atom —and above all, how ready should he be to cast every lofty imagination away from him when he thinks of the God who, on the simple foundation of His word, has reared the whole of this stately architecture, and by the force of His preserving hand, continues to uphold it; and should the word again come out from Him that this world shall pass away, and a portion of the heavens that are around it, shall fall back into the annihilation from which He at first summoned them—what an impressive rebuke does it bring on the swelling vanity of science to think that the whole field of its most ambitious enterprises may be swept away altogether, and still there remain before the eye of Him who sitteth on the throne an untravelled immensity which He hath filled with innumerable splendours, and over the whole face of which He hath inscribed the evidence of His high attributes in all their might and in all their manifestations.

"But man has a great deal more to keep him humble of his understanding than a mere sense of that boundary which skirts and which terminates the material field of his contemplations. He ought also to feel how within that boundary the vast majority of things is mysterious and unknown to him, that even in the inner chamber of his own consciousness, where so much lies hidden from the observation of others, there is also to himself a little world of incomprehensibles; that if stepping beyond the limits of this familiar home he look no further than to the members of his family, there is much in the cast and colour of every mind that is beyond his power of divination; that in proportion as he recedes from the centre of his own personal experience, there is a cloud of ignorance and secrecy which spreads and thickens and throws a deep and impenetrable veil over the intricacies of every one department of human contemplation; that of all around him his knowledge is naked and superficial, and confined to a few of those more conspicuous lineaments which strike upon his senses; that the whole face, both of nature and of society, presents him with questions which he cannot unriddle, and tells him that beneath the surface of all that the eye can rest upon there lies the profoundness of a most unsearchable latency; and should he in some lofty enterprise of thought leave this world and shoot afar into those tracks of speculation which astronomy has opened—should he, baffled by the mysteries which beset his footsteps on earth, attempt an ambitious flight towards the mysteries of heaven—let him go, but let the justness of a pious and philosophical modesty go with him: let him forget not that from the moment his mind has taken its ascending way for a few little miles above the world he treads on, his every sense abandons him but one—that number and motion and magnitude and figure make up all the bareness of its elementary informations—that these orbs have sent him scarce another message than that told by their feeble glimmering upon his eye, the simple fact of their existence—that he sees not the landscape of other worlds, that he knows not the moral system of any one of them, nor athwart the long and trackless vacancy which lies between does there fall upon his listening ear the hum of their mighty populations."

Another very noble and touching passage from the discourse entitled "Sympathy felt for man in distant places of Creation," begins with the hypothesis that this earth is probably the only sphere astray in all the immense universe. "For anything we know, every planet that rolls in the immensity around us may be a land of righteousness: and be a member of the household of God: and have her secure dwelling-place within that ample limit which embraces His great and universal family. But we know at least of one wanderer, and how wofully she has strayed from peace and purity." Following out this idea, he represents the universal feeling which would be excited by such an exception to the rule—

"And here we cannot but remark how fine a harmony there is between the law of sympathetic nature in heaven and the most touching exhibitions of it on the face of our world. When one of a numerous family droops under the power of disease, is not that the one to whom all tenderness is turned, and who in a manner monopolizes the inquiries of his neighbourhood and the care of his family? When the sighing of the midnight storm sends a dismal foreboding into the mother's heart, to whom of all her offspring, we would ask, are her thoughts and her anxieties then wandering? Is it not to her sailor-boy, whom her fancy has placed amid the rude and angry surges of the ocean? Does not this, the hour of his apprehended danger, concentrate upon him the whole force of her wakeful meditations, and does not he engross for a season her every sensibility and her every prayer? We sometimes hear of ship-wrecked passengers thrown upon a barbarous shore, and seized upon by its prowling inhabitants, and hurried away through the tracks of a dreary and unknown wilderness, and sold into captivity, and loaded with the fetters of irrecoverable bondage, and who, stripped of every other liberty but the liberty of thought, feel even this to be another ingredient of wretchedness, for what can they think of but home? and as all its kind and tender imagery comes upon their remembrance, how can they think of it but in the bitterness of despair? Oh, tell us when the force of this disaster reaches his family, who is the member of it to whom is directed the full tide of its griefs and of its sympathies? Who is it that for weeks and for months usurps their every feeling, and calls out their largest sacrifices and sets them to the busiest expedients for getting him back? Who is it that makes them forgetful of themselves and of all around them? and tell us if you can assign a limit to the pains and the surrenders which afflicted parents and weeping sisters would make to seek and to save him?

"Now conceive, as we are warranted to do by the parables of this chapter, the principles of all these earthly exhibitions to be in full operation around the throne of God. Conceive the universe to be one secure and rejoicing family, and that this alienated world is the only strayed or only captive member belonging to it, and we shall cease to wonder that from the first period of the captivity of our species down to the consummation of their history in time, there should be such a movement in heaven: or that angels should so often have sped their commissioned way on the errand of our recovery: or that the Son of God should have bowed Himself down to the burden of our mysterious atonement: or that the Spirit of God should now, by the busy variety of His all-powerful influences, be carrying forward that dispensation of grace which is to make us meet for re-admission into the mansions of the celestial. Only think of love as of the reigning principle there: of love as sending forth its energies and aspirations to the quarter where its object is in most danger of being for ever lost to it: of love as called forth by this single circumstance to its uttermost exertion, and the most exquisite feeling of its tenderness; and then shall we come to a distinct and familiar explanation of the whole mystery: nor shall we resist by our incredulity the gospel message any longer, though it tells us that throughout the whole of this world's history—long in our eyes, but only a little month in the high periods of immortality—so much of the vigilance and so much of the earnestness of heaven should have been expended on the recovery of its guilty population."

We may add the solemn warning with which at the end of this series the preacher addressed the crowded and remarkable audience which had sat at his feet during their delivery. It was a very remarkable audience indeed—the most busy, the most energetic citizens of one of the greatest centres of industry and enterprise in the empire, laying aside work and plans and accounts in the very heart and freshness of the working-day, in order to listen to these great speculations and penetrate with the preacher into the arcana of the heavens, and the almost more impressive mysteries of the human heart. The picture that is given us of the reading-room opposite, and the Glasgow merchants, newspaper in hand, waiting for the moment to cross the street and take up their places in the familiar Sunday pews, so seldom occupied in the busy morn of a working-day, is very curious and characteristic; and it would have been strange indeed if these men, and the hosts of clerks and tradesmen who were set free for the same purpose, should not have felt at least a momentary elevation of mind as if they themselves had made a palpable advance, and a certain complacency in the sacrifice which they had made and the great thoughts which they had shared. The preacher, as he wound up this series of discourses, compares first the emotion excited by music, by "the deep and solemn oratorio," and then the influence of habits of piety, and finally the temporary chastening and impression of sorrow which brings many for a time to perceive the beauty and like the consolations of faith. But he adds—

"The deep and tender impression of a family bereavement is not religion: the love of established decencies is not religion. The charm of all that sentimentalism which is associated with many of its solemn and affecting services is not religion. The man whom death has widowed may abandon himself to the movements of that grief, which for a time will claim an ascendancy over him; and amongst the multitude of his other reveries may love to hear of the eternity where sorrow and separation are unknown. He who has been trained from his infant days to remember the Sabbath may love the holiness of its aspect, and associate himself with all its observances, and take a delighted share in the mechanism of its forms. But let not these think, because the tastes and sensibilities which engross them may be blended with religion, that they indicate either its strength or its existence within them. We recur to the test. We press its imperious exactions upon you. We call for fruit and demand the permanency of a religious influence on the habits and the history. How many are there who take a flattering unction to their souls, when they think of their amiable feelings and their becoming observations, with whom this severe touchstone would, like the head of Medusa, put to flight all their complacency! The afflictive dispensation is forgotten, and he on whom it is laid is practically as indifferent to God and to eternity as before. The Sabbath services come to a close, and they are followed by the same routine of week-day worldliness as before. In neither the one case nor the other do we see more of the radical influence of Christianity than in the sublime and melting influence of sacred music on the soul; and all this tide of emotion is found to die away from the bosom like the pathos or the loveliness of a song.

"The instances may be multiplied without number. A man may have a taste for eloquence, and eloquence the most touching or sublime may lift her pleading voice on the side of religion. A man may love to have his understanding stimulated by the ingenuities or the resistless urgencies of an argument: and argument the most profound and the most overbearing may put forth all the might of a constraining vehemence on behalf of religion. A man may feel the rejoicings of a conscious elevation when some ideal scene of magnificence is laid before him: and where are these scenes so readily to be met with as when led to expatiate in thought over the track of eternity, or survey the wonders of creation, or to look to the magnitude of those great and universal influences which lie within the compass of religion? A man may have his attention riveted and regaled by that power of imitative description which brings all the recollections of his own experience before him: which presents him with a faithful analysis of his own heart: which embodies in language such intimacies of observation and of feeling as have often passed before his own eyes or played within his bosom, but had never been so truly or so ably pictured to the view of his remembrance. We will venture to say on the strength of these illustrations that as much delight may emanate from the pulpit on an arrested audience beneath it, as ever emanated from the boards of a theatre; and with as total a disjunction of mind too in the one case as in the other from the essence or the habit of religion. We recur to the test: we make our appeal to experience; and we put it to you all whether your finding upon the subject does not agree with our saying about it, that a man may weep and admire and have many of his faculties put on the stretch of their most intense gratification, his judgment established, and his fancy enlivened and his feelings overpowered, and his hearing charmed as by the accents of heavenly persuasion, and all within feasted by the rich and varied luxuries of an intellectual banquet. Oh, it is cruel to frown unmannerly in the midst of so much satisfaction! But I must not forget that truth has her authority as well as her sternness, and she forces me to affirm that after all has been felt and gone through, there might not be one principle which lies at the turning-point of conversion that has experienced a single movement, not one of its purposes be conceived, not one of its doings be accomplished, not one step of that repentance, which if we have not we perish, so much as entered upon, not one announcement of that faith by which we are saved admitted into a real and actual possession by the inner man. He has had his hour's entertainment, and willingly does he accord this homage to the performer, that he hath a pleasant voice and can play well on an instrument—but in another hour it fleets away from his remembrance, and goes all to nothing like the loveliness of a song."

These sermons were completed and ready for publication in January 1817, when Chalmers had been about a year and a half in Glasgow. The publication of sermons is not considered a very lucrative branch of the publishing trade, and Mr. Smith, Chalmers' first publisher, had proposed the adoption of the usual method in such cases, publication by subscription. It was not a suggestion that pleased the preacher. "It is far more agreeable to my feelings," he said, "that the book should be introduced to the general market and sell on the public estimation of it, than that the neighbourhood here should be plied in all the shops with subscription papers, and as much as possible wrung out of their partialities for the author." As it turned out, there was little need indeed for any such proposal. The little volume was published on the 28th January, and in April six thousand copies had been sold, with an increasing demand for more. Within the year the publication had run into nine editions of more than two thousand each. "Never previously, nor ever since, has any volume of sermons met with such immediate and general acceptance," says Dr. Hanna. "The *Tales of my Landlord* had a month's start in the date of publication, and even with such a competitor it ran an almost equal race. Not a few curious observers were struck with the novel competition, and watched with lively curiosity how the great Scottish preacher and the great Scottish novelist kept for a whole year so nearly abreast of one another." The world had become unaccustomed to think of sermons which were literature, and which presented that "loveliness of a song" which their immediate audience had so fully recognized, and the ready acceptance of such a happy combination was at once apparent. Curiously enough, the critics, or at least the specially religious critics, assailed a book which gave so little occasion for any cavilling. In the *Eclectic Review*, John Foster, the essayist, a writer then of the greatest reputation, found fault with the author of the Astronomical Discourses "for dragging into notice a stale and impotent objection against the truth of the Christian religion, and giving a wide spread by his discourses to an argument which, so so far as we can find, is almost unknown." The *British Review* had "never encountered this argument against the Christian doctrine," or had "given it no heed on account of its apparent inconsistency," whatever may have been meant by that. "It may be doubted whether the objection to which he has devoted his powers ever obtained a currency sufficient to render it deserving of so elaborate a refutation," said the *Christian Observer*. The *Monthly Review*, bolder still, denounced the discourses as "impotent in point of argument, and vicious in point of style." "The doctor," said this critic, "has acquired an ephemeral reputation, but it can only be ephemeral, at least in the southern part of our island, for it possesses none of the constituents of lasting fame. His mind is neither vigorous nor comprehensive; his sentiments are often grovelling and intolerant; and his diction never permanently attracts by real beauty or nobly elevates by true sublimity." The authorities in pure literature were happily of another mind. The vigorous and eloquent critic of *Blackwood's Magazine*, Christopher North, as he chose to call himself, a writer little given to sermons, but open to almost everything truly noble in contemporary letters, took up this subject in another strain.

"The objections which he combats," says this prince of criticism, "are not so much the clear, distinct, and decided averments of infidelity as they are the confused, glimmering, and disturbing fears and apprehensions of noble souls bewildered among the magnificence of the universe. Perhaps there is no mind of any strength, no soul of any nobility that has not often in the darkness of the night been beset by some of these majestic terrors. We may never have communicated them even to our dearest friends, for when they are gone they are unutterable; like the imagined shadows of ghosts, they come and go silently and trackless; but an awe is left in the haunted mansion of the soul, and with all the deepest gratitude of a perturbed imagination we listen to the holy and the lofty voice which scares away the unholy visitants, and once more fills the midnight stillness with dreams of a peaceful and of a heavenly happiness."

We cannot but feel after such a sentence how much more real is the inspiration of kindred genius than that of professional criticism, and that true Art has a wiser and finer comprehension of most subjects than religious or any other brethren. Another critic, less great than Wilson, but of a very keen and penetrating discrimination, added his testimony in a similar tone. "We remember," Hazlitt says, "finding the volume in the orchard of the inn at Burford Bridge near Boxhill, and passing a whole and very delightful morning in reading it without quitting the shade of an apple-tree." Orchards and apple-trees are no longer very common characteristics even of country inns, and the combination is piquant when we think of this particular volume lying out in the summer atmosphere for such a reader. "These sermons," he adds, "ran like wild-fire through the country." We fear that if not forgotten now, they have at least fallen much out of the knowledge of the younger generations, all occupied with the abounding prelections, smart "New" criticism, and complacent explanation of everything, which are their own. But no one worthy will find this volume, if not in an orchard yet in a library, without falling under that spell more or less, and receiving from these faded pages the echoes of a noble voice.

CHAPTER III.

THIS record, with all its excitements and labours, and the hum of a multitude which goes through it, was however the merest surface of Chalmers' life. His thoughts were occupied far less with the people who crowded the Tron Kirk and besieged others, creeping in through church windows and clambering over scaffoldings to hear him, than with those who had no desire to hear him, who stood behind in gloomy or ignorant indifference, unmoved by the impulse which swept all other classes towards that point of attraction. It was not the mere fact of their indifference which stimulated him, though that is an incitement not unknown to those who achieve easy triumphs on every side but one. There was, however, a far deeper motive. When Chalmers came to Glasgow he was in every fibre of his being a countryman, a country minister, accustomed to that universal rural acquaintance and influence which even the most easy-going head of a rural parish must die or else attain. And his was no easy mind taking things quietly, but a masterful and sympathetic spirit unable to let things or people alone. In his early days, before he had yet discovered how much higher and more vital a message he had to deliver, he had insisted upon opening the wonders of chemistry to his gaping rustic folk, and teaching the old wives of the village to make a pot boil without fire. Now he had a much greater work in hand, and it galled his spirit to think that there were thousands of his people, his own parishioners, those over whom he felt himself ordained, whom he never saw, and did not know, and could not reach by any of the usual means. The weavers of the Saltmarket had no seats in church. They came to no meetings, if not to a revolutionary assemblage now and then on the Green; and showed themselves in no public places, if not on a summer evening saunter across that Green, where their minister was far too busy to go. But it irked him to his very soul to be spending his strength, almost ornamentally, as it were, making the sound of one who played cunningly upon an instrument to add an additional pleasure to the well-off and prosperous, while his true charge, his real object, lay untouched. The parish economy of Scotland is unlike that in the other parts of the British Islands. It is a very marked and individual system, democratic, oligarchic, whatever name may please the reader best. The minister is at its head, but he is no absolute sovereign reigning alone. His power is shared and his actions in many ways controlled by the Kirk Session—consisting of elders ordained, like himself, with a solemnity little short of his own vows, to rule and guide, and aid in all things the parish priest. Heaven forbid that we should attribute that title savouring of popery and sacerdotal pretension to the Scotch minister! Yet religion and humanity are bigger than system and doctrine, and the office is one and the same. The elders in the ideal system are like Electors Palatine round their emperor. In many actual cases they are merely his agents, if not like an ill-humoured churchwarden here and there, his critics and opponents among the people. In a careless age they were chiefly the guardians of the Plate, an institution also purely Scottish. This is a vessel placed in the church porch, into which, great and small, every worshipper as he enters places his customary and entirely voluntary coin; while two respectable figures stand behind, lending the dignity of their presence to the old-world familiar practice—sometimes with a little ostentation of not observing whether the coins are silver or copper that most abound, more often with the indifference of habit performing their part as it has been performed for some three hundred years. We who remember the childish flutter of excitement, whatever else might be wanting, to have one's penny ready for the plate, when one was hardly high enough to reach it, would rather part with much impedimenta of doctrine than see that plate disappear from the church door, with its attendant warders—the kindly elder who gives a grave smile to his little acquaintances as they pass, or the solemn elder of whom they are afraid.

It may be that a stranger might pass that homely object by without any thought of the significance of the Plate. It means more than an offertory, more than the embroidered bag or brass trenchard which goes the round of the congregation, the "alms and oblations" which are for general purposes, and mean no long-established and weighty institution. The big *Suisse* and the fine lady who perform *la quête* in a French cathedral are not half so imposing. The Plate was instituted to mean, and did still mean in Chalmers' days, the whole system of public charity in Scotland, a better Poor-Law, a nobler beneficence than any represented by assessments. The childrens' pennies, the sixpences of father and mother—that offering which Scotch families blushed to omit, and in the utmost penury still managed to maintain—were indeed for several centuries all that Scotland knew as a permanent provision for the poor. It was nothing for those who gave, but with the aid of stern independence and neighbourly kindness, it was sufficient for those who received, and had been so for many generations before Chalmers. It was enough for Kilmany—enough even for Anstruther—combined with the private benefit of a sea-box or other institution of mutual help among the sailors. To Chalmers it seemed that it was enough for the Tron parish or any parish in the world. In these days the Poor-Laws were under hot discussion, and in the very act of being re-formed in England; while in Scotland they were only beginning to be thought of, to be introduced in big towns where the poor had outgrown the revenue of the Plate. When Chalmers came upon the scene, a complicated system of charity existed in Glasgow by which he thought much harm was done, and wholesome primitive virtue injured or destroyed among the people. Among the many impatiences of his strong and somewhat imperious, though always brotherly, soul, was an indignant antipathy to have questions of personal profit combined with those of religious instruction. Dr. Hanna tells an amusing story of his reception of a visitor who introduced himself as under great distress of mind owing to his inability to satisfy himself of the Divine origin of

Christianity, and especially of the trouble he had to understand what is said of Melchizedek. Chalmers addressed himself seriously to this problem, and when he had to all appearances impressed if not convinced the doubter, the latter declaring himself much relieved in mind, suggested that he was very badly off, and that perhaps a little money—— "Not a penny, sir, not a penny!" cried the indignant divine, suddenly enlightened. "It's too bad; too bad! And to haul in your hypocrisy on the shoulders of Melchizedek." A similar sentiment is in the following grave account which was made before a committee of the House of Commons on the subject of the Poor-Laws. He had been questioned as to the state of his parish on his arrival in Glasgow, and had described his withdrawal altogether from the management of its pauperism, finding that quite false in principle and alien to his character as a Christian teacher. "In the eyes of the population," he said, "the minister stood connected, not merely with the administration of this compulsory fund, but with the administration of a great many such charities as we call mortifications in Scotland, which are endowments for indigence left by benevolent citizens, who generally constitute the clergy their trustees."

"Among the earliest movements I made through the families, I was very much surprised at the unexpected cordiality of my welcome, the people thronging about me, and requesting me to enter their houses. I remember I could hardly make my way to the bottom of a close in the Saltmarket, I was so extremely thronged by the people: but I soon perceived this was in consequence of my imagined influence in the distribution of these charities; and I certainly did feel a very great recoil, for it was so different from the principle upon which I had been received with cordiality in my country parish, where the topic of their temporal necessities was scarcely ever mentioned. I therefore resolved to dissever myself from the administration of these charities altogether. I soon made the people understand that I only dealt in one article, that of Christian instruction, and that if they chose to receive me on this footing, I should be glad to visit them. I can vouch for it that the cordiality of the people was not only enhanced, but very much refined in its principle after this became the general understanding: that of ten thousand entries made of different times into the houses of the poor of Glasgow, I cannot recollect a dozen instances in which I was not received with welcome."

Thus it was odious to him at all times, and in all circumstances, that Christian instruction should be sought for the sake of pecuniary relief, or a petition for a little money hauled in on the shoulders of Melchizedek. He had his own great way of making prayer and alms aid each other in the succour of the people, but it was not this; and that the Church should interfere with the money levied from the ratepayers, or the minister become the official dispenser of public charity, was not only to him a false principle, but an odious imposition. His doctrines and views on this point might even seem severe to the reader. He was not alone a parish minister, but a moral philosopher, a political economist, a born statesman and legislator. From one point of view he was a determined, even harsh, opponent of public charity. The reader must again be reminded that the time of which we are writing was that in which the old Poor-Law of England, with its facile allowances and large measure of outdoor relief, was being remodelled, and the country was ringing with discussions upon the subject, some strongly defending that mode of action, and some insisting that parish relief should be made not an easy but a displeasing thing, dispensed not by means of little subsidies spent at home, which raised no feeling of degradation, but by the stern workhouse and all its separations and humiliations. Dr. Chalmers was in favour of neither, and his views, which we shall immediately quote, were of the most distinct and determined character.

"We have long thought," he says, in the preface to his *Christian and Civic Economy of Large Towns,* "that by a legal provision for indigence two principles of our moral nature have been confounded, which are radically distinct from each other—distinct both objectively in the ethical system of virtue, and subjectively in the laws and workings of the human constitution. These two principles are humanity and justice, whereof the latter is the only proper object of legislation—which, by attempting the enforcement of the former, has outstepped altogether its own rightful boundaries. It is right that justice should be enforced by law, but compassion ought to go free; and the mischief that has practically ensued from the violation of this obvious propriety strikingly evinces the harmony of the abstract with the concrete in the constitution of our actual world, insomuch that derangement and disorder will inevitably follow wherever the natural laws of that microcosm, which each man carries in his own heart, are thwarted by the dissonancy of those civil or political laws by which it is so often vainly attempted to improve on the designs of the great Architect, when the inventions of man are suffered to supersede the great principles of truth and nature in the mechanism of human society.

"Pauperism, in so far as sustained on the principle that each man solely because he exists holds a right on other men or on society for existence, is a thing not to be regulated, but destroyed. Any attempt to amend the system which reposes on such a basis will present us with but another modification of that which is essentially and radically evil. Whatever the calls may be which the poverty of a human being may have on the compassion of his fellows, it has no claim whatever upon their justice. The confusion of these two virtues in the ethical system will tend to actual confusion and disorder where introduced into the laws and administration of human society. The proper remedy, or remedy of nature, for the wretchedness of the few is the kindness of the many. But when the heterogeneous imagination of a right is introduced into this department of human affairs, and the imagination is sanctioned by the laws of the country, then one of two things must follow—either an indefinite encroachment on property so as ultimately to reduce to a sort of agrarian level all the families of the land; or, if to postpone this consequence a rigid dispensation be adopted, the disappointment of a people who have been taught to feel themselves aggrieved, the innumerable heart-burnings which law itself has conjured up, and no administration of that law, however skilful, can appease.

"If the many thousand applicants for public charity in England really do have a right to the relief of their wants, why should not that right, as a right, be fully and openly and cheerfully conceded to them? Why should they be scared away from the assertion of this right by any circumstances of hardship or degeneration or violence to the affections of nature being associated therewith? Should the avenue to justice be obstructed, and that too by the very pains and penalties which are laid on those who trample justice under foot? Yet every approximation of an alms-house to a jail, of a house of charity to a house of correction, but exemplifies this grievous paralogism; nor can we wonder, when the rulers of England have led its people so grievously astray, that elements of conflict are now afloat which destroy the well-being and even threaten the stability of society.

"It is playing fast and loose with a people, first to make a declaration of their right, and then to plant obstacles in the way of their making it good. There is an utter incongruity here of the practice with the principle which betrays a secret misgiving as if the principle was not felt to be a sound one. The truth is, that it is such a principle as will not bear to be fully and consistently acted upon. The economy of a legal provision for the poor can only be upheld in a country by a compensation of errors, an expedient which might do in mathematics, but which can never be made to do prosperously or well in the management of human nature."

It is amazing to hear this sweeping condemnation of a system and a principle which we have all been accustomed to see in full action, and to recognize from our cradles; nor is it less astounding to discover that the system which this man of genius, sense, and insight proposed to substitute for it, was that of a Scotch parish, the old economy of the middle ages, wrought to a kind of perfection (imperfect he would have no doubt admitted in the carrying out, as are all things human) in the sixteenth century, when the Scotch reformation was accomplished in fire and flame. The spectator of to-day will probably laugh at the "devout imagination," as the nobles of the Reformation laughed grimly at John Knox; but we can none of us refuse to allow that the evils which Chalmers anticipated have been more or less carried out, that the "encroachment on property," which he spoke of as probable yet problematic, has now come to a very advanced state of propagation, as a doctrine at least, and "the agrarian level" becomes daily a more firmly established ideal and hope among the masses, who are more and more sure of their right to be supported when in want, and more and more angry and impatient with the degradation and insults of the workhouse. As for Chalmers' remedy, he proved its success triumphantly for several years in circumstances as little adapted to be regulated by so simple a theory as can be conceived, which gives him at least as good a right to be heard on the matter as any man can have. We must now proceed to give, as well as is possible, an account of what he attempted and what he accomplished in the parish of St. John—to which, a newly-separated district erected into a parish of "at least ten thousand inhabitants composed almost entirely of operatives," he was "translated," according to Scotch phraseology, with the express purpose of making his great experiment, the magistrates of Glasgow having no power to interfere with the economy of the old parishes, but being "prepared to go so far along with Dr. Chalmers as to enable him in this new parish to try those schemes of reformation which he was known to have so much at heart." First, however, we may attempt to show how he had spent his four years of previous work, from 1815 to 1819, in the parish of the Tron, though that was not the independent kingdom and territory over which he ruled, the noblest kind of despot, in the later period of his career in Glasgow. The Tron was bound in all the bonds of those restrictions which had grown up about a city parish, with all its "mortifications," hospitals, and municipal rights and duties, and it was not there that the great experiment could be made.

Chalmers, though a philosopher and social economist, and, in the higher sense of the word, politician—moral politician, if we may invent a phrase—was above all a Christian minister, to whom the work of religious instruction was the great and only work, to which all others were subservient. His economy was indeed part of his Christianity, as he sets forth in the preface, which we have already quoted, to his *Christian and Civic Economy*. No two classes of men stand more apart from each other, he says, than the clergyman, whose office it is by prayer and labour to build up a high average character for the people, and the economists, whose office it is to investigate the law of dependence between character and comfort. "Nevertheless," he adds, "it is not the less true that between a high tone of character and a high rate of wages there is a most intimate alliance; and while it is for the economists alone to speculate aright on the action and reaction of these two elements, it is for the ministers of the gospel alone, by the influence of that faith which they teach, to elevate the morality of the common people, and so to carry into practical fulfilment that glorious connexion which is ever found between a well-principled and a well-conditioned peasantry." The parish of the Tron lies in the very heart of Glasgow, in what no doubt was once the merchants' centre, the Saltmarket, as already noted, being part of it; but is now, and already was in 1815, occupied by working-people, from the comfortable artisan to the lowest labourer. The people were lodged in large houses let in flats and subdivision of flats, according to the system still practised in Glasgow, as in all foreign countries. It is a system which has been introduced into England in some small degree in later days, but except in fashionable mansions, or in model lodging-houses, has not attained any acceptance. Great houses of five or six storeys, inhabited by tribes of people, wholesome and unwholesome, clean and dirty, decent and the reverse, with dark staircases seldom attended to, reeking with humanity in its least pleasing atmosphere and emanations, each the common habitation of a crowd of families, were the homes of this overgrown parish. The church was thronged Sundays and week-days, whenever Chalmers preached, by crowds which had nothing to do with these rabbit-warrens of population—the "best people" in Glasgow, the merchant princes, the great manufacturers, the professors, students, clerks, all the intelligent portion of the community; but by very few of the parishioners, who would have been sadly disconcerted, had they been in the habit of coming to their parish kirk, by such an invasion. But they had not been in the habit of coming, and their silent existence, lying all around, invisible, scarcely represented at all, while their parish minister poured out his best to others, was a thing intolerable to that minister if to no one else. It is to be remembered that the Tron Church was built for the very classes who occupied it, who were drawn back into the centre of the city to hear the great preacher, but who had long departed from the region where it stood, the centre of a population which had ebbed away. If not Dr. Chalmers but an ordinary man had been there, it would have been partially empty—the official church of magistrates and a few old-fashioned people, not of the existing Saltmarket and Gallowgate. But nevertheless the parishioners were there, and it was the duty of the minister to know every one of them, according to all the rules of a Scotch parish. From this rule Chalmers had no thought of withdrawing. He was obliged to modify it: he could not pause in every house to exhort or to pray: but neither could he neglect his first duty. He visited every house, inquiring into its religious habits, which generally were nil, and into the condition of its children, who were or were not at school, and so with a kind word and grasp of many hard-working hands, passed on to neighbour after neighbour, inviting them to meet him in the evening of that or another day in a convenient room close at hand. In this way all his afternoons and most of his evenings were occupied. He kept the morning for study and composition, dined not later than three o'clock, after a custom not unusual in those days, and then "sallied forth and expatiated at the bottom of the

Saltmarket till seven." On another day, after hard work in his study till two, he took a stroll through a neighbour's garden, then "came back to my beefsteak, and after it I had another round of visitation at the head of the Green, and after going amongst the houses, drank tea with a Mr. M'Leary, and assembled the people in a weaver's, who came to the amount of a hundred and twenty-five hearers. This is truly gratifying work, and I feel that if unmolested I shall have great pleasure in it. The cordialities of the people are quite unbounded." On another day he "had a visitation along with Mr. C. Went through Norris's Land. Drank a hurried tea in the parish with Mr. Ure, and went back to Norris's Land at eight, where I held forth to a motley assemblage of a hundred people at least. I had great freedom and satisfaction in this work."

The same account is repeated day by day. It is taken from a series of journal letters to his wife, then absent: and the time of the year was high summer, when all the genteel persons and good society in Glasgow were absent too, and the smells and close air of the "Lands," which is the name given to the great tenement houses in Scotland, would be at their height. "Met Mr. John Brown, elder, and took him and Mr. Montgomery to a visitation in the proportion of the latter. Went through two hundred and thirty people, and drank tea at Mr. Brown's, then at eight delivered an address in one of the houses to an assemblage consisting of eighty-five people. Have great comfort in this work." His glee in getting off from a number of tourist visitors to hurry "to the Saltmarket, where I spent four or five hours among my old people;" his sudden remark, accompanied by no special tenderness—(for he signs himself, as already remarked, "Yours truly" to his wife—as, indeed, what could a man say more?—and writes to his most beloved friends as "My dear sir")—"Nothing but the complete filling up of my time by useful employment would render our separation tolerable;" his wrathful indignation at the meeting of a society which had lost him "two complete days, one in preparing for it, and another exhibiting for it. You will see how utterly this distraction is at variance with my best and dearest, and, I think, most valuable objects"—show us the man in the manner and with the object of his existence in a remarkable way. They are not like the similar letters of Irving, full of the tender revelations of a high-toned and sensitive spirit; but their brief and unadorned record gives us a view into a life which is full of duty, and love of that duty, without a single word of self-consciousness or expansion. The other is the more lovable and attractive. It may be doubted whether this is not the highest record.

But this hurried kind of visitation by no means satisfied the ardent apostle. "I know," he said to a respectable elder, toiling after him up a long dark stair, "that if you were to speak your mind, you would say that we are putting the butter very thinly upon the bread." He himself longed to "expatiate," according to his own humorous solemnity of expression, among the closes and wynds as he had done among the green lanes at Kilmany, making every cottager a friend, and becoming learned in all the beautiful obscure thinkings and all the quaint whims and prejudices of an uneducated but intelligent people. What he desired was to know the weavers and cotton-spinners as he had known John Bonthron and all the worthies of the East-Neuk. That, however, was impossible to one man, and he soon perceived that without a large body of coadjutors very little could be done. An English rector might have gathered round him a troop of curates, but this was entirely out of the thoughts or possibilities of a Scotch minister, to whom indeed the help of an "assistant" was presently proffered, but who knew what he believed to be a more excellent way, not only of reaching the poor, but of linking them with their more fortunate neighbours. Before his second year in Glasgow he had presided at the ordination as elders, of a new class, not the respectable seniors of a comfortable and satisfied community, but men like himself, still young and eager, full of work and full of fight, and pervaded by the enthusiasm of the leader, who had roused them to a fuller conception of the nobler duties of life, and the claims upon them of the neglected and poor. His address to these elders at their ordination—which was a rite little less solemn than the ordination of the minister himself, and preceded by the same vows—is admirable in its practical advice, which is such as every worker among the poor might well lay to heart. He reminds them first of the duty of spiritual instruction and help, which, according to all Scotch Church law and tradition, was the first duty of the elders as well as of the clergy, but proceeds afterwards to counsel them as to their intercourse in the way of benevolence and help-giving with the population under their care. At a period when service of this kind is so much more general, these advices are well worthy repetition. The reader will remark that they were not addressed to a humble company of district visitors, but to men, some of whom were of the first consequence in their great community, and holding an office fully recognized there.

"I shall venture on three observations relative to this department of your services.

"My first is that the poor will feel themselves greatly soothed and conciliated by your ready attention, by your friendly counsel, by your acts of advice and assistance as to the conduct of their little affairs, by the mere civility and courteousness which mark your transactions with them, and that these will positively go further to gladden their hearts and endear your person to them, than all the money you may find it necessary to award for the support of their indigent families.

"My second remark is counterpart to my former one. It will be said that by this unrestricted facility of manner you will lay yourselves open to the inroads of the unworthy and undeserving. In answer to this, I ask if there be not room enough in a man's character for the wisdom of the serpent along with the gentleness of the dove? That we may ward off the undeserving poor, is it necessary to put on a stern and repulsive front against all the poor who offer themselves to our observation? The way I apprehend is to put forth patience and attention, and to be in the ready attitude of prepared and immediate service for all cases and applications in the first instance: to conduct every examination with temper and kindness—and surely it is possible to do this and at the same time to conduct it with vigilance. Exercise will soon sharpen your discrimination in these matters, and when you have got at a thoroughly ascertained statement of the claim which has been advanced, and you find it is not a valid one, then put forth your firmness, then make a display of calm and settled determination, then show your people that you have judgment as well as feeling, and that you know how to combine the habit of justice to the public by not squandering their money on unsuitable objects, with the habit of sympathy for genuine distress and of ready attention to the merits of every application. . . . Your people will not like you the worse when they see you acting in a sound, judicious, and experimental way with them. They know how to appreciate good sense as well as we, and they admire it, and they actually have a liking for it. They are scandalized when they see kindness lavished on the unworthy. Though they like attention and sympathy, they have a greater esteem for them when they see them conjoined with the wisdom of judgment and a good understanding; and in proportion as you evince yourselves to have the faculty of rejecting those claims which are groundless, in that very proportion will a real sufferer esteem that act of preference by which you have had the discernment to single out his claim, and the benevolence most soothingly and most sympathizingly and most amply to provide for it.

"I have just one remark more to submit to you. I know not a more interesting case that can be submitted to you in this way than when an applicant proposes for the first time to draw relief from a public charity. This he is often compelled to do from some temporary distress that hangs over his family; and if the emergency could be got over without a public and a degrading exposure of him who labours under it, there would both be a most substantial saving of the public fund and a most soothing act of kindness rendered to the person who is applying to you. I am very far from urging anything upon you. I merely throw this out as a hint and suggestion. If by your own influence, or that of your friends, work could be provided for a man in such circumstances, or some private and delicate mode of relief be devised for him, then I know not in what other way you would more effectually establish yourselves as the most valuable servants of the public, and as the best and kindest friends of your own immediate population."

Long ago, in ancient Florence, there was an order of men bound in love and honour to the Service of the Poveri Vergognosi—the shamefaced poor—those to whom asking was not easy nor the bread of charity sweet. Might not these advices have been given forth from their dignified head-quarters to the mediæval gentlemen in their cloaks and plumes who undertook this most Christian of offices? Dr. Chalmers would not have found it easy to recognize his like among the slaves of Papistry and in the depths of what he would have called the Dark Ages, nor could the honest Glasgow elders have made any show among the civic nobles of the old Republic; but let us thank heaven that makes the differences always so much less than the resemblances, and vindicates the nobler motives, the higher instincts of our nature everywhere in all ages and all complexions of mankind.

Notwithstanding the work thus begun, however, and the assistance thus secured, Chalmers could do little more than shape his plans for after action, and try the mettle of his blade in the Tron Kirk. The reader must recollect that in those days none, or very few, of the countless agencies now at work in every poor parish or district of every English or Scotch city existed at all. Sunday-schools, of which so many of us are half-contemptuous now by dint of over-familiarity, were rare. There was in Glasgow a Sabbath-school Society which planted a school here and there at the pleasure and convenience of the few teachers, but without any special connexion with any church or district. Chalmers saw the capabilities of the instrument thus lying at his hand, and with a swift glance of his statesmanlike genius, perceived how it could be used with some real effect. The very earliest adaptation of what was afterwards entitled, with a little Scotch grandiloquence, the Territorial scheme, was caught at and taken up by a flash of insight in this simplest way. Instead of a school for general and languid use, or even a parish Sunday-school dedicated to the 11,000 people over whom he had charge, he planted one of his men-at-arms in a Glasgow close—or "land"—to devote himself to that little corner of the alas! very stony and neglected vineyard. The idea seized possession of him in the following way. He had secured a new Sabbath-school teacher, and set out to find him pupils, accompanied by an elder.

"They secured a room at the entrance of a long close. After going through the families living in this single lane, and summing up the number of children, there were found to be twenty-eight who had promised to attend. 'I think,' said Mr. Thomson, 'that we have got plenty.' The idea of a separate school in and for a single close pleased Dr. Chalmers amazingly. 'Yes,' he exclaimed, 'this is the true local plan: we will just fix R——down to this close: we will make it his parish: let him visit all the families here and look after all the children: that will be an effectual preaching of the gospel from door to door.'"

This was the nucleus of all his future undertakings; he had caught the principle; the parish system, yet something more minute and more practicable than any mere general parish system in a population of 11,000 people. His Sunday-schools multiplied on every hand, and in every little district—or "proportion," as he called them, loving always a bigger word: and wherever these little schools were established, there was a little theocracy at once established also, a world within the world, a little section of society taken possession of by the Church, with all the charities both of earth and heaven brought to bear upon it. What good these Sunday-schools accomplished of themselves we need not inquire, but the voluntary teacher coming and going, suggesting and urging the week-day school as well, finding places for the elder boys, encouraging economy, promoting order, gaining confidence, was a still greater advantage. It furnished him at once with the idea of the future agency for a greater undertaking still.

Chalmers had been four years in Glasgow when he was appointed to the new parish of St. John's, formed especially for him, that he might have the independence necessary to carry out the great schemes which had been forming in his mind. It is needless to say that nobody but a very exceptional man would have induced the magistrates of a great city to take such a step, and virtually deliver over a portion of their town to his sovereign sway—which, along with the fact that his great scheme continued to exist only while the force of the original impulse lasted, places his experiment more or less in the position of a Utopia, though one that such another man, as influential, as powerful, and as clear-headed, might again carry out. He had, as we have seen, been greatly moved by the subject of the Poor-Laws as lately remodelled in England, disapproving of them highly on principle, and feeling that kindness, and not legal right—sympathy and compassion and brotherhood, not doles of money, nor the dreadful expedient of a workhouse—were the things to neutralize and more or less abolish destitution and want. His system was, in administrating, to abolish public charity altogether, an idea that will seem very strange to the reader, habituated as we are now to the ideas and theories against which Chalmers so stoutly struggled.

It was in the end of September 1819 that he entered into possession of his kingdom, he and the large body of "Agents," his court and officials, all bent upon making this wilderness blossom as the rose. The new parish was not only one of the largest, it was the very poorest parish in the city. Weavers, labourers, factory-workers, and other operatives made up its population. The radical and revolutionary element, which was in one of its ebullitions at this time, was very strong in it. The people who came to church were not a hundredth part of the population. There were no schools, nothing at all of the machinery of a parish, no foundation to work upon—but only a mass of poor houses, poor families, cognizant of little in Christianity but vague, half-superstitious hopes of consolation in sickness and help in want. The tradition of the seemliness and use of the minister's presence at a death-bed, as a sort of passport and warrant of a good end, was almost as strong among them, though so different, as the desire of the Irish peasant for his priest to send him assoilzied on the same dread journey: but religion meant little more to them than this. That the subsidies of public charity were of supreme importance in such a district, it is unnecessary to say. Chalmers, however, accepted the living on the condition that all connexion with these public charities should be broken in the new parish. He demanded that it should be severed from the rest of the city in respect to all assessments and public provision for the poor, as if it had been removed a hundred miles away, and that the entire control of the parish should be made over to himself and his session, so far as its pauperism was concerned. He gave up all interest and all claim to any share in the poor-rates or general funds of the city, and undertook on his part to provide for every need of this kind in his parish, so as "never to add to the general burden." It was a very extraordinary bargain to be made between a modern municipality and a city incumbent, and we repeat that nothing but the extraordinary faith which all Glasgow had in this man, and the influence he exercised over mind and imagination, could have made it possible. But it was done—with no doubt many speculations of the profane as to the chaos in which this devout imagination must result.

To provide for the "submerged" of that population of 10,000 poor and labouring people, subject to all the fluctuations of daily work and those accidents which constantly convert the poor, who can just keep the wolf from the door and no more, into recipients of charity, Chalmers, for all his revenue, had the Plate at the church door. No poor-rate was levied in that parish, nor even any spasmodic effort made by a great subscription to provide an extraordinary fund. The Plate and no more: the unasked, natural offering, to which every one was accustomed—not emphasized even by so much as the sending round of a bag, or what in Scotch country parishes is called "the ladle": the entirely voluntary, unfelt, infinitesimal contribution of every one, from the smallest child proud of its halfpenny to the respectable shilling of manhood well-to-do. There are many changes nowadays in the outward forms of piety in Scotland, attempts to harmonize its sober absence of ritual to the higher organization of public religious services on the other side of the Tweed, but we hope that if the tradition of three hundred years needs any strengthening, the memory of Chalmers and his great experiment will always be enough to protect the Plate, that wise and simple institution, so entwined with every association, and so harmonious with its place and sphere.

"My confidence in a successful result is not at all founded on the expected magnitude of my future collections, but upon the care and attention with which the distribution of the fund will be conducted. . . . At the same time, I can also with such an arrangement stimulate more effectually than before the liberality of my congregation; and with this twofold advantage I am hopeful, not merely of being able to overtake the whole pauperism of St. John's, but of having a large surplus applicable to other objects connected with the best interests of the population in that district of the city."

These are Chalmers' words in anticipation of the new *régime* which he was about to inaugurate. He stipulated besides that this ideal kingdom of his should be guarded by the usual "law of residence" between parish and parish. "I am quite willing that every parish should have protection by this law from the ingress of my poor, in return for the protection of my parish from the ingress of theirs." At the same time he desired that it should be distinctly understood that, "I do not consider the revenue of the Kirk Session to be at all applicable to those extraordinary cases which are produced by any sudden and unlooked-for depression in the state of our manufactures. Nor, if ever there shall be a call for pecuniary aid on this particular ground, do I undertake to provide for it out of our ordinary means, but will either meet it by a parochial subscription or by taking a full share of any such general measures as may be thought expedient under such an emergency."

All these stipulations and conditions were the cause of a great deal of turmoil, agitation, and struggle. The magistrates freely granted that the pauperism of St. John's should be taken off the general fund and provided for within the parish: but to surround that parish with a cordon of protection from the invasion of paupers from other places, and to give up all control of its revenue and expenditure, was a thing over which both the Municipal Court and the public officials of charities hesitated long. It was, however, accomplished at last, and Chalmers and his "agency," his elders and deacons (the latter an order founded upon the suggestion of St. Peter "to serve tables," *i. e.* to attend to the external economy of the community, and without any spiritual charge, which is the Scotch and Presbyterian meaning of the word), got fairly into possession of their kingdom, and began the great experiment over which no doubt many a heart quaked, but not that of the leader, in whose determination and confidence every man of his helpers took refuge as in a citadel of boundless certainty and strength.

We are led to dwell upon this scheme and its triumphant realization all the more from the fact that all theories and efforts of this kind are of supreme interest at the present moment, when we are every day brought more and more closely in contact with those great problems, the solution of which is the chief public anxiety of the age. There are almost as many theories nowadays on the subject as there are charitable societies and benevolent persons; yet we do not seem to come any nearer to the root of the trouble. And we do not know that there is much possibility, in an age which has piled upon all its movements many more impedimenta in the shape of conventional systems and burdens since the age of Chalmers, of renewing such a great experiment, which indeed in all its conditions is Scotch, and closely connected with the parochial system which once was the pride of the northern kingdom, but which like other things has, we believe, been modified in many respects by a closer connexion with its powerful neighbour. But at all events the subject is one which is of the highest interest to all who have to deal with the questions of poverty and its help and relief. To Chalmers the whole matter was founded on religion, and by that only was made a practicable scheme. His agents were men all penetrated by that form of duty and love to one's neighbour which is the other side, the reflex and natural issue, of duty and love to God. The homely statement that "between a high tone of character and a high rate of wages there is a most intimate alliance," was the inspiration of leader and followers alike. The "high rate of wages" was secondary in an almost infinite degree to the other, but yet naturally proceeded from the other along with every other virtue and advantage It was a scheme for reducing and eventually destroying pauperism—that is true: but it was first a scheme for making men Christians, in the sure and certain hope that everything good would follow—one of the efforts continually repeated, continually foiled, but never, thank heaven, wholly given up, to persuade the world that the one great and simple expedient of being good, which i will never consent to try, is the solution of the grea problem and the only one. "What need of war and bloody crusades against the Moslem?" said our old and dear father in God, Francis of Assisi; "let me but go and convert them." "I will be good," said the littl Princess Victoria in the awe of hearing that she wa to be queen. It is the phrase of the nursery, thoug even there how hard to carry out! It is the only answe to all our questionings. "Let him that sinneth, sin n more." Alas, a Utopia more hard to establish than an conventional one! Yet the aim of all wisdom, howeve we may differ as to how it is to be brought about.

The manner in which Chalmers organized his paris was as follows. It was divided into twenty-five district or proportions as they are called, each embracing fro

ixty to a hundred families, and each placed in charge
f an elder and deacon, the first for spiritual help, the
econd for temporal. The whole management of the
auperism of the parish was confided to the deacons.
n each district was also planted one Sabbath-school
t least, sometimes more, the number of teachers being
etween forty and fifty. There were thus about a
undred persons employed day by day in the parish,
all for love and nothing for reward," knowing every-
ody and everybody's circumstances, behind the scenes
f all that teeming life, and ready for every office of
indness and watchfulness. We are told of one gentle-
nan, a wealthy merchant, with a beautiful house amid
he woods and waters which even then were so ready
f access, near Glasgow, who spent "two hours every
ay" in his proportion—and he was but an example of
nany. It must be remembered, however, that the aim
f all this, as over and over again repeated by Chalmers,
vas not as in so many instances to coddle and caress
chosen and favourite population with excessive kind-
ess, which is a thing not unfrequently seen, and
erhaps a greater danger in a well-managed parish
uled by kindness, than neglect. The autocrat of St.
ohn's was as kind as heaven, but as inexorable as fate.
Iis object was not to keep his poor people fictitiously
omfortable, but at any cost, even of discomfort, even of
omplaint, to keep them independent, to preserve them
y every strenuous art from becoming poor in the
echnical sense of the word, or depending on charity at
ll. It was an object very apt to be misunderstood,
nd indeed very difficult to understand at all, by those
o whom the limp ideal of religious charity had been
lmost indiscriminate giving. Chalmers hated giving

almost as a miser does, though for ends so different
His whole scheme of charity was to extinguish charity
His "agents," each man in his sphere, were inspired t
this instead: to find work where work was wanting
to stimulate mutual help and self-denial, to administe
private aid, neighbourly, in secret, removing obstacles
tiding over a special emergency, as friend may do with
friend—and above all to save the poor from the sham
of pauper-allowances and receiving of alms. Ther
was of course, as in all undertakings of a similar kind
disappointment on one hand and impatience on anothe
to be encountered and surmounted. But fortunatel
an idea so great, accompanied by all the friendly huma
warmth of constant contact, has a way of penetratin
a crowd, and it was not long before the reservation
as well as the bounties of the new system were unde
stood. Some curious instances in which tender Charit
thus stood by with a blank countenance, pretending a
austerity which on the surface seemed almost unkin
in order to let finer influences work, are very remark
able. There is something of the imagination of
poet in this mode of dealing with the vulgar detai
of penury, very apt to be misconceived, yet very nob
when the secret was known. Chalmers had the ac
ditional power of not being afraid of misconception
popular reproach. The following instances are fro
the notes of one of the workers—

"Typhus fever made its deadly inroads into a weaver
family, who, though he had sixpence a day as a pensio
was reduced to extreme and obvious distress. The cas
was reported to Dr. Chalmers, but no movement towar
any sessional relief was made—entire confidence wa

herished in the kind offices of the immediate neigh-
ourhood. A cry, however, of neglect was raised, an
ctual investigation of what the man had received in
he period of his distress was undertaken, and it was
ound that ten times more than any legal fund would
ave allowed him had been supplied willingly and with-
ut any sacrifice to the offerers.—A mother and daughter,
ole occupiers of a single room, were both afflicted with
ancer, for which the one had to undergo an operation:
he other was incurable. Nothing would have been
asier than to have brought the liberalities of the rich
o bear upon such a case; but this was rendered un-
ecessary by the willing contributions of food and service
f those living near this habitation of distress. 'Were
t right,' asks Dr. Chalmers, 'that any legal charity
vhatever should arrest a process so beautiful?' I
ever, during my whole experience in Glasgow, knew
single instance of distress which was not followed by
he most timely forthgoing of aid and sympathy from
he neighbours. I never found it otherwise, though I
ave often distinctly observed that whenever there was
stensible relief obtruded upon the eyes of the popu-
ation, they did feel themselves discharged from a re-
ponsibility for each other's wants and released from
he duty of being each other's keepers. One particular
ase of distress met the observation of the Female
Society at Glasgow, which society operates upon the
eneral population, and with a revenue of some
undreds a year, from which it can afford very little
n each individual instance, besides the impossibility of
aving that minute and thorough acquaintance with
he cases that obtains under a local management. I
emember having heard that a lady, an agent of that

society, went up-stairs to relieve this widow, and gave all that the Female Society empowered her to give, which was just five shillings. The people, observing this movement, felt that the poor woman was in sufficient hands, and that they were now discharged from all further responsibility, so that the opening-up of this ostensible source of relief closed up far more effectual sources that, I am sure, would never have failed her."

With this seeming sternness, but constant watchfulness, the system was carried on with the most triumphant and extraordinary success. Objection after objection was answered in the most overwhelming way by practical results. Thus one argument—which was that though the wealthy people who thronged to hear Dr. Chalmers on every available occasion filled the Plate with unusual offerings, that source of supply would cease when another less remarkable man occupied his place—was met, being foreseen, by the appropriation solely of the offertory (we apologize in such a connexion for using a word quite foreign to Scotch customs, simply because it is the most convenient) contributed at the evening service, when the church was reserved for the parishioners and the richer visitors were absent—"the pennies of the poor" thus sufficing for the parish charities. Another was that the doctor's scheme would starve the poor out of his own parish, and drive them into the adjoining districts—a possible insinuation which he had also guarded against by requesting that the law of residence should be rigorously enforced, his own impression being that instead of an "afflux out of his parish there would be an influx into it," and that "the poor themselves would be much better pleased with a system which, while it would do nothing for the idle and dissolute, brought human sympathy and kindness and all friendly aids to industry into the dwellings of those who were in real want." His foresight was fully justified: at the end of four years, it was found that fifteen had removed out of St. John's parish against the almost double number of twenty-nine removing into it, an evidence which could not be gainsaid. The last remaining argument, which is one which we are disposed to view with indulgence, was the plea of objectors who attributed the success of the scheme to 'the extraordinary eloquence and zeal of its author, and to the strenuous management of that select body of agents which he had gathered from all quarters of the city, and whom, by his presence and his impulsive energy, he had kept working at a rate of vigilant activity altogether unprecedented." Nothing could be more reasonable than this supposition, but even that, it appears, was not justified by the facts. The scheme continued to be worked for fourteen years after Chalmers left Glasgow. The testimony of his successor, Dr. Macfarlane, comes in with an amusing touch of self-satisfaction on this point: "I was agreeably disappointed," says this good man, "at finding that Dr. Chalmers was not the only person having sufficient influence to obtain the aid of the respectable members of his congregation in administering the affairs of the poor. I had not the smallest difficulty in procuring a sufficient number of deacons for that purpose." The practical result was that the pauper population of St. John's, which had cost the city a yearly subsidy of £1400, was, under the new scheme, provided for at a cost of £384; "or, deducting the expense for lunatics and deserted children, which, owing to peculiar circumstances, had come to press heavily upon the parish," £232—the largest sum being not much more than a fourth part of the original expenditure. This remarkable result was indeed only a small part of the advantages gained. "With an income from collections not much exceeding £300 a year," says the same Dr. Macfarlane, whom we have already quoted, "we kept down the pauperism of a parish containing a population of 10,000; and I know from actual observation that the poor were in better condition, and, excepting the worthless and profligate, who were refused assistance, even more contented and happy than the poor in the other parishes of Glasgow." An English Poor-Law Commissioner, Mr. Tufnell, who visited Glasgow in 1833, and made a thorough examination of the condition of the parish of St. John's, adds to all this his emphatic testimony—

"This system has been attended by the most triumphant success," he says, and adds a half-bewildered statement of the causes of that success, which must indeed have been curiously difficult for the official mind to grasp. "This personal attention of the rich to the poor seems to be one of the most efficient means of preventing pauperism. It is a subject of perpetual complaint that the poor do not receive the charities of the rich with gratitude. The reason of this appears to be, that the donation of a few shillings from a rich man to a poor man is no subtraction from the giver's comfort, and consequently is no proof of his interest in the other's welfare. If the rich give their time to the poor, they part with a commodity which the poor see is valuable to the givers, and consequently esteem the attention the more, as it implies an interest in their prosperity, and a feeling seems to be engendered in their minds of unwillingness to press on the kindness of those who thus prove themselves willing to sympathize with them in distress, and to do their utmost to relieve it. This feeling acts as a spur to the exertions of the poor; their efforts to depend on their own resources is greater, and consequently the chance of their becoming dependent on the bounty of others less."

Thus confused, and not knowing how to believe in, yet forced to accept a conclusion so different from all the usual laws as seen by a Poor-Law Commissioner, the visitor attempts to explain, by sentimental reasons curiously inadequate, what Chalmers calls "nature's own simple mechanism," the "process so beautiful" of mutual help, succour, and brotherly kindness, which the economist and philosopher, being at the same time a poet in deed if not in verse, would not allow to be interfered with by miserable alms and doles of charity. We do not pretend to say that Chalmers' great experiment was the origin of the wonderful parish agencies which between that time and this have grown up almost in every district of the United Kingdom; but it certainly was so in Scotland, and very likely may have had some share in pervading the atmosphere further south with that fertile seed. Nowhere else, however, was the same great effort of Christian statesmanship ever accomplished or even attempted, perhaps because nobody has ever had the courage to dare it, or the influence to push aside obstacles out of the way, and so make it possible to begin. And in point of fact these outside obstacles did push into the way again when there was no longer any one powerful enough to meet them. The stipulation as to the law of residence was disregarded, and the parish of St. John, notwithstanding that it had relieved the funds of Glasgow to so great an extent, was called upon to pay poor-rates for the benefit of the rest of the city. Under these and other encroachments of the authorities, which Chalmers, had he been there, would no doubt have found means of staving off, the managers of his system succumbed. The story of this brief but brilliant experiment remains accordingly only an episode in the history of the Church and the city, and as remarkable a one as has ever been recorded.

In the midst of all our higher admiration of these statesmanlike efforts for the good and elevation of the people, one turns at the same time with a whimsical relief to the doings of the young preacher who had come to be "the doctor's" assistant in his pulpit and parish, a certain tall, dark young man from the Border, Edward Irving by name, who, it is told, receiving a legacy at the moment when all these forces were in full operation, took it out in small coins, which he placed in a drawer, putting so much in his pocket every day till the little fund was exhausted, and sowing these surreptitious shillings through the parish wherever he moved. The wise doctor foresaw that too, and did not object, loving the dew of kindness wherever it fell, though he would have no formal irrigation of the soil.

In the meantime, by the side of all this deeply important secular work, Chalmers' own exertions were given to the spiritual instruction of his parish without stint. An English clergyman of the present day, possessed with the same enthusiasms of work, would multiply daily services and the administration of the rites of the Church to an extent which would have been inconceivable in that day. But at no time would the Scotch Churchman think of this. His ideal is not of daily matins in the church, but of daily "worship" in the family. He would rather hear the wavering psalm out of tune, the solemn, monotonous reading of "the chapter," the confused prayer, half formal yet much from the heart, rising from a poor room in a Glasgow "land," than the finest Church service. And that ideal still lingered in Scotland with all the force of a tradition still unexhausted. When Chalmers first set up his Sabbath-schools, the objection to them was that they would interfere with home catechizing, the spiritual instruction which it was the duty of parents at their own firesides to give to their children. Imagine the spiritual instruction likely to be conveyed around the domestic hearth in St. Giles's or in Clerkenwell! and the Gallowgate was scarcely a more refined abode. How strong, however, this feeling was may be divined from an expression in a newspaper report of the opening of St. John's Church. As we have already said, there were three services there every Sunday instead of the usual morning and evening "diet of worship." The first two services were for the great congregation which had followed Dr. Chalmers from the Tron, as they would have followed him anywhere, who paid a high rent for their pews, and thus indemnified the authorities for the building and expenses of the new church, and consisted of the "best families" in Glasgow and its neighbourhood. The last was for the parishioners of that very poor locality. This is how the *Glasgow Herald*, of the 27th September, 1819, recounts these details—

"From the intimations previously given, it was understood that the last of these services was meant for the exclusive benefit of the inhabitants of the parish, who are enabled by a wise and liberal arrangement on the part of the magistrates and council to obtain as good a right of occupation to the evening seats as is held by any other sitters among the day congregations of our city. The decidedly parochial aspect of the evening congregation was scarcely, if at all, impaired by any great admixture of hearers from the general and indiscriminate public. The impression was much heightened upon observing that the great body of the population on retiring from church, when they had reached the bottom of Macfarlane Street, turned in nearly an unbroken stream to the east, along the Gallowgate, or in the direction which leads to the main bulk of the parish and its inhabitants. It gives us pleasure to observe that the hour of meeting for the evening sitters is so early as four in the afternoon, thereby giving to this parochial diet the character and convenience of a day service, and enabling the hearers to spend an unbroken Sabbath evening in the bosom of their own families."

This reads almost like a satire in the present day, when the highest hope of many anxious and hardworking religious teachers is to organize, with abundant music and many details which suggest something like a religious entertainment, evening services which will "keep the men out of the public-house." The Gallowgate, we fear, did not even in these days present so many edifying scenes of family communion around tranquil firesides as are implied in the above description; but it shows at least that at that time the ancient tradition was not as yet entirely worked out.

And certainly, if incessant care and labour would have made it again a living rule, Chalmers' labours might have done so. When other people took their holidays in the high summer, when Clyde and all its beautiful coasts and outlets is so glorious, and every loch along the west coast opens its little paradise of woods and mountains for the refreshment of the hard-worked toilers of the darker year, Chalmers settled himself down, with an air of content and a long-drawn breath of relief and satisfaction in having got rid of all dinner-givers and disturbers of his peace, to the full enjoyment of the parish and its labours, the Gallowgate, and the Saltmarket. His wife and children even were away, and it is to this that we owe the details of an existence which is as wonderful as any other part of the story. Instead of going to the "Saut-water"—which is, or used to be, the graphic Glasgow description of sea-bathing quarters—"the doctor" with glee "rented a small apartment within the bounds of the parish." The description is a little grand, but what it meant was one small prophet's chamber in "Mrs. Hamilton's lodgings," the homeliness of which may be realized by the description. "I take one room from her, and the bed is to be put up on Monday. I took a lesson from you, and determined to settle beforehand about the rent. She said that would be according to the trouble, and condescended upon six or seven [1]

[1] It is amusing to note the Scotch peculiarities of phrase in this sentence. To "cast out" is to quarrel; to "condescend upon,"

shillings a week, but that we would not cast out. After such a moderate condescension as that, I do think that there is very little danger." Here, accordingly, the most popular preacher in Scotland, the hero-leader of the great city, whose name was known from one end of the kingdom to the other, settled down while his wife was absent, resorting to his own house only when parish business called him to that more habitable region. "This," he says, "will be a mighty improvement in any of my future parochial lodgments; and I feel and perceive the mighty charm of being much among the people in the capacity of their next-door neighbour."

We can scarcely wonder at the consternation of a visitor—an old Anglo-Indian, Dr. Bell, the founder of the Madras College in St. Andrews, and the system of education which has its head-quarters there—when ushered into this little room in the lodging-house, where the minister of St. John's was still in bed. "Is this the room of the great Dr. Chalmers?" said the astonished caller. How Chalmers occupied himself there we shall now see.

"I spend four days a week visiting the people, in company with the agents of the various districts over which I expatiate. I last week overtook between 700 and 800 people, and have great pleasure in the move-

---

to come to particulars. A "diet of worship" is a religious service. Dr. Chalmers was fond of describing himself as "expatiating" in his parish, not as may be supposed in words as describing or eulogizing it, but as roaming through it from street to street, and house to house. Another still more curious twist of meaning is when he speaks of the population of the Gallowgate as "peasantry," using the word as if it included all classes of the poorer inhabitants.

ment. At nine I go out to family worship in some house belonging to the district of my present residence, where I assemble the people of the land or close vicinity, and expect in this way to overtake the whole of that district. I furthermore have an address every Friday night to the people of my vicinity in the Calton Lancastrian school-room, and a weekly address will be necessary for each of the four weeks in St. John's Church to the people whom I have gone over in regular visitation. Add to all this the missionary meeting held yesternight, and you will find that without one particle of study I am in full occupation. My parochial operations are now at their most interesting crisis, and I do not feel that there is any church or congregation in Scotland that should tempt me to abandon them. There is a prodigious excess of day scholars (he had already built one school in the parish), insomuch that another fabric has been resolved upon, and measures have been taken to prosecute a subscription for it among the sitters, and we have already got four patrons of £25 each. The subscription is still in its infancy, and promises extremely well."

The meetings and services thus held for the benefit of the persons visited during the day became a very important part of the system, and were, according to the following account, of the most interesting description.

"These local week-day undress congregations, assembled in a cotton-mill, or the workshop of a mechanic, or the kitchen of some kindly accommodating neighbour, had a special charm for Dr. Chalmers, and all alive to the peculiar interest and urgency of such opportunities, he stirred up every faculty that was in him while he urged upon the consciences and hearts of such auditors the high claims of Christian salvation. His chosen and beloved friend, Mr. Collins, often accompanied Dr. Chalmers to these evening meetings; and we have his reiterated and emphatic testimony that no bursts of that oratory which rolled over admiring thousands in the Tron Church or in St. John's even equalled in all the highest qualities of eloquence many of these premeditated but unwritten addresses in which, free from all restraints and intent upon the one object of winning souls to the Saviour, that heart which glowed with such intense desires for the present and eternal welfare of the working-classes unbosomed in the midst of them all the fullness of its Christian sympathies."

We may quote here, however, Chalmers' own idea of these working-classes, and what the object of his constant labours among them was, which shows at once the high ideal of his view, his hearty, human recognition of that only equality which can really exist between man and man, and his often-stated conviction of the dependence of well-being on well-doing—the alliance between "high character and high wages," according to its homeliest scientific statement. He was then pleading for his newly-erected schools, which were apparently at that time a new idea in Glasgow—

"There will, I prophesy, if the world is to stand, be a great amelioration in the life of general humanity. The labouring classes are destined to attain a far more secure place of comfort and independence in the commonwealth than they have ever yet occupied, and this will come about, not as the fruit of any victory gained on the arena of angry and discordant politics, but far more surely as the result of growing virtue and intelligence among themselves. I trust the time is coming when humble life will be dignified, both by leisure and by literature; when the work of the day will be succeeded by the reading and the improving conversations of the evening; when many a lettered sage, as well as many an enlightened Christian, will be met with even in the very lowest walks of society; when the elements of science and philanthropy and high scholarship will so refine throughout the general mind of the country as to exalt it prodigiously above the level of its present character and attainments."

What would Dr. Chalmers have thought, we wonder, of Trades Unionism and those methods of attaining "reading and improving conversation" which have come less, we fear, through the influence of "growing virtue and intelligence" than by more vulgar means, universal debating clubs, and the flaming rhetoric which makes out all poverty to be an injury and all property an oppression? Human prophecy purchases its gleam of insight often by wonderful and wistful worlds of mistake. But the wish and desires of the philanthropist and reformer, the friend and lover of the poor, was towards a higher ideal than any dreamt of in the Trades Unions. He deprecates the thought that the object of his scheme of education was to "stir up a restless appetite for being removed from one sphere of earthliness to another sphere of earthliness."

"That object is to refine alike and to dignify alike every condition of earthliness. It is to give us the comfortable feeling, as we move through the swarms of population that issue from the manufactory and workshop, that instead of a rude mass of ignorance and its companion profligacy, we are in fact passing through a most respectable assemblage of human worth and human accomplishment. This has been verified in many individual instances, and did we only do what we ought, it will be verified thoughout the whole mass in the course of another generation. A most delightful eminence of mental cultivation has been attained by the ploughman of a country parish and by the mechanic of a city parish. It is clear as day to all who have been much in contact with those classes of society that there are among them the full capabilities for thus adorning their own condition with all the graces of cultured and well-taught humanity. And I repeat it, the main object of pouring a more copious and rich supply of education among them, is not to furnish them with the means of abandoning their status, but to furnish them with the means of morally and intellectually exalting it. It is not to raise them on the artificial scale of life, but to raise them on that far nobler scale which has respect to the virtues of the mind and the prospects of immortality. It is to confer a truer dignity upon each than if the crown of an earthly potentate were bestowed upon him. It is to pour the stores of knowledge into his understanding, and more especially of that sacred knowledge by the possession of which he becomes rich in faith and heir of that kingdom which God hath prepared for those that love Him."

Chalmers, however, was happier in some of his other previsions than he was in this noble statement of his hopes. It is the fault of human nature, and not of the philosopher, if education has not done so much as he desired and anticipated for the labouring man. From his two little schools in St. John's parish to the colossal system of free education, what an immense and incalculable progress! and yet it is to be feared that the "delightful eminence of mental cultivation" which Chalmers generously boasted to have seen attained by ploughmen and mechanics, has not spread through the whole mass as he fondly hoped it would. It has led to what a smattering of education so often leads to—an increase rather than a diminution of prejudice and hasty conclusions and mistaken principles. But in other ways his great sagacity and understanding carried him forward to conclusions which legislators arrived at much later, as well as to some which still are as devout imaginations to the wisest. At a time when the revolutionary spirit was abroad, and there was even a miserable attempt at insurrection, and the great city of Glasgow passed at least one day in the same mingled hush of resolution and alarm which made the threatened outburst of the Chartists so memorable in London, Chalmers was one of the first to suggest an expedient not adopted till long after, but which has been so long a part of the law of the land that we begin now, in this inevitable whirligig of time, to question whether we might not have been better without it. He writes as follows to Mr. Wilberforce, in December 1819—

"It were greatly more desirable to sweeten the spirits of the disaffected than to subdue them; and while I approve very much of certain minor expedients for this object—such as the repeal of the cottage-tax and of the taxes on the first necessaries of life to be commuted into an income-tax upon the wealthier classes—yet from my extensive minglings with the people I am quite confident in affirming the power of another expedient to be such that it would operate with all the quickness and effect of a charm in lulling their agitated spirits. I mean the repeal of the Corn Bill. I have ever been in the habit of disliking the interference of the Legislature in matters of trade, saving for the purpose of a revenue. The interference in question is perhaps of all others the one by which Government has incurred the greatest waste of popularity with the least return of advantage to the country; nor could they take a readier step than by recalling this measure to soothe the manufacturing districts of the country."

It was about a quarter of a century after this before the Government, forced by one of the strongest of popular movements, took the step which Chalmers suggested. It was a step which had become inevitable at the time—one wonders whether the time will ever come when a reconsideration of this question will be forced upon a legislature, more and more dependent upon the multitude, by an agitated and excited people again?

Had we taken the character of Chalmers as an ideal one, and here worked out its future career upon the ordinary laws of human development, we should have pictured him as accepting his reign in Glasgow as at once the climax of his righteous ambition, and the large sphere for which his large nature longed. He was not the model of a mild and benevolent pastor and apostle, nor was the ideal of a dispassionate legislator—occupied above all the tides of sentiment, with a profound study of the best and highest principles upon which men were to be ruled and guided for their own best advantage—his. He was of an imperious nature, born to command, not unready to fight, impatient of interruption and misconception, accustomed to carry through his purpose, whatever it was, with a high hand, to mould everything around him to his will; a natural despot, though a most genial and friendly one. There was not air enough for him to breathe (one would have said) in any limited sphere; and that the bigness of the enterprises in which he was engaged, the devotion with which he was regarded, the surrounding and following of just such men as this best class of Glasgow citizens afforded him—men not too intellectual, but recipient to the highest degree, open to the influences of an eloquence which was powerful enough to draw them out of themselves, and ready to catch fire at the enthusiasm of great things to be done—was all that he wanted and preferred. The strong practical side of his nature, his capacity for almost endless work, was not only called forth by a gigantic work to do, but by the practical force as well as the ready response of his friends, strong men like himself, who might have been contemptuous of all the petty machinery of parish economics, but sprang to the crusade on so large a scale against those giant forces on the other side which make a great city a hotbed of misery and crime. All this was in favour of the continuance of Chalmers' imperious and splendid career. He was a sort of Prince Bishop of Glasgow, whom it was impossible to oppose, whom magistrates and municipality trembled before, and who swept away like cobwebs every obstacle on his great impetuous and imposing way. That he was, on the other hand, the most reasonable man, ready to listen to any practical suggestion, and respecting the experience of his "agency" as a wise despot respects the wisdom of his councillors, are facts which take nothing from the great individuality of his character, which was all heroic, the embodiment of irresistible and characteristic force and power.

This is what we should have said, judging according to the laws of human nature. Never was man so qualified for his sphere. The size and impetus and uncontrollableness of him, even his impatience and often indifference to common methods, the great sweep and wind of his going, seemed to fit him above all others for this position, in which he was paramount and supreme. And we confess that all our ideas of what is life-like in nature are suddenly confounded when we find this great and energetic figure suddenly pause in the career thus shaped for him, like a ship in full sail with the most favourable winds sweeping her along upon her course, yet arrested in a moment in mid seas, and turning aside to some little haven where only the stress of storms would naturally drive such a vessel. Such is the effect produced upon the mind when we find Chalmers stop, at the height of his noble venture and in the flush of his triumphant success. It is hard to imagine even now how it was. There had not come the faintest shadow upon his success in any way. Wherever his voice was heard it seemed to bring forth a crowd as from the desert itself; whatever he laid his hand upon prospered. In London, in Edinburgh—wherever he went—there needed no trumpet to be blown before him, the mere whisper of his name was enough. His little kingdom, his ten thousand folk, were lifting gradually out of chaos into a nobler life; his little army was faithful to a man; his great plan, working so that it bade fair to vindicate every theory, and to prove the real way of salvation from pauperism and want. Why, then, did this great leader withdraw himself from his work, throw down his truncheon of command, leave his forces to the chances of a new general—not likely to be such a man as himself, and certainly not possessed by the scheme as he was who originated it—and withdraw into the quiet, into seclusion from all that had charmed and upheld him, the struggle with a national evil, the heroic triumphs of a holy war?

We are completely unable to give any answer to this question. Dr. Hanna, the biographer of Dr. Chalmers and his son-in-law, a man of admirable intelligence and with perfect command of all possible information, does not even attempt to throw any light upon this problem. We can scarcely imagine that it was merely a caprice of a mind so strong, and above the sway of circumstances. Yet there was a class of circumstances by which Chalmers was so fretted, and of which he was so impatient, that they no doubt influenced him to some degree in his strange decision. If he was impatient of the public business of an official character which hampered the path of a minister and occupied the time which ought to be devoted to more sacred duties, he was still more impatient of those hindrances which gather round the social life of every man who has the misfortune to be overwhelmingly popular, whose company is sought in all directions, and whom everybody desires to meet.

These troubles are generally surmounted with great magnanimity by the ordinary popular preacher; but to Chalmers they were an insufferable burden. He had been afraid of them when he came to Glasgow, and though he held in many cases his would-be entertainers very much at bay, there were times when this was difficult and his impatience overflowed. The following notes from his journal will show what his feelings were when this annoyance was coupled with the jealousy which so easily arises in every such competition for social favour—

"Mr. Falconer called between eleven and twelve. He told me that he had been dining lately with Mr. ——, who had complained bitterly of my neglect towards his family, and compared it with my attentions to Mr. B——, whom, by the way, I have only spent a single hour with in the evening for a whole half year: and Mr. Falconer concluded with recommending it to me to make up for my bygone negligence. I should have heard this with the utmost patience and charity, in which I am sorry to say that I failed. I should bear all things, and do all without murmurings or disputings, and be meek and gentle with all men. But at the same time it is obviously impossible that I can be dragged or dragooned into Mr. ——'s house in his present humour, or pay an attention extorted from one in the spirit of a jealous exactor; nor do I think it my duty to dine at my hearers' tables whenever they choose to let out an invitation. I must try to keep a charitable spirit towards him; and I am sure that my absence from his house bears no more reference to him particularly than it does to the hundred others who have kept asking and asking at me, and have just as good a right to be angry as he that I have never moved a single footstep to them. This is really a vulgarism which must be abolished. . . . They have conceived themselves to be grievously insulted by the neglect of unconscious me, who all the while was prosecuting my own affairs without the slightest intention either of offending them or any other body —who spoke when I was spoken to, and went to the church when the bell rang."

This may be considered as a glimpse into the nature of those smaller annoyances which are as the mosquitoes of life. Chalmers had many other and better reasons for desiring a change from the overwhelming occupations of his existence. He had pleaded vehemently against the official business which had threatened to overwhelm him in the beginning of his Glasgow life, urging his conviction of the necessity for time and study to a due performance of his duties as a preacher; while, on the other hand, he had felt his duties as the pastor of so large a parish demanded incessant labour, and would, if fully performed, leave no time for anything else. In addition to this, latterly he had been drawn into questions and thoughts of still wider interest: he had been led by his scheme of legislation for St. John's to a study of the English Poor-Laws and pauperism generally, to the consideration of the character and necessities of city populations, and to the mode of redemption from the ruin which he believed to be involved in the charity of the State—which were of larger scope than anything affecting a single parish. How was he to reconcile all these conflicting claims? And throughout everything, both the immediate circle of parish duties and all the greater schemes and subjects to which he felt his mind drawn —he was hampered and held down by chains of custom and conventional necessity; like Gulliver, bound to earth by innumerable minute cords. He had indeed succeeded in making of his parish a little kingdom, ruled by an economy of its own; but when he had laid the foundations, and established the framework of that system, and overcome all those difficulties which had been pronounced insuperable, Chalmers' great spirit longed for fresh woods and pastures new. He had been offered the charge of Stirling at an early period of his Glasgow career, with a playful proviso that the guns of the castle should be turned towards his gates to keep all intruders at a distance: but he had not entertained the idea of that or any other proposal which would have interfered with the carrying out of his great experiment. Later, when all the weariness and conflicts—"the fatigue and the sore vexation of Glasgow" were beginning to tell, he was offered by the magistrates of Edinburgh a church vacant there, which he declined in the following terms—

"You know that all my personal tastes and partialities are on the side of Edinburgh: nor, were it righ to indulge an earthly perspective, can I figure an sort of *beau idéal* that more regales my imaginatio than to retire from the fatigue and distraction c my present habits to the literature and intellectua society of our cultivated metropolis. Any situatio of superior Christian usefulness to the one that I no occupy, and which would at the same time affor tranquillity and leisure for the prosecution of theological learning, I should feel, in spite of all the ties that bind me to Glasgow, to be quite irresistible. But this is what I cannot look for in the mere exchange from one parish to another."

Chalmers, however, ended this letter of refusal by a very significant note. He thanked the magistrates of Edinburgh for their offer, and expressed his sincere desire to do nothing which should "disoblige or alienate a single individual among them." "The truth is," he added, "that there is not a body of men in the kingdom to whose patronage I should feel greater satisfaction in being indebted for such a retreat from the manifold activities of a parish as would not withdraw me at the same time from the service of Christianity, but only enable me to exchange the personal for the literary abours of my profession."

This intimation that he would accept a professorship —most of the chairs of the Edinburgh University eing curiously enough in the gift of the Lord Provost nd Bailies—is very distinct, and it was not forgotten hen the time came. Whether it was through this, or rom any other hint of his wishes, that the Principal of St. Andrews conceived the strange idea that a man so popular and so great might be approached with the offer f a modest chair, not even theological, in that small University, we have no means of knowing. It seems, ithout some such reason, the most presumptuous and reposterous notion that so extraordinarily influential nd successful a man as Chalmers should give up he really splendid and authoritative position which he eld as minister of St. John's to retire into the silence and gossip of a small community, and to teach Moral Philosophy to a small number of very youthful students, even though it was in his native county, and the University from which he had derived his own education. Preposterous as it was, however, we can scarcely say less than that Chalmers "jumped at" the proposal. He accepted it instantly, and without hesitation. The income of the chair was £300 a year, the most modest of stipends. On that side, assuredly, the most malicious of critics could not say that there was any inducement. Nor was there either ambition or opportunity, as far as could be seen, to justify the change. It might be in his power to add a higher tone, to introduce a more religious feeling into his expositions of the science of thought. But it was not even to the sacred subjects, which he felt to be highest in the world, that he could direct the minds of the handful of young men who were to replace for him the community of Glasgow, with all its far-reaching influences, and the still infant scheme which might have revolutionized the whole country and turned every parish in Scotland into a more excellent way. We confess that to ourselves the motives of Chalmers in this step were inexplicable. Fatigue and vexation there might be, but he was in the prime of life, forty two, a man of unbroken health and all the vigou of a sturdy and unexhausted race. The reasons which he gave to his astounded and distracted "agency" were no doubt genuine enough, and the desire i his mind to shake himself free of his labours an cares was indisputable in its vehemence and sincerity but still the step remains unaccountable. He told hi elders and deacons he was unable to combine due attention to his sermons with the innumerable calls of his personal and pastoral work. "My very last attempt at exertion out-of-doors has been followed up by several weeks of utter incapacity for fixed thoughts," he says. He explains how he had been led into "the fields of civic and economic speculation . . . . not because I knowingly turned me away from the objects of Christian usefulness, but because I apprehended that I there saw these objects before me; but the field has widened as I have advanced upon it, insomuch that I cannot longer retain the office which I now hold without injustice to my parish and congregation." Finally, he added that he held "even a literary office in a university, through which the future ministers of our parishes pass in numerous succession every year, to be a higher office in the vineyard even of Christian usefulness than the office of a single minister of a single congregation."

We cannot but feel something apologetic, even something sophistical, in these reasons for his change. And we return to the evident fact that it was the determined will of Chalmers to make this change, and that he did so with no sense of regret as for a great post abandoned and a great work relinquished at the most critical moment. Whether it might have been better for Scotland had he wrought out his great experiment and perhaps extended it over the country, an undertaking which would have been highly beneficial had it been, as there is every reason to believe, successful, not to Scotland alone—it is not for us to decide. There are many who may think that the work which occupied his later life was of more importance than this great re-organization of the country; while there are also many upon whom the disadvantages attending that work may more strongly impress themselves, and who will feel that the rending asunder of the venerable Church of Scotland was a kind of silent revenge of time for the abandonment of a more beneficent revolution. We can only record what did happen; but at this period of Chalmers' life with a great dissatisfaction and inability to enter into his motives, and with much regret.

CHAPTER IV.

It must be added, however, to the regrets and astonishment which we have ventured to express, that Chalmers' career in Glasgow was not unaccompanied by disappointment, and that one of his schemes, the building of a chapel-of-ease for the service of a section of his great parish, with the hope that this might eventually develop into an independent parish of its own, did not in any way fulfil his hopes. It was, what strikes us very strangely in these days, a proprietary chapel built by shareholders, who hoped by this means not only to serve the highest of causes, but to secure a certain interest for their money. It is very curious to find such a man as Chalmers not only embarking in such a speculation, but setting it on foot. The commercialism of his surroundings must have affected his thoughts in a singular way to lead to such an enterprise, and the whole conception is marked with that special unwisdom of the wise which is so much more elaborate and less excusable than the foolishness of the foolish; for while the chapel was erected in a poor district, and for the benefit specially of the poor, it was intended that the seat-rents should at once provide a stipend for the minister and pay the interest on the shares subscribed. Chalmers himself was the largest shareholder, and consequently the greatest loser by this curious scheme; and the mingling of the just but incongruous disappointment of an investor, with the sorrow of a Christian philanthropist over an unsuccessful effort, is disagreeable and very disturbing to the ideal. It was not till several years after his removal from Glasgow that the failure became fully apparent: when it was commented upon by himself in a letter of great severity and sternness to the unfortunate minister who, alas! we must say it, had not made the enterprise pay. We have no right to omit this jarring note.

Glasgow was overwhelmed by the loss of the great preacher, who had done almost what he liked with the economy and the heart of the city. The community was wounded, angry, outraged, like a cast-off lover. To leave that great field upon the wants of which he had expatiated so often, the swarms of helpers, the well-organized band which he had formed to fight all that penury and misery, the rich who gave almost whatever he wanted, and the enthusiastic whose sympathy surrounded him like a genial atmosphere—for what?—a little University, a small town with its coteries and gossip, a limited class-room, a little circle of only half-understanding students—it was no wonder if the greater sphere, the thronged and eager city, was astounded, and could not believe its ears. One thing could not be said, and that was the familiar and often-repeated accusation constantly put forth against a clergyman who leaves one position for another, that it was the worldly considerations of increased income or advantage that moved him. It was against his interest, against his importance, a voluntary withdrawal from applause and fame. The great city was confused, humbled, mortified, disappointed—there was a brief interval almost of estrangement, of hot discussion, attack and defence. But finally every other sentiment sank in one universal sense of loss and regret. When he took his farewell of Glasgow, the soldiers had to be called out to keep the church doors, which were being carried by assault of the crowd. Every homage that admiration and affection could give were heaped upon him; but he went away to his little Alma Mater, to his insignificant class-room, to the quiet, and so far as was possible, obscure place which he had chosen for himself, through an atmosphere vibrating with the clamours and magnetism of the multitude with a sigh of relief.

> "Who is the Happy Warrior?—who is he
> That every man in arms would wish to be?
> It is the generous spirit who, when brought
> Among the tasks of real life, hath wrought
> Upon the plan that pleased his boyish thought."

Notwithstanding all his schemes of legislation, and that great gift of eloquence which can never be so fitly exercised as in the large atmosphere of the world, this had been his ideal all his life.

It is curious to add that his study of political economy, in which his mind was so deeply interested, and which he twice brought forward publicly as one of his chief reasons for withdrawing into the quiet and leisure where he could pursue his investigations most fitly, dropped from him almost as soon as he attained that leisure and quiet. He published, indeed, the third volume of the *Christian and Civic Economy of Great Cities*, in which his view of various questions, still hotly debated at the present moment, is full of interest, as of wisdom. His chief object was still the new Poor-Laws, and in particular one regulation, much canvassed and criticized, by which public charity was used to make up the wages of working-men when subject to any depression of trade or failure of work. This interference with the laws of trade, and with the natural restrictions of supply and demand, was against every principle of his philosophy, and was denounced by him with great effect—so much so that his biographer considers his publication to have had much to do with the abolition of this rule. A question more important still, and which now occupies so much of the foreground of politics, the question of Trades Unions, was then in its earliest dawn. The repeal of the Combination Laws had made the league of workmen for mutual support a possible thing. "For a few months," says Dr. Hanna, unprescient of much trouble to come, "the effects of this repeal were most disastrous. Under the delusion that some new power had been given to them of coercing their masters, the workmen formed into monstrous combinations all over the country, ceasing in some instances for weeks and months together from all labour, and not only threatening, but executing violence upon those who consented to work. The alarm excited was excessive."

"Dr. Chalmers threw himself as an arbiter between parties driven into a temporary and ill-judged warfare. The occasion offered him a good opportunity for bringing forward some general speculations upon the proper province of legislation in such questions, and upon the natural and artificial influences by which the wages of labour are regulated: upon the principle that nothing should be ordained to be a crime by the legislature which is not felt to be a crime by man's natural conscience—that workmen should be left as free in the employment of their labour as their masters are in the employment of their capital. Dr. Chalmers loudly applauded the repeal of the Combination Laws. But while he strongly urged that no law should be enacted against combinations as such, he as strongly contended that the severest penalties should be visited upon everything, whether in the form of threat or force, by which the perfect freedom of the individual labourer was violated."

Thus Chalmers formed his opinions while yet the materials of judgment were small, and the greatness of the danger which now rends the foundations of society unknown. What would he think now of those "monstrous combinations" which threaten more and more every day to become one of the greatest tyrannies which the world has ever known—tyrannies which would seem to be so strong a necessity of human nature that under one form or another they are continually reappearing, balking every law of freedom? Strikes were but infantile and struck no awe into the general heart in those days; but the far-seeing judgment and wise instincts of the man who saw that they were inevitable conditions of a new *régime*, yet sought to secure the strongest safeguards for personal freedom, so darkly menaced by them, are very remarkable.

But when he had published this volume, Chalmers withdrew from a region in which he seemed so well qualified to exercise a commanding influence. The quiet for which he had longed, stifled and silenced him. He withdrew from all the larger questions of public life. It is true that he never failed in personal labours, nor, above all, in those evangelical enterprises which were so dear to his heart; but even in these his sphere was small, his work subdued and obscure. He had a class in his house on Sundays, at first for the children of a district in St. Andrews, which he worked like one of his faithful retainers in Glasgow—and afterwards for the students; but nothing on a grander scale was possible in the little place which he soon found was no haven of rest. All around him were constituted rights, forbidding interference: and the close contact of a small community is not always made more easy or without friction by the existence of a high level of intellectual life among them. It does not seem to us that in any way the experiment of Chalmers was a successful one, and certainly one of the chief objects for which it was made, dropped from him with that single publication, and was seen no more.

This is not, however, to say that the five years of his residence in St. Andrews was either without fruit or without comfort. Dr. Hanna tells us that his residence in that very characteristic little town, so full of all the traditions of Scotch humour, wit, and clear-headedness, little given to sentiment, and much to strong expressions and acute criticism, transformed the place, and created a softened atmosphere of piety and fervour amid its population, intellectual and otherwise. Dr. Chalmers, in his own journals, scarcely however bears out this impression. The leisure and continual social intercourse, so humorous, often full of the keenest interchanges of satire and of jest, as well as of high thinking and serious meaning, which we have learned to know in later generations and to enjoy at second-hand as one of the most characteristic phases of Scotch society, were not of a kind to please this large and serious individual soul, who could not be still, or saunter, or spend hours in talk: and though he loved a quiet round at golf, and the free-and-easy comments of the caddies describing how "the Principal tappit every ball," he soon gave it up because he thought it impaired his power for work. Perhaps it was a more common rule in St. Andrews at that period to do in the way of work as little as was indispensable, and enjoy the quiet life which Providence had accorded, without being disturbed by zealous dreams of toil uncalled-for. The religion of the district was "Moderate," that admirable title, descriptive of a state of sober feeling, in which there was, no doubt, much reserve of genuine belief and piety, but little demonstration of that faith which can move mountains. It is a name which was used, and was intended to be used, in a derogatory sense, an epithet of contempt, and as such was bandied about in Scotland till the use of it became a kind of anathema. We do not take up the defence of that substratum of Scotch religious character. It has always been in the background, carrying out no ideal of the national imagination. At all events it was at the very antipodes of feeling from the vehement, absolute, and impatient spirit of Chalmers, and this alone was enough to take all the enchantment from the scene.

Amid this effacement of himself and withdrawal from the busy scenes which he had so largely filled, there were, however, some appearances of note in the General Assembly, where he began to take a more and more important part. One great question, that of pluralism, had been long a subject of the greatest interest to him.

The pluralism possible to a Scotch minister was of a very limited kind. He could not hold a string of livings, as had been, during one dreary period, common enough in the Church of England, nor add anything like a fat-prebend or cathedral stall to his cure. He could, however, which was still less appropriate, as involving a much greater amount of occupation and labour, distinct from his most important charge, combine a professorship with his incumbency. Chalmers, as the reader will recollect, had himself done so, and had defended his position with all the vehemence of his hot-headed youth, before he had realized what it was to hold a cure of souls. He had opposed the conjunction with equal vehemence after the change in his views, and had been for many years its strongest opponent. At the end of his career in Glasgow the question had been strongly revived by the appointment of the Principal of the University there to the High Church of Glasgow, a large and important parish. This appointment was strongly opposed, and as strongly defended, the Evangelical party in the Church, in which Chalmers was already conspicuous as a leader, straining every nerve against it: and the question was carried by appeal from one Church Court to another, and finally to the General Assembly, where the appointment was sustained to the great grief of the reforming party. Though there was at the moment little prevision of a still greater controversy which was to follow, and which was destined to shake the Church of Scotland to its foundations, there was already a note of warning in the speech of Chalmers on this occasion, which may be remarked. The most persistent tradition of the Scotch Church was that of her own self-government and absolute authority in all internal matters. She had never yet come into absolute collision with the State on any of these questions, partly no doubt because of the "Moderate" character, the cautious avoidance of any such conflict, which had prevailed for a long time within her borders. But the question of the appointment of the Principal of Glasgow University to a city church was precisely one which might have brought about that collision, since, had the Assembly opposed it, it was quite possible that the Glasgow authorities might have pressed their nomination, and forced their presentee into outward possession of what are called in Scotland the "temporalities," the stipend, and the ecclesiastical buildings, even in opposition to the decision, hitherto considered in theory as supreme, of the Church. "We can never dream," said Chalmers in his speech on the subject, "that this final sentence, if given in our favour, is not to be effective." It was the first sound of the trumpet in a war which had not yet begun. And he proceeds with a serious anticipation of an inevitable conflict.

"But if it could possibly be otherwise—if on the plea that the Church hath overstepped her boundaries, it is found that there are a right and force in the mere presentation which shall carry it over all your resistance, then I cannot imagine a feebler instrument, a more crippled and incompetent machinery than our Church is for the professed objects of its institution: nor do I see how, if struck with impotency like this, it can lift an arm of any efficacy to protect our Establishment from many great evils, or to stay the progress of a very sore corruption within our borders."

This question, however, had not as yet come among the controversies of the ecclesiastical parliament. And in the meantime the question of Pluralities was that on which the position of Chalmers as leader was most definite. He brought forward a motion for their abolition in the following year, and it was in the course of the debate which followed that a remarkable and picturesque incident occurred. The discussion had lasted one whole day till midnight, and the second day was nearing its close, when one of the speakers on the opposite side produced, and quoted from an anonymous pamphlet, in which the author declared that from what was to him the highest of all authority—the authority of his own experience—he could assert that "after the satisfactory discharge of his parish duties a minister may enjoy five days in the week of uninterrupted leisure for the prosecution of any science in which his taste may dispose him to engage." It was a perfectly legitimate use against himself of the early utterance of his youth, an expedient which has been not unfrequently resorted to in debate, but never, that we can remember, with such an overwhelming force of reply. Chalmers rose amid the breathless silence of the House to make his defence. And this was what he said—

"Sir, that pamphlet I now declare to have been a production of my own, published twenty years ago. I was indeed much surprised to hear it brought forward and quoted this evening. But since that gentleman has brought it forward in the face of this House, I can assure him that I feel grateful to him from the bottom of my heart for the opportunity he has now afforded me of making a public recantation of the sentiments it contains. I now confess myself to have been guilty of a heinous crime, and I now stand a repentant culprit before the bar of this venerable Assembly. The circumstances attending the publication of my pamphlet were shortly as follows: As far back as twenty years ago I was ambitious enough to aspire to be successor to Professor Playfair in the mathematical chair of the University of Edinburgh. During the discussion which took place relative to the person who might be appointed his successor, there appeared a letter from Professor Playfair to the magistrates on the subject, in which he stated it was his conviction that no person could be found competent to discharge the duties of the mathematical chair among the clergymen of the Church of Scotland. I was at that time, sir, more devoted to mathematics than to the literature of my profession; and feeling grieved and indignant at what I conceived an undue reflection on the abilities and education of our clergy, I came forward with that pamphlet to rescue them from what I deemed an undeserved reproach, by maintaining that a devoted and exclusive attention to the study of mathematics was not dissonant to the proper habits of a clergyman. Alas, sir, so I thought in my ignorance and pride. I have now no reserve in saying that the sentiment was wrong, and that in the utterance of it I penned what was most outrageously wrong. Strangely blinded that I was! What, sir, is the object of mathematical science? Magnitude, and the proportions of magnitude. But then, sir, I had forgotten two magnitudes. I thought not of the littleness of time—I recklessly thought not of the greatness of eternity!"

The effect of this apology was extraordinary; the House listened in profound silence, with mingled awe and sympathy, to so impressive a confession. But he did not carry his motion, though he increased that enthusiasm and faith in him which was to become more and more a power in the nation and the Church.

He was not happy, however, in his changed and limited sphere. Doubts whether he had after all been right in accepting it seem to have assailed him in the quiet. "Visited with melancholy thoughts," he writes in his journal, "when I dwell on the uncongeniality of my present neighbourhood, on the prospect of next winter, on the fancied decay of my talents, on the decline of my circumstances (my regular income not being adequate), and on the review of my splendid correspondence a few years ago. Against all this desire to be fortified by the sublime hopes and associations of eternity." He was not, however, left very long in this partial obscurity; his influence, and the public consciousness of the great power thus within reach for great uses, grew in the progress of these quiet years. After spending five years in St. Andrews, in 182 Chalmers entered upon a new sphere. He had been appointed to the Chair of Divinity in the University of Edinburgh in the previous year. He declined, as he always did, to seek the appointment in any way, but was so congenial to all his wishes that he had no hesitation in accepting it when it was offered to him. The student of his life cannot but feel a sensation of relief and exhilaration when Chalmers thus returns to the larger sphere for which he was in every way fitted. The results of his five years in St. Andrews, if they did not bring to him the comfort and repose he had hoped for, were in many other ways of high importance and encouragement. His power of teaching and influencing youth—the class which he thought of all others the most important, the future clergy of the country—was proved, and he had the gratification of feeling that he had carried with him in the fullest degree the enthusiasm and sympathy of the young men about him, leavening their intellectual fervour with profound Christian sentiment, and leading them into the work he himself delighted in, the culture and elevation of the poor. One remarkable result of his work was the great number of his students—among them the distinguished missionary, Dr. Duff—who devoted themselves to missionary labours in India and elsewhere.

In Edinburgh Chalmers at once assumed his natural place as a great leader of the Church and one of the most important personages in Scotland. Not only were his footsteps followed by crowds wherever he made any personal appearance, but he was consulted with the most remarkable deference by the public authorities and the statesmen of the time. Appointments were made by Government on the almost sole ground that hey were agreeable to this prince of the Church, and his support and advocacy of the most important measures were solicited by the highest functionaries of the realm, n terms which show their consciousness of his authority lmost as if it were that of an independent power. n this way his help was appealed to on the great ubject of Catholic Emancipation, and, still more remarkable, he was called to London to give his opinion nd aid to a Parliamentary Committee sitting in council pon the great and never-exhausted subject of Irish distress, though his knowledge of Ireland was little more than that which could be obtained on a holiday journey. It is amazing when we look back to see how strangely different from the present was the then state of the country and the public questions which occupied it. Parliamentary Reform and Catholic Emancipation were both questions hotly discussed, and still capable of different solutions to those which we have known all our lives. The very conditions upon which our present life is founded did not exist. The trade of the country was bound by the Corn Laws, and by the existence of many monopolies; the Poor-Laws were a rife and continual subject of discussion; there were no factory laws or regulation of labour. The Churches of England and Scotland, the Universities, and many public appointments, were defended (as was supposed) by the Test and Corporation Laws, which made a participation in the most sacred rite of Christianity, according to one or another form, a necessary preliminary of office. It is very difficult for us, amid the broader lines of our present living, to realize that condition of affairs in which all this network of bonds and restrictions caugh the feet at every turn.

Chalmers was one of the bold and manly reformer who opposed them all. He wanted no pains an penalties to surround the bulwarks of religion. H desired no bondage of tariff or impost upon trade. H had confidence in the force of both, but especially th first, to make way against all resistance and all difficult One of his early efforts in the Assembly after his settl ment in Edinburgh was to lead that venerable body t express publicly by an address of congratulation to th King the gratitude of the Church and country for th repeal of the Test and Corporation Acts, a measure which he spoke of as "this delightful Bill." He did not succeed in this, but he at least expressed very plainly his own sentiments and those of the ever-growing party which looked up to him as its leader. Still more notable was his utterance in respect to Catholic Emancipation. Before the Bill was brought in he received a letter from Sir James Mackintosh, anxiously appealing to him for support, to which he replied with characteristic appreciation of one side at least of the matter: "I have never had but one sentiment on the subject of the Catholic disabilities, and it is that the Protestant cause has been laid by them under very heavy disadvantages, and that we shall gain prodigiously from the moment that, by the removal of them, the question between us and our opponents is reduced to a pure contest between truth and error." He amplified this view of the subject, which was one perhaps not taken very much account of by statesmen, at a great public meeting in Edinburgh, to petition in favour of the Bill—

"We are not hostile, neither are we indifferent to the holy cause of Protestantism. I cannot answer for others, but in vindication of myself, I can at least say it is in the spirit of devotedness to that cause that I come here, and because in this emancipation of Papists I see for Protestants a still greater and more glorious emancipation. The truth is, that these disabilities have hung as a dead-weight around the Protestant cause for more than a century. They have enlisted in opposition to it some of the most unconquerable principles of nature: resentment because of injury, and the pride of adherence to a suffering cause. They have transformed the whole nature of the contest, and by so doing they have rooted and given tenfold obstinacy to error. They have given to one side the hateful aspect of tyranny; while on theirs we behold a generous and high-minded resistance to what they deem to be oppression. They have transformed a nation of heretics into a nation of heroes. We could have refuted and shamed the heretic out of his errors, but we cannot bring down the hero from his altitude; and thus it is that from the first introduction of this heterogeneous element into the question, the cause of truth has gone backward. It has ever since been met by the unyielding defiance of a people irritated but not crushed under a sense of indignity; and this notable expedient for keeping down the Popery of Ireland has only compressed it into a firmness and closed it into a phalanx which, till opened up by emancipation, we shall find tc be impenetrable.

"Gentlemen would draw arguments from history against us, but there is one passage in history whicl they can never dispose of. How comes it that Protestantism made such triumphant progress in these realms when it had pains and penalties to struggle with? and how came this progress to be arrested fron the moment it laid on these pains and penalties in it turn? What have all the enactments of the statute book done for the cause of Protestantism in Ireland and how is it, when single-handed truth walked througl our island with the might and prowess of a conqueror so soon as propped up by the authority of the Stat and the armour of intolerance was given to her, th brilliant career of her victories was ended? It wa when she took up the carnal and laid down the spiritual weapon—it was then that her strength went out of her. She was struck with impotency on the instant that from a warfare of principle it became a warfare of politics. With the pains and penalties to fight against, the cause of the Reformation did almost everything in Britain. With the pains and penalties on its side, it has done nothing and worse than nothing in Ireland."

Chalmers' prophecy that when these restrictions were removed the question, "reduced to a pure contest between truth and error," would soon be solved in the most desirable way by the conversion of Ireland to a more enlightened faith, has turned out to be one of those devout imaginations which are not justified by events; but it was at least a noble and generous way of considering a question which tore the nation asunder, and which many good people regarded with very different feelings. His ideas in respect to the condition of Ireland—alas! a question so constantly discussed, the problem of all recent generations, and still so far from being settled—are more remarkable still. They are of a character which never becomes old-fashioned, nor perhaps ever ceases to be visionary. What Chalmers advocated was the same rule which Bishop Berkeley would fain have applied—the remedy for all things which the world has never yet tried among all its expedients—to make the people good, that simplest, all-embracing, unquestionable remedy! The great Scotch preacher stood before the bar of the Committee assembled to consider that question, and propounded his case with the noble gravity of his strong conviction. With what sentiments they listened to him, and what they thought of his method, we are not informed; but it is interesting to quote what this high optimist, this Christian reformer, said. One of the questions immediately before the Committee was the expediency of introducing the English system of Poor-Laws into Ireland. Chalmers was not called in the usual authoritative way, but invited, "if not entirely inconsistent with other duties and engagements," to give them the benefit of his experience, which, the question being so near his heart, he was very ready to do. His examination proceeded as follows—

"The population of Ireland being chiefly potato-fed, which is a crop attended with great fluctuations and casualties, do you consider that those fluctuations and casualties would render a system of compulsory relief advisable?"

"Quite the reverse."

"In what respect do you consider the assessment principle would be productive of evil under the circumstances?"

"I think it would just add to the recklessness and improvidence of the people, and so land the country in a still greater population without increased means of maintaining them. If I may be permitted, I will advert to a principle which I think may be called the pervading fallacy in the speculations of those who advocate the establishment of a poor-rate in Ireland, and is founded on the observation of a connexion between a high state of character and a high state of economic comfort. It is quite palpable that so it is in fact; but there seems to be an important mistake in the order of causation. It is often conceived that comfort is the cause, and character the effect; now I hold that character is the cause, and comfort the effect. It does not appear that if you lay hold of a man thirty or forty years old, with his inveterate habits, and improve his economic condition by giving him through a poor-rate or otherwise three or four pounds a year more, it does not appear to me that this man will be translated thereby into other habits or higher tastes, but he will dissipate it generally in the same reckless and sordid kind of indulgence to which he had been previously accustomed; whereas, if instead of taking hold of the man and attempting to elevate him by the improvement of his economic condition, you take hold of the boy and attempt to infuse into him the other element, which I conceive to be the causal one, by means of education, then you will, through the medium of character, work out an improvement in his economic condition. What I should advise is, that education should be made universal in Ireland, and that you should weather for a season the annoyance of Ireland's mendicity, and the annoyance of that pressure which I conceive to be altogether temporary. This appears to me the only principle upon which Ireland can be securely and effectually brought to a higher standard of enjoyment, and into the state of a well-habited and well-conditioned peasantry. I think that, if patiently waited for, very great results might be looked for ere another generation pass away; but then the establishment of a Poor-Law would throw a very heavy obstruction indeed on that educational process to which alone I look for a permanent improvement in the state of Ireland."

It is this to which he turns again and again in the course of his examination. High character first, economical improvement afterwards. Improvidence, over-population, everything, he conceives, is to be ameliorated by these means ; not by emigration—except as perhaps "an auxiliary to the cure"—not by any artificial method. "The people are in an uneducated state, with perhaps no great infusion of Christian principle in their minds; it is this which produces misery and a low economic condition." The thing for England, for the Government, for all the friends of Ireland to do was to make the people good—simplest yet most impossible of all actions. If it could but be done, how certain the issue; how well to wait and have patience with Ireland's mendicity or any other trouble in the world! But the speaker, who had but a short time before confessed his misconception of two magnitudes, had again fallen into the same blunder in a far more magnanimous way. He had forgotten the waywardness of human nature, that great incalculable force which cannot be moulded according to any wish. He had forgotten the fallibility of all human modes of instruction. Nevertheless, his lofty and generous opinions, his visionary yet so practicable advice remains, like a unused lighthouse over those dark waters, catching in all its reflectors, if not the lights of earthly manufacture, yet the sunshine of heaven.

During this period, in January 1832, Chalmers published what he wished to be his great work. "My chief earthly ambition," he had written five years before in the privacy of his journal, "is to finish a treatise on Political Economy, as the commencement of a series of future publications on Moral Philosophy and

Theology. Consecrate this ambition and purge it of all sin and selfishness, O God." This work embodied in still fuller force of expression those ideas and opinions to which he had already given vent on every practicable occasion, as his scheme for the redemption of the country. It came into the world at an inauspicious moment, just when the climax and outcome of a period of great national agitation had produced the Reform Bill—a measure in which, as in so many since, the mass of an uneducated people believed as in a charm, which was to bid not only all the tempests and clamours of political trouble, but all the seethings of poverty and distress, and all the problems of advancing yet crushing civilization, cease. We are all well enough aware now that the franchise does not do very much for any one, and that the springs of well-being lie deeper down in nature than anything that can be touched by a vote. But it was the first time this panacea had been tried, and it was not perhaps much wonder that in the perplexity of men's minds it was looked upon as a cure for all the troubles of the time. Chalmers was too good a philosopher to put faith in any such easy method, and therefore we are told that he was "not in favour of the Reform Bill." It was the first measure for what was supposed to be the good of the people of which he had not been in favour, and no doubt his distrust of it arose simply from his sense that as a panacea it was naught, and touched none of the deeper principles in which the springs of well-being and moral recovery are.

"He had studied long and closely the question how the great mass of the labouring population of the country, in so many instances toil-worn and over-driven, could be sustained in sufficiency and comfort, could be prevented from sinking, as he saw many of them doing, into greater straitness of circumstances, and into the necessity of severer toil. He heard it on all hands asserted that this great change in the mode of electing representatives was to effect a mighty amelioration upon the economic condition of the people. He utterly disbelieved such assertions; and more particularly as to that class of the community on whose behalf his own labours and sympathies had for years been expended. He was satisfied that it was to build up the labouring man of Britain in an egregious and misleading delusion, to direct him to the mode in which the members of the House of Commons were appointed, or to the measures which they might adopt, as to the main fountain of any great and permanent improvement in his economic condition."

There are few thinkers now who would be out of accord with the conclusion of Chalmers on this question, though the delusion has spread downwards in ever wider and wider circles, and what is called the enlightened working-man of to-day has gone back to the wild folly of public workshops and employment provided by the State, to take the place of all economic principles whatever, and all the spontaneous action of wholesome and independent life. But it is not for us to enter into any discussion of such matters. We have the word of John Stuart Mill, no mean authority, nor at all likely to have any bias in favour of a Christian philosophy, that "the simple explanation" of the fluctuations and recoveries of wealth "was never given by any political economist before Dr. Chalmers, a writer many of whose opinions I think erroneous, but who has always the merit of studying phenomena at first hand, and expressing them in a language of his own which often uncovers aspects of the truth that the received phraseologies only tend to hide."

We are not called upon either to enter into any discussion of this work, which was not received with the popularity or respect which had attended the former productions of Chalmers. The head of the country was turned by its supposed great and intoxicating progress, in the opening of the way which has had so many further developments since—and it did not care, in its excitement, to hear the sober voice which bade it put no trust in any external remedy. Dr. Chalmers' cure for national ills was not a sudden and dazzling one. "The highway to this is education." "Education is the specific" are the sign-posts erected through these pages. "Character is the parent of comfort, the best creator, preserver, distributor of wealth." The country in the flush of a new development, in the supposed triumph of every liberal principle over the effete and antiquated, was scarcely in a humour to accept such conclusions as these. Whether they are to be relied upon even now, and if the panacea of education will do more than the other panaceas, it remains to be seen, and the indications are perhaps not so hopeful as were the prognostics of Chalmers. But it is a noble faith which thus proclaims its unfaltering dependence upon a higher revolution to come.

"It will be the aggregate effect of a higher taste, a higher intelligence, and, above all, a widespread

Christianity throughout the mass of the population; and thus the most efficient ministers of that gospel which opens to them the door of heaven, will be also the most efficient ministers of their temporal comfort and prosperity upon earth. Next to the salvation of their souls, one of our fondest aspirations in behalf of the general peasantry is that they shall be admitted to a larger share of this world's abundance than now falls to their lot. But we feel assured that there is no method by which this can be wrested from the hands of the wealthier classes. It can only be won from them by the insensible growth of their own virtue. The triumph will be a glorious, but to be effectual and enduring, it must be a pacific one—won not on the field of blood or amid the uproar of furious and discordant politics. It will be a sure but a silent victory, the fruit of a moral warfare, whose weapons are not carnal but spiritual; and which shall at length come to a prosperous termination, not in strife and anarchy and commotion, but in showers of grace from on high upon the prayers and labours of the good."

Another piece of literary work undertaken by Chalmers during this calm period of his life was a Bridgewater Treatise, which he was invited by the Bishop of London to contribute to that series. *On the Adaptation of External Nature to the Moral and Intellectual Constitution of Man* was the subject he chose, and it was received with much favour by the public. His reign as a preacher was by no means impaired by the fact that he had no pulpit of his own where his appearances were punctual and certain, but was only to be heard occasionally and at special moments. Many invitations were addressed to him to induce him to resume the charge of a parish, among others that of the West Church in Greenock, one of the few prizes of the Scotch Church. Dr. Chalmers heartily thanks the patron, Sir Michael Shaw Stewart, for the offer of "the most lucrative ecclesiastical living in Scotland, whose endowments, I believe, are nearly double those of the one which I now occupy." "You have, in fact," he says, "conferred upon me a substantial favour by having placed within my reach a benefice so lucrative. You have enabled me to say, in language which cannot be mistaken, in what estimation I hold the professorships of theology throughout Scotland; and in pleading whether for the virtuous patronage or for the adequate endowment of these high offices, your offer of the parish of Greenock will effectually shield me from any ungenerous imputation to which I might otherwise have been exposed."

Thus he held his place, glad only to have it, proud that gain was not what he sought, the always ready, vulgar indictment against clergymen in general—and exercising a sway which is beyond all the privileges of wealth or position over the thoughts and impulses of his country. The great conflict of his life and time, the most remarkable struggle and event in the recent history of Scotland, was about to begin, and to sweep him away in the progress of its development from much that he held most dear. We linger with regret on the milder period in which all issues were less tragic, when the unity was disturbed only by natural divisions such as exist always in every human society, divergences of opinion, differences of constitution and thought; but when no rent had been made in the garment of the Church, and it was one not only in faith and doctrine, as it has always remained, but in economy and outward form. That period, perhaps, like other periods of the past, takes

> "A glory from its being far,
> And orbs into the perfect star
> We saw not when we walked therein":

but looking back upon it, the philosophic reader will not be able to refrain from a regret, nor the patriot from a sigh, nor perhaps the more hot-headed spectator from an unauthorized anathema of denunciation against the trifling persons unknown to any other human record, whose struggle against all the laws of their Church for promotion and a living brought about a catastrophe which no persecutions nor oppositions of power had been able to effect, and which has left a wound in the heart of Scotland which, so far as can be foreseen, nothing is likely to heal.

CHAPTER V.

BEFORE we enter upon the great question which presently was to tear both Scotland and the Church in two, and in which Dr. Chalmers was so much instrumental, and took so great a part that it figures in the estimation of many as the principal point in his life, we must refer to a matter much more truly expressing the greatest pre-occupation and desire of that life, the system of Church Extension, which to him meant the redemption of Scotland both morally and physically. The reader, who has seen his exertions in Glasgow, and been made aware of his impassioned conviction that the work of the Church, and the constitution of the parish, were the only, or at least the far better way of reclaiming a population which had exceeded all the old boundaries, will understand with what a vehemence of desire and warmth of advocacy he threw himself into the scheme of reorganizing Scotland, especially in the great towns, and placing within reach of every district, however poor, the Church, the parish institutions, the school, the parochial scheme of charity, in which all his hopes, both as a Christian and a patriot, were embodied. The one consistent endeavour in his life all through, from the time when

N

he learned its alphabet in humble Kilmany in his first experiments, until that in which, close upon the threshold of the grave, he gave his best attention to the "territorial Church," built by his exertions and called by his name in one of the poorest districts of Edinburgh, had been this. The Non-Intrusion controversy, the Disruption, the organization of the Free Church, which occupy so much room in the history of his later days, may almost be called accidents in his career —accidents of the most important kind, yet more or less forced upon him, unpremeditated and undesired—but his inspiration, his enthusiasm, his whole heart of work and longing were for this. He believed in the gospel as the one means of saving and elevating the masses which in every country are so apt to fall into both moral and physical degradation, especially in the crowded streets of quickly-growing towns, where they herd together and entrench themselves in ignorance and penury and want, with at once a sense of neglect and a sense of resistance, bitterly resenting the one, yet fiercely setting up the other against efforts made in their behalf. Chalmers had that preference for the poor which it is not at all unusual to find among clergymen who feel the superior ease of access to them, and the absence of ceremony and precaution, to be a great relief amid those complications of society which make so many people in a different sphere irritated rather than attracted by exertions for their individual spiritual well-being. He who was happy in his little lodging among the Glasgow slums, where he could feel himself on terms of next-door neighbourship with his weavers and cotton-spinners, believed in that way, having himself tried it, of driving out the demons, and bringing in all the charities and beneficent influences of a higher life. A small parish, a little church, an active minister, always about the cluster of streets which formed his domain, a dozen or so of elders and of deacons, and the Plate at the church doors—with these conditions he was ready to face the world, and to pledge his hearty and generous word to Queen and Government that there should be, instead of vice, pauperism, and discontent, purity and peace and honest labour in every division of the realm. It was a great thing to undertake, but it was the absolute belief of this man who knew what he was saying, who was no theorist, but had personally tried the method which he had advocated. This was the real and true object of his life: to have the Scotland of the nineteenth century mapped out as primitive Scotland had been, while Glasgow was still but a small place, and crowded streets were almost non-existent: and to bring to bear upon each handful of people the ancient laws and economy of the parish, the system which had made of Scotland in more primitive times the best educated and the most independent and self-helping of kingdoms. It was a system which had been triumphantly successful in these early times. It had been triumphantly successful under extraordinarily different circumstances, when fully and honestly tried, in St. John's parish in Glasgow. He had no doubt whatever of its success everywhere, when fully and honestly tried. There would be no finer and nobler work for any man, and this was the true and lasting inspiration of Chalmers' life.

He had proposed that his plan should be tried in Glasgow while he was still there, but it had not met with any general approval. And perhaps his own immediate surroundings were too much absorbed in their great exertions for St. John's parish to be prepared to undertake the greater work. But thirteen years after, the seed he had sown suddenly came to fruit. Mr. Collins, one of Chalmers' agency in St. John's, his devoted friend, a man of the highest character and reputation, was the head of the new effort. There had been many obstacles in the way—not only the want of money, which in rich Glasgow, and among the band of wealthy men who had been taught their duty and responsibility by Dr. Chalmers, was a less hindrance than in most places, but difficulties with the law both of the Church and the land. The ecclesiastical difficulty was that ministers appointed to these mission churches were not recognized as parish ministers, had no place in the Presbytery, and no power to form a Kirk Session—in short, were only recognized as the incumbents of chapels-of-ease, the Church having no power to multiply parishes at her pleasure; while the difficulty with Government arose from the law of patronage, which held that, according to the doctrine of the primitive Irish in St. Columba's time, every calf belonged to the cow, and the patronage of the new church must pass to the original patron of the parish from which it had been separated. In the Assembly of 1834, however, the Church passed an Act admitting such ministers, who had hitherto been only *quoad sacra*, to the full privileges of parish ministers, while a Bill in Parliament of the same year "relieved all newly-created parishes from the claim to patronage vested previously in the patron of the original parish." The Church Building Society of Glasgow immediately proceeded to carry out their long thought-of plan. They resolved to build twenty new churches in that town, but not to begin the work until £20,000 was subscribed. This was done in a few months, and the work began.

This practical step roused the Church in general to action. The year 1834 was the first in which the Evangelical party, of which Chalmers was the most prominent leader, attained a majority in the Assembly. And the work of Church Extension, with all the sanctions of the highest authority, was put into his hand. He was appointed, in Scotch phraseology, Convenor of the Committee, which had been appointed for some time for this object, but which had hitherto found little opening for active work. He was no sooner at its head, however, than work was begun with all the force of his influence and energy, and something of the impetuosity and impatience of all delay which were in his character. It was a twofold effort which he organized, the one part consisting of an appeal to the country for money, an appeal addressed to all classes, from the Glasgow millionaire, who cheerfully gave forth his thousand pounds for the Doctor's great scheme, to the poor household which pledged its loyalty by the penny a week which Chalmers had learned to know was a subsidy of the utmost importance, not only by its capabilities of production, but by its power to interest and bind together the givers. The other branch of his schemes related to permanent endowment, and was an appeal to Government for a provision for the ministers of the new churches about to be built. This, as the more difficult portion of the work, and that on which he was ultimately defeated, we must explain in his own words, taken from the letter of guidance and direction which he wrote (not being able to accompany them) to a member of the deputation which went to London to bring it formally under the notice of the Government, of which at this moment Lord Melbourne was the head.

"I hold it of great importance that if a grant should be obtained, it should be accompanied by such conditions as may at once make plain, both to Government and the public, the main objects of the grant, and this will best justify both the measure itself and our application for it.

"The chief object, then—and let this stand palpably forth, and be expressly provided for in the constitution of the grant—is a cheap Christian education for the common people. Now a simple and unqualified grant does not secure this object. It may secure an additional £100 a year to each of our present unendowed ministers; but it is of the utmost importance its being distinctly understood that an appetency for this addition to their income is not in truth the animating principle either of their or our application. For this £100 a year, or whatever the allowance shall be, there should be the stipulation of a *quid pro quo*. It ought to be given on the part of the Government in return for such a regulation of the seat-rents as shall make the means of Christian instruction accessible to the great mass of the community. We want our present unendowed ministers to obtain £100 a year each: but for that they should be required to give up their present high seat-rents. The grants, so far from enriching, would at this rate make some of them poorer than they are at present. But this cannot be helped. The character of your application, be it known to all, is not a personal but a public and patriotic one; it being for a boon, not to the ministers of our unendowed churches, but for a boon to the plebeian families of their parishes. This furnishes the principle of the first article or condition which is specified.

"But there is a second condition nearly as indispensable as the first one: and that is, that a preference for the sittings shall be given to those who reside within the parish of the newly-endowed church—this preference at the terms stipulated for when the endowment was made, in favour of the church becoming the permanent and inalienable right of the parishioners. . . . The third condition, if it could be obtained, would prove an inestimable moral blessing to Scotland, and earn for Government the lasting gratitude of her people. It is that the grant of, say £100 a year, should be extended to all the churches of new parishes that may hereafter be erected. On the one hand, it would be the means of ultimately making our Church commensurate with our population; while, on the other hand, the increase of these churches would proceed gently and gradually, and without any immediate or, even after the process is completed, without any great or sensible pressure. I suppose the churches to be erected at the expense of individuals, and the endowments sought for to be provided by Government—a security, therefore, that the claim will never be preferred until a great previous sacrifice has been incurred—the best proof of the existence of the great and real necessity which demanded it."

These proposals received at first from Government a

favourable reception, and the prospect was very cheering before the eager workers, in whose eyes, between the interests and liberality of the people and the apparent good intentions and amiabilities of the State, their project seemed half accomplished. But it was not long before storms arose. Dissent in Scotland has never been like Dissent anywhere else. It was no divergence in doctrine, no difference of theological belief that had carried one band after another out of the Established Church. The "Relief," one of the first of these bands, was, to give it its full name, a "Relief from Patronage" —the "Secession," *par excellence*, was a secession for the same reason. A stranger might have gone in those days from one church to another in Edinburgh or Glasgow, and would never have discovered by any sign which was Dissent and which was the Established Church—as indeed he might still do now, except in so far as the tendency to what is considered an improved ritual may perhaps be more prominent in the latter. The same peculiarity perhaps has secured to Dissenters in Scotland a very different position and estimation from that held by them in England. There is little difference, if any, in credit and rank between a Dissenting minister and his brother of the Church. But by that natural advance in the chosen way, whether to the right or the left, which happens inevitably to every community, there had developed among the Dissenters the new doctrine of the voluntary principle, a doctrine unknown to their fathers. Driven to it in the first place by the exigencies of their position, and finding it in towns very successful, affording to a popular preacher large means of living and working, they had come by degrees, and against all the traditions in which they had taken their origin, to an adoption of the new principle—that only voluntary offerings were acceptable to God and appropriate as a provision for His worship, which was really the first distinctive and original doctrine of their own which distinguished them from the Church—with great enthusiasm. The idea that there was injustice in appropriating the public funds to the support of one division of the Church more than another was the political view of the same question, and this had lately come into great prominence in Edinburgh in consequence of the conflict on the so-called Annuity Tax, which was the fund (originally a commutation of tithes) out of which the stipends of the Edinburgh ministers had been provided. As soon as the proposals of Dr. Chalmers for additional endowment was laid before the Government, a fierce agitation broke out on the side of the Dissenters. Their main plea was, that while additional churches, ministers, and endowments were thus demanded, a large number of seats were unoccupied in the existing churches, and that consequently any addition to church accommodation or provision for new workers was uncalled for. There was a speciousness about the argument which staggered many minds, and brought a Government entirely indifferent to the question, and with imperfect means of judging, to a pause—but that it was an entirely fallacious one, it requires but little examination to perceive. It was the same as to say: There is plenty of room in the churches of Bloomsbury and Belgravia; why, then, ask for new places of worship in St. Giles's or Bethnal Green? But the outcry was hot, and the question a new one, puzzling to the unreflective mind. The very idea was new of carrying in this fashion the teaching and the ministrations of religion to every man's door: and the strong Conservative principle of leaving things alone, and bidding every man go to the church in which there was room for him, whether it suited him or not, mingled with and gave force to the new Radical principle that it was an injustice to give the money of the State to one division of religious teachers rather than another. In face of the sudden rise of these forces, the Government paused. No Government is ever willing to spend money where it can be avoided, nor has there yet been any Government which could allow itself to judge of the abstract right and wrong in such a matter. After many delays, it appointed a Commission to inquire into the subject, and it really does not appear what in all the convolutions of circumstance it could have done more.

Chalmers, however, was highly discontented with this result. He disapproved of the Commission: of the members of it, who were neither important men nor such as could be supposed to have any real knowledge of the subject; and of the object, which seemed to him to be that of an inquisitorial examination into the parochial system of Scotland, bringing each individual minister to the bar—thus changing the question from an inquiry into the wants of an increased population to an inquiry "as to how the Church of Scotland performs its duty," an investigation which, to a Church so jealous of all State interference, was insulting in the highest degree. It is evident that political feeling at the same time soon came to mingle with the real question on both sides. As it happened, although as it seems involuntarily, the deputation sent to press the claims of the Church—after long delay, and after the report of the Commission had made it manifest that the representation of the needs of Scotland in respect to church accommodation was genuine—was almost entirely composed of Conservatives, while the Government was Whig. As a matter of fact, the Tory party was, and had always proved, the support of the Church, so that this was natural enough; but it was not likely to conciliate the party in power. In addition to these drawbacks, there was the still more serious one that Chalmers did not even carry his own party in the Church with him in this effort. Dr. Guthrie, in his *Autobiography,* states very clearly that the movement was premature, that it was hurried on and pressed upon Government to its own defeat, and that, great as was the influence of Chalmers, many of his own chief followers were of this opinion. Guthrie himself, on his own much lower practical standing-ground, explains the opposition of the Dissenters from a homely matter-of-fact point of view, which is curious. He describes their sudden vehemence in favour of the Voluntary principle as the fruit of the exasperation and consternation with which Dr. Chalmers' great scheme filled them. "If this 'Church Extension,' as it was called, succeeded, it would cut out the ground below a large number of the Dissenting Churches in the country; since the people, in the popular election of their ministers, would enjoy all the privileges of Dissent without having to pay for them by maintaining ministers and ordinances at their own expense."

"This was driving" (adds Dr. Guthrie) "the Dissenting or Voluntary Churches into a corner. The bread of their ministers and their very existence was in danger, so they were driven desperate, ready rather than be pulled down themselves to pull down all establishments. In forcing the Dissenters into this desperate position, I thought the Church wrong in points both of principle and policy. The Dissenters had preserved religion and made up for her lack of service for many years in many parts of the country; and I would have had these services practically acknowledged by our asking the Government, when we sought the endowments for the purpose of extending the Church, to endow any or every party who, though seceders from the Church of Scotland, adhered to her standards. But this, which at that early period would have taken off the edge of Dissenting opposition to the extension of the Church as contemplated by Dr. Chalmers, and would thus have been as consistent with policy as with principle, was not done."

Nothing can bring more clearly into evidence the true statesmanship of Chalmers' mind and scheme than the side-light upon it thrown by such a curious exposition of supposed motive and meaning as this. To imagine the Voluntary principle to be no principle at all, but a fictitious plea set up to conceal a sordid alarm and self-interest, which could be silenced by a bribe, is a poor view indeed of the opponents to whom this champion imagines himself to be more tolerant and kindly than was the large-souled and clear-sighted, if impetuous, leader who pursued his great object without any thought of the Dissenters, in the full conviction that their methods were not sufficient for the emergency any more than the old provisions of the Church, which a greatly increased population had outgrown. To cut the ground from under the feet of any workers was not in Chalmers' thought. It was the wastes where no man worked which were in his mind. He felt himself in face of the problem of a great need which those who were destitute did not feel, and had no desire to have supplied to them. The ignorant and degraded, and those who are born and bred in the dark purlieus of great towns, where education was not or Christian teaching, do not seek, do not wish for the moral training and spiritual light which alone can raise them from those depths. This was the argument which was strong in the mind of Chalmers, and stated over and over again with all the force of the strongest conviction throughout his whole career. The people for whom he laboured were not conscious of what they wanted most. It was necessary to carry the light to them, to their very doors, not to expect them to be already so enlightened as to come and seek it for themselves. Those who have reached this point do not remain long in the darkness. But the darkness which he sought to pierce was not moved by any desire of electing its own ministers or of having ministers at all, or teachers, or light or air, or any improving and elevating thing. The principle of carrying religious instruction to every man's door, of bringing its teachers into personal contact with all, the most unwilling to be taught, of persuading, entreating them to hear, by every charm of human loving-kindness and brotherliness—this was the inspiration of Chalmers' life. He thought it could best be done by that aid of the State to which the National Church had a right according to all the stipulations of the constitution—the aid of a modest provision which procured little more than that the man who devoted himself to such work should not actually starve in the doing of it.

When he found that this was not to be obtained, and when the storms of the ensuing period had passed over his head, and he was free again to think of his chief object and most real, he threw himself upon Christian charity to carry out that beloved aim. To do it was his desire, not to quarrel over the modes of doing it: to do it by such methods as were possible, if not in what he thought the best and surest way, then in the next best. No doubt it was a profound disappointment to Chalmers that his great scheme was not carried out. As a preacher of the gospel, believing that the only means of salvation: as a Christian philosopher, believing that to elevate the character of the people was the only way really to improve their position: as a philanthropist, bound to do away with the ills of poverty and confident in the power of his system to do so—he was disappointed, and over again disappointed, by the careless reception, careless rejection of his noble and well-thought-out scheme. He was impetuous, no one could deny it, and impatient of delay and tergiversation. A statesman ought not perhaps to be so human, he ought to have patience beyond all assault; but no statesman could have conceived a finer scheme, nor shown a wider comprehension, a more absolute grasp of the matter in hand.

The conclusion was, that Government refusing the aid asked for, Chalmers, encouraged by the large liberality of some of his old Glasgow friends, took upon himself a tour through the country to raise the public interest and gain from private gifts the amount that was needed for the erection of the churches in question. The enterprise, undertaken at first while peace and unity reigned more or less in the Church, fell upon troublous days, and was carried out in the face of a new and vehement conflict, which withdrew men's minds from the general question and concentrated all their energies on an internecine struggle; and the result of his labours was another immediate disappointment in the amount of money provided. Yet, at the end of seven years' of arduous work, from 1834 to 1841, he had the satisfaction of seeing two hundred and twenty-two churches added to the force of the Establishment, with so many additional ministers, kirk sessions, and the full machinery of the parish system—no inconsiderable achievement. His opinion of the means by which he and his colleagues attained this remarkable result is worth quoting. It is from the report of a speech before the Assembly, in which he asks to be relieved of his laborious post at the head of the movement.

"While he rejoices in the experimental confirmation which the history of these few years has afforded him of the resources and capabilities of the Voluntary system, to which, as hitherto, unfostered by the paternal care of Government, the scheme of Church Extension is indebted for all its progress, it still remains his unshaken conviction of that system notwithstanding, that it should only be resorted to as a supplement, and never, but in times when the powers of infidelity and intolerance are linked together in hostile combination against the sacred prerogatives of the Church, should it once be thought of as a substitute for a national establishment of Christianity. In days of darkness and disquietude it may open a temporary resource either for a virtuous secession or an ejected Church to fall back upon; but a far more glorious consummation is when the State puts forth its hand to sustain and not to subjugate the Church, and the two, bent on moral conquests alone, walk together as fellow-helpers towards the achievement of that great pacific triumph, the Christian education of the people."

Thus while he attained his object to a certain extent, he did it, not by the means he approved, but by means with which he was destined thereafter to work with greater success, and to depend upon more entirely than any religious leader who had gone before him. It is a curious position in which to stand, and his future efforts were all in the direction of making that voluntary principle which he had no faith in, yet was compelled to adopt, as unlike a voluntary principle as possible. This curious contradiction and paradox throws a transverse light as strange as it is interesting upon the latter part of this great man's actions and career.

While this work was going on, Dr. Chalmers was invited to deliver a series of lectures in London upon Church Establishment, which produced a great effect There was much in the commotions of the time which resembled the present unsettled conditions of though and project; and the Church was supposed to be in danger, as she has so often been supposed to be, withou any corresponding catastrophe. Under these circum stances, the appearance of an orator so well known and popular was of special importance, and excited much attention. Why he should have lectured to what i called "a picked audience," and in so restrained a space as that of the Hanover Square Rooms, does not appear since "dukes, marquises, earls, baronets, bishops, and members of parliament," of whom his hearers are said to have chiefly consisted, did not need to be convinced of the advantages of national support to religion, nor of the error of withholding it. A bystander relates how the speaker when he appeared was received and welcomed "with clappings and shouts of applause, that grew more and more intense, till the noise became almost deafening." "The tide that had been rising and swelling each succeeding day," it is added in describing the last of these orations, "now burst all bounds. Carried away by the impassioned utterances of the speaker long ere the close of his finest passages were reached, the voice of the lecturer was drowned in applause, the audience rising from their seats, waving their hats above their heads, and breaking out into tumultuous approbation." The unusual attitude which he assumed, seated at a table, according to his custom as a professor, a little startled his audience at first, yet occasionally added to the force of his address, since he himself sometimes sprang unconsciously to his feet, carried away by his own fervour, while the whole audience rose with him in a sympathetic climax of excitement, responding in a "whirlwind of enthusiasm" such as has rarely been seen in any public assembly. "Near us were the reporters," says another of Chalmers' companions. "One seemed to leave the room every five minutes with what he had written, so that by the time the lecture was finished it was nearly all in print."

The oration ended about half-past three o'clock, and at five it was issued to the world in the pages of the *Globe*, as if it had been a statement of imperial policy or a declaration of war. Never, either before or after, has the appearance of a Scotch minister so forced and riveted the attention of the greater and richer Church of the South, or so stirred the interest of the public. He was an ally whose gifts and power were unique, called to the aid of a community in danger, to whom his strange tongue, his vehement gestures, and his bold and distinct difference of doctrine were as nothing in comparison with his heroic championship. His theme before that audience of bishops and potentates was not the imposing aspect of the Church or its high influence in public life: it was that parish system which he loved, its efficacy to meet all circumstances, its adaptation to all national needs, its pervasion everywhere with the right of a national institution, and the freedom of an agency independent of the approbation of the crowd. When he had come to the end of his subject, in the last of his addresses, with "nine bishops," as his biographer proudly describes, among his hearers, the orator, who had ventured to warn the great Church of England that she must "come down from all that is transcendental and mysterious in her pretensions," in order to become "the great standard and rallying-post for all that would unite their efforts and sacrifices in that mighty cause," turned to the case of his own Church, and proclaimed her distinctive quality of spiritual independence with fond and proud enthusiasm. "We," he cried in the fervour of his eloquence, "own no head of the Church but the Lord Jesus Christ. Whatever is done ecclesiastically is done by our ministers as acting in His name, and in perfect submission to His authority." His hearers were of that great Church which owns as its earthly head the Sovereign of the realm, and whose power of action is limited on all hands by law, and tradition under the safeguard of law. The impetuous Scot was capable as a Christian of many self-denials, yet could not refrain as he stood up before them all of one boast and proclamation of the superiority in spiritual independence of the Church of his fathers.

"It should never be forgotten that in things ecclesiastical the highest power of our Church is amenable to no higher power on earth for its decisions. It can exclude: it can deprive: it can depose at pleasure. External force might make an obnoxious individual the holder of a benefice; but there is no external force in these realms that could make him a minister of the Church of Scotland. There is not one thing which the State can do to our independent and indestructible Church but strip her of her temporalities. The magistrate might withdraw his protection, and she cease to be an Establishment; but in all the high matters of sacred and spiritual jurisdiction she would be the same as before. With or without an Establishment she, in them, is the unfettered mistress of her doings. The King by himself, or by his representative, may be the spectator of our proceedings; but what Lord Chatham said of the poor man's house is true in all its parts of the Church to which I have the honour to belong. 'In England every man's house is his castle: not that it is surrounded with walls and battlements: it may be a straw-built shed, every wind of heaven may whistle round it, every element of heaven may enter it—but the King cannot, the King dare not.'"

Thus, with a fervour of enthusiasm which was received with an almost wild response of applause, Chalmers waved aloft the banner of his Church in the presence of the representatives of that other great national establishment, whose highest councils could not nominate or place a member of the hierarchy without the royal *congé d'élire.* It was generous of his English audience to allow itself to be thus moved by the stranger's eloquence; but what could be more strange than to see the champion of the Church of Scotland on the very verge of the precipice which was soon to break beneath his feet, separating him from the Sion he loved, and turning his boast into a mockery—thus proclaiming as with the voice of a trumpet the independence which was so soon to be proved a fiction, and the superiority of a freedom which even then was threatened by every hostile power?

It would not be fair, however, to Dr. Chalmers' fame, while showing his deep attachment to the principles of an Established Church, and strong sense of its necessity, not to show also the feeling with which he regarded the Nonconformists, with whom he was much brought in contact in his visits to England. On one occasion, in the neighbourhood of Bristol, he was asked to open a church of the Independent or Congregationalist community. When he reached Bristol he found a strong feeling against the Established Church to prevail in this community, a feeling with which he was very unwilling to identify himself in any way. He thought it his duty accordingly, at the close of his sermon, to clear his conscience by a declaration of his faith, which must have been somewhat astonishing in such an atmosphere. "I hold the Establishment to be not only a great Christian good, but one indispensable to the upholding of a diffused Christianity throughout the land," he said, with what fluttering of the dove-cots around one can imagine. We have already said that Dissent in Scotland occupies an entirely different position from Dissent in England, and Chalmers in all probability was unaware of that additional burst of feeling. He went on in a tone of judicial calm, stating the case from grounds much unlike those which English Nonconformists are in the habit of hearing.

"We think it might be demonstrated that, were the ministrations of your Established Church to be done away, they would never be replaced by all the zeal, energy, and talent of private adventurers. Instead of the frequent parish church — that most beauteous spectacle to a truly Christian heart, because to him the richest in moral associations, with its tower peeping forth from amidst the verdure of the trees in which it is embosomed—there would be presented to the eye of the traveller only rare and thinly-scattered meeting-houses. The cities might indeed continue to be supplied with regular preaching, but innumerable villages and hamlets left dependent on a precarious itinerancy would be speedily reduced to the condition of a moral waste. . . . But we are far from regarding with a jealous eye the zeal and exertions of other orthodox religious bodies. In connexion with our Establishment we wish ever to see an able, vigorous, and flourishing dissenterism. The services of Dissenters are needed to supplement the deficiencies and to correct and compensate for the vices of an Establishment, as far as that Establishment has the misfortune to labour under the evil of a lax and negligent ministration, a corrupt and impure patronage. Such wholesome dissent is a purifier, and, because a purifier, a strengthener of the

Church. I am willing to profess everywhere, and upon all occasions, my sense of the usefulness of such Dissenters, and of the worth of their services."

Perhaps a moral relation so elevated and impartial, so full of the true unity, so unlike the belligerent attitude of two strongly opposed and mutually hostile camps, is an ecclesiastical Utopia scarcely to be realized while men continue as they are. But it was at least a noble ideal of that variety yet harmony, that one great object pursued in many ways, that spiritual unity beyond and above every divergence of opinion, which ought to be the inspiration of all Christian teachers and faithful servants of God and man.

CHAPTER VI.

It is with reluctance that we approach the great controversy which rent Scotland and the Church in two, and which is so complicated, so lengthened, and so full of names and things which have fallen out of recollection even in Scotland—and out of Scotland are always difficult to understand—that the task of explaining and setting it forth to the general reader is a very difficult one. The public interest which was largely called out by the conclusion of that controversy, one of the most startling and the most picturesque historical events that have happened in our age, has long ago dropped, and the monotony of commonplace life and routine has fallen with the course of half a century upon the romance and the heroism of the Disruption. That heroism indeed has become dim even in the success which made it less of a catastrophe than a triumph for those most involved; while all manner of after considerations have tempered the enthusiasm which at the moment carried the sympathy of all spectators with the astonishing romance of a renunciation unparalleled in modern times. The effect produced in England in 1662 by the Act of Uniformity was even more great; but it was accomplished piece-meal, and not with the union and completeness, impressive to the senses as well as the mind, of the later event. We must now endeavour to give as brief a summary as possible of the condition of the Scotch Church from 1840 to the great climax of the agitation in 1843, the constitutional principles involved, and the reasons which actuated some half of its ministers to withdraw solemnly, shaking the dust from their feet, from what they considered its desecrated and outraged sanctuary.

The principle which, as we have just said, Chalmers had proclaimed at the end of his lecture upon Church Establishment, as the distinction and the pride of Scotland, the fact that its Church recognized no head but Christ, that "the King could not, the King dared not" enter its sacred enclosure with any power or authority there, was the principle upon which its entire ecclesiastical system was built. The Lord High Commissioner, as he is called, the Queen's representative, sits in the highest council of the Church, the General Assembly, still, as he has done since the Revolution of 1688, but he is a mere pageant, taking no part, having no word in the matter—a symbol of State, representing the fact that the Church has its special approbation and favour, but no more. The wildest imagination has never originated so mad an idea as that this functionary should interfere in the business or presume to express an opinion even upon the proceedings of the "Right Reverend and Right Honourable" representatives and rulers of the Church, who sit there in their parliament. In the deepest depths of the reign of the "Moderates," as well as in the times when what is now the Free Church was supreme, such an impossible proceeding would have been regarded with the same feeling; such an interference never has been, and never could for a moment be permitted to be. This fact will perhaps, better than anything else, explain the position to the reader unacquainted with the subject. In England, the secular authority is the final judge in ecclesiastical matters, and the Anglican hierarchy has never claimed to rule in its own sphere with the independence claimed by the Presbyterian: but that independence has always been one of the most precious possessions of the Church of Scotland, sealed and secured by jealous stipulations ever since the union of the two crowns. It is, we believe, the first act demanded of every British Sovereign, after he or she has taken the Coronation oaths, to swear to maintain inviolate the independence and privileges of the Church of Scotland; and there has never been, so far as we are aware, any doubt in respect to these privileges, so far as principle is concerned. That of unfettered action within her own sphere, of power to make her own laws, to rule her own members, to pull down and to set up according to the ancient laws and traditions within her own boundaries, has never ceased to be her ideal and her claim.

There has been one hindrance and one alone upon this freedom, and that was the institution (or rather the restoration) of Patronage, which dates from the time of Queen Anne. The Revolution Settlement, upon which the privileges of the Church of Scotland, which the Sovereign swears to preserve, were founded, knows nothing of this law. It was a piece of additional legislation added when the waves of national disquiet had fallen to make up for a little of the lost way which the Crown and the State had endured in Scotland. We have already said that this law had been the cause of every secession from the Church of Scotland, from the time it was instituted. No breach of doctrine, no change of ritual had affected the minds of the men who had broken off from her authority. They had rebelled against patronage, and against that alone. And the Church herself, as she became more and more pervaded by the great awakening and revivals of life, had in her turn rebelled. During the eighteenth century there had been great indifference on the subject throughout Scotland. The reign of the party which is called "the Moderates" was in full force—if such words can ever be used of the slumbrous reign of routine which existed in the Church. It was perhaps good for her outward aspect; for the minister who had been the laird's tutor, and accustomed more or less to such society as was to be had in his little circle, was more distinctly a member of the rural aristocracy than the minister called by the suffrages of the people, and more akin to them than to the higher class; but it was not good for her saving strength as the guardian of an increasing and multiplying race. In the old quiet days the patron was largely moved by influence, by friendship, by connexion, as it was very natural he should be; and though a wise and sensible man would no doubt endeavour to select the best incumbent he could find, and to show a certain regard for the good of the parish and the credit of the Church, he was by no means compelled so to do. We all know that sentimental pleas have always been not only valid but laudable in the distribution of benefices. Mr. Quiverful has a perennial claim upon the kindness of a friend who has a living to bestow, and who can find fault theoretically with the good feeling which assures the future of an early friend, a sympathetic teacher perhaps, in this natural and becoming way? Such preferments have always been common and are unquestioned to this day in England. If the man does not suit the parish, does not work it, is not popular in it, so much the worse for the parish; and even popular sentiment has gone no further than this in the Church of England.

But in the Church of Scotland it was not so; all her forms conveyed a different idea and supported a different principle. In the established and never altered method of appointing a new clergyman to a vacant parish, the two distinct jurisdictions were always brought clearly before the world—the one active, the other passive. The patron indeed took the first step by nominating an individual either already in full orders, or a licentiate of the Church, corresponding to the deacons' orders of England. This was all he had to do. The Presbytery of the county or district, consisting of all the ministers and elders within its bounds, then took the matter in hand, and held a meeting in the parish, according to Scotch phraseology, "to moderate in a call"; in other words, to preside over the invitation of the people supposed to be given on their own initiative to the presentee. In by far the greater number of cases this invitation was given with more or less unanimity, and the settlement made by full consent of all parties involved. But in a few cases this was not so; the presentee was sometimes offensive, sometimes so strongly disliked that no pretence of assent could be procured from the people, nothing indeed but protests more or less solemn. In some few detached cases the parish rose in rebellion, and the hated minister had been known to be put in by force of arms, by a detachment from the nearest garrison, curious officers of religion. In such circumstances it may be believed that the effect upon the parish was not conducive to religious life or progress. Those who were piously disposed made their laborious way to other parish churches, or set up little conventicles among themselves. The indifferent remained indifferent, or threw off the bonds of religion altogether.

> "A cauld day December blew,
> A cauld kirk and in 't but few,
> A caulder minister never spak,
> They'll a' be warm or I gang back,"

was the picture presented by many rural churches and the sentiment in many minds, brought up in all the reverence for the Church and with every tradition in favour of church-going, and the observance of all pious decorums, if nothing more.

But when the warm tide of Evangelical life burst into the Church of Scotland, this grievance, as was natural, came at once into the foreground as a thing insupportable. The Evangelical party, the Low Church as it has been called in England, has scarcely occupied the highest place there, even in its fullest tide of influence. It is not the ideal of an Episcopal and hierarchical Church; it is always more or less a rebellion, an innovation, a new thing, breaking down the higher claims of Apostolical succession, making light of ritual, offending many of the tastes and instincts of the people. But in Scotland this again has not been so. The ideal and the tradition of that Church have all gone with the fervour, the zeal, the uncompromising doctrine, the indifference to form, and intense pre-occupation with spiritual necessities, which are the features of this party. "A cauld kirk" is the last thing in the world to please or to attach the people, who are so much more apt to have opinions of their own on such subjects than in other nations. The passion of ritual has never taken root on Scotch soil—never at least in modern times—but the passion of earnest religious feeling, the warmth of that burning appeal, "Now is the accepted time, now is the day of salvation," has been a universal charm, and has penetrated, as nothing else could, into the heart of the country as the highest manifestation of religion and its greatest office. The Evangelical party possessed at the same time the highest intellect of the Church, and the greatest gifts. Such an orator as Chalmers, a man entirely after its own heart, embodying at once the enthusiasm and the practical character of its genius, patriotic above all things, forming all his schemes and expending all his powers for Scotland, was such a leader as few could resist. The Moderates, who loved a quiet life, and the cultivation of the milder virtues, fell back under his influence, and that of the whole young living world of power and feeling which he drew with him, into the minority in the Church and in the world. They were the High and dry, the Church and State men, the "cauld kirk" unexpanding, unadvancing; while the others were the Highflyers, at once the new life and the representatives of the Covenant and the Reformation. All Scotch tradition and distinctive principle thus went with the Evangelical party.

And as has been said, the one great popular and national grievance came at once into the foreground. To a people as to a leader so profoundly attached to the parochial system, and seeing in it not only the stronghold of the past but the highest possibility of the future, the desecration and outrage of a forced settlement, the introduction into the Church and manse, those strongholds of influence, of a man detested by the parish and refused by them, was intolerable. In 1834, when the Evangelicals first began to get the upper hand, there was passed by the General Assembly a law giving to the heads of families in each parish a veto—that is, a right by their dissent and protest properly expressed, to stop the proceedings in the case of a distasteful minister, and return to the patron his presentee, that he might be replaced by another more acceptable. No idea of interference with the patron's right was in this step, or proposal to transfer the power of appointment to another. It was not even, we believe, ever alleged to have been used wantonly, or without sufficient reason, and the patron retained the full right to make a new presentation. Nothing could seem more simple, more according to all the principles of the Church, or less a hardship to any side. It was, however, the cause of a vehement and long-continued controversy. Those who supported the veto were called the Non-Intrusion party; the others, who upheld the absolute rights of the patron, the Intrusionists (in all the party names of this period of strife, the Evangelical party had the best of it, as will be seen, which is much in a popular movement). This was the plain, practical matter and claim: that no man should be forced upon an unwilling parish as its minister to whom there was already a well-founded aversion in the mind of the people. It expanded a little afterwards in the natural course of agitation, when the one side asserted, and the other, while denying, almost allowed, that any aversion, however unfounded, was enough to call forth this veto, and that the objectors, who were not compelled to formulate their objection, might shut out an excellent clergyman from a living because he had red hair! which was the *reductio ad absurdum* of the question. The higher doctrinal statement involved the whole basis and standing-ground of the Church. The Veto Act, in this point of view, was the assertion of the right of the Church to govern itself by its own laws and officers independent of the State, and, still more solemn, of the Supreme Headship of Christ, the only Head acknowledged by the Church of Scotland, in Whose name and by Whose authority these laws existed, and these officers exercised their various faculties. This had been the position of the Church throughout all its history. It was no new thing.

It must be added that in all this a careful separation was made between things temporal and things spiritual. The most pronounced Non-Intrusion champion never asserted rights on the part of the people to secure the stipend, manse, or other privileges of the legal presentee for another, or indeed to take any steps to replace that presentee with another in contradiction to the legal rights of the patron. The "temporalities" were carefully excluded from all part in the question. It was the right of the patron to retain them, to bestow them on whom he would. His presentee might enjoy the stipend, live in the manse, if he so willed; but he could have the rank and office of minister of the parish only by the agency of the Presbytery, the acknowledged local court of the Church, and that agency could not act contrary to the will or without the consent of the people. Thus the position of the Church as supreme in all sacred things was carefully guarded from interference with rights and property in things not sacred.

That this state of passive opposition between two such powers could go on long without an actual encounter was not to be expected. It is an unfortunate peculiarity of such internecine wars that they are often brought about, and carried out to the disaster and almost ruin of the community in the midst of which they are waged, by some agent of the most insignificant kind. When a Church and country are thrown out of gear for such a great figure as a Becket or a Wolsey, there is something sufficient in the cause, some compensation for the loss; but when the touch which precipitates change and rends a world asunder is given by some perfectly obscure hand, and for the advantage of a trifling individual of no note or importance to any one but his insignificant self, a certain exasperation mingles with our regret. The whole fabric of the Church of Scotland was thus shaken, and infinite disaster brought about, by the determination of a certain Mr. Young, altogether unknown to fame, to get himself put into possession of the parish of Auchterarder, in Perthshire, to which in the year 1834 he was presented by the Earl of Kinnoull. When in the ordinary course of precedence the Presbytery met at Strathbogie to preside over the signing of the "call," it was found that in a parish containing three thousand souls, and out of the number of three hundred male heads of families entitled to take part in this formal invitation, two individuals alone presented themselves to do so, while two hundred and eighty-seven expressed their dissent. The Presbytery, after conference with the people, adjourned its meeting for a fortnight to allow time for further consideration. At the adjourned meeting, however, the determination of the parish remained unchanged.

We hear nothing about Mr. Young, who he was or what, or in what way the people had formed so invincible a feeling against him; he appears out of chaos in order to give the fatal touch to the swiftly revolving wheel of events, and then disappears again. The Presbytery's embarrassed situation was happily relieved by an appeal to the Synod of Perth and Stirling, the next higher court, which one cannot but feel must have been a great relief to the first reverend body brought face to face with this responsibility. From the Synod it was carried to the General Assembly, the supreme court of the Church. The Assembly could do no more than retransmit the matter to the Presbytery, directing it to proceed in the matter according to the "Interim Act of last Assembly"—that is, the Veto Act. The Presbytery, carrying out the instructions of the highest authority in the Church, proceeded again to the consideration of the question as between the presentee and the parish. The veto secured to them by this law having been exercised by the people, and their opposition to the presentee remaining as strong as ever, the Presbytery, according to the law of the Church, rejected Mr. Young, and invited the patron to choose another and more acceptable person for the charge. "Against this rejection the presentee entered an appeal to the Synod, which he afterwards abandoned; and it was with mingled curiosity and alarm that the Church learned that, in conjunction with the patron, he had raised an action against the Presbytery before the Supreme Civil Court, the Court of Session."

"As the action was originally laid, the Court was asked to review the proceedings of the Presbytery solely with the view of determining the destination of the benefice, and declaring that the just and legal right to the stipend still lay with the rejected presentee. The case, however, had not been in Court more than a few weeks when an ominous change was made upon the whole character of the action. This change, technically denominated 'an amendment of the libel,' was affected by the introduction of new clauses, in which the Court was asked to find and declare that the rejection of Mr. Young, expressly on the ground of a veto by the parishioners, was illegal, being contrary to statute, and that the Presbytery was still bound under statutory obligation to take Mr. Young on trial, and if found qualified, to ordain him as minister of the parish."

Thus the battle was engaged. The Church, it may be said, had taken the first step by meeting the popular grievance with a new law, which, though embodying a principle always held by the Church, was yet not a part of its acknowledged constitution. It might be just and right and necessary, but that was not the question—it was a new thing: and whether the Church had a right to enact such a law, and thus introduce a new popular privilege hitherto not formulated by any enactment, was open to discussion. The Court of Session gave a decision against that right. It is impossible for us in the limited space at our disposal to enter into the long course of litigation and discussion that followed. The question was finally carried to the House of Lords, where it was decided not only that the Church had no power to make a new law on the subject, but that as a matter of fact she had no right to reject any man presented by the legal patron, or to test or judge him in any particular except as to whether he was qualified in "life, literature, and morals" for the position of a clergyman. The process followed the course we have seen in more recent cases in the Church of England, where practices that have existed for ages have, on sharp legal examination, been discovered to have no foundation in actual law, and therefore to be untenable; while other practices, which can be made out to have some hold upon an obscure legal stipulation, are endowed with sudden force. The question in this case was much more practically important than the distinction between having candles unlighted upon the altar, which was permitted, and having them lighted, which was not. It went against the universal practice of the Church—exercised so often that the precedent itself might have entitled it to rank as law—a practice supported by both parties in the Church, the leader of the Moderate party having himself "strenuously affirmed," as Dr. Hanna says, "that the Church regarded qualification as including much more than learning, moral character, and sound doctrine—as extending in effect to the fitness of the presentees in all respects for the particular situation to which they are appointed." The decision of the House of Lords was therefore entirely unexpected, and took Scotland by surprise. It was such a decision as extended far beyond the immediate question, and changed altogether the aspect, not only of that question, but of the Church's position altogether in a country where she had hitherto and always held her own independence as complete and supreme.

It is not a question easily comprehensible in England, where no such idea existed, and, save in a few extraordinary cases, where the right of popular election to a living has been found to be attended by all the evils of political elections in the most corrupt times, and to occasion little less than a public scandal—the action of a congregation in the choice of their spiritual instructor has never been thought of. Nor, we presume, would it be very intelligible in the only other country likely to enter into this subject, in America, where the general choice is the only principle upon which the selection of clergymen to individual charges rests. Scotland stood between the two, holding very strongly by its ideal of a National Church with its (very modest) endowments and privileges, yet with equal force to its own power of regulating the appointments made for its benefit and use. One subtle and important difference, however, between the apparent indifference on this subject in England, and the passion with which it was regarded in Scotland, is stated by Dr. Chalmers in one of his great speeches to consist in the fact that, whereas in England admission into Holy Orders is given without reference to any local position, in Scotland a minister is ordained to the special church he is designed to occupy, so that it might be pleaded that the Church was coerced even in the very act of ordination by this new decision of the law—an argument which may be stated for what it is worth, perhaps not so great after examination as at the first glance. We are tempted to quote, however, his exposition of the "true theory of the connexion between Church and State."

"When this alliance was first entered upon, the first movement was made by the State. The overture came from them, on what motive, whether of piety or patriotism or any other cause, it matters not; if it was such an overture as could be righteously, in that case it might be most rejoicingly consented to by the Church, who might bless God in orisons of the devoutest gratitude, in that by the aid of the civil magistrate a way had been opened up for the lessons of the gospel, for the words and message of eternal life to all the population. The boon on one side was a maintenance for the Church's labourers, who might be distributed over the length and breadth of the land, and act each as the herald of salvation on his own assigned portion of the territory. The return on the other side was an immense blessing to the State, that best security, not for the temporal and eternal happiness of individuals only, but for the moral and political and the economic well-being of every community—a universal Christian education. Such, then, is the precise footing on which the Church enters into that alliance with the State, by which it becomes what is termed a National Church, or an Established Church, or a Religious National Establishment. It may have subsisted for many ages as a Christian Church with all its tenets and its usages, not as prescribed by human authority, but as founded either on the Word of God or on their own independent views of Christian expediency, meaning by this their own views of what is best for the good of imperishable souls. None of these things were given up to the State at the time when the Church entered into an alliance with it; but one and all of them remained as intact and inviolable after this alliance as before it. She did not make over her liberties to the State at the time when she entered into fellowship with it in this new character of a National Establishment, she only made over her services. . . .

There are certain obligations incumbent upon her *quasi* a Christian Church, and there are certain privileges which belong to her *quasi* an Establishment. I hold it to be quite an axiom, a first and elementary truth, that we are never in any instance to depart from the obligations that lie upon a Christian Church for the sake either of obtaining or perpetuating the privileges which belong to us as an Established Church. But though on the one hand we cannot either rescind or refrain from enacting what we hold to be vital, ere we make a voluntary withdrawal of ourselves from the State we should make every effort to obtain its concurrence, and that in order to avert the calamity of a disruption betwixt us; and this too in the face of every ungenerous misinterpretation to which our desire of preserving the connexion between the parties with all its advantages is liable. But, meanwhile, till we make this out, we have nothing for it but to administer our own affairs in conformity with and under the guidance of our own statute-book."

That this view is a very reasonable and true one, in theory, few people will deny; nor will those who know the Church of Scotland hesitate to allow that it has always been her principle. Whether it is legitimate, while thus claiming no absolute Divine authority for the laws of the Church, but admitting the ecclesiastical system to be more or less founded on "Christian expediency," that Dr. Chalmers and his party should have taken the very high ground of asserting the Headship of Christ to be involved, and His Divine authority to be dishonoured by the compliances required of them, it is perhaps more difficult to see. Yet that this was the view taken up with the highest passion and enthusiasm by a large part of the population of Scotland, both clergy and people, there can be no reasonable doubt; nor that the acts of the legal party which followed, against all precedent or tradition, were in every sense of the word tyrannical and oppressive, a sort of law gone mad, and running amuck among all the sentiments and prepossessions most dear to the country thus arbitrarily brought to bay.

The struggle which followed was twofold, accompanied often by circumstances of the highest exasperation, and an arbitrary exercise of authority on both sides, despotic on the part of the law courts, defiant on that of the Church, both perhaps having that strain of the absolute and uncompromising which is a characteristic of Scotsmen in every great period of excitement. The calmer English temper would never, we believe, have come to such a struggle. That conciliation and caution were the first necessities in so critical and important a crisis, ought to have been perceived on both sides; the law courts however, it seems to us, in initiating a course of procedure quite beyond all previous rule and precedent, were most to blame. But the hurry of events altogether unforeseen, and that curious heat and fluster of quickly-rising excitement which seems now and then on the eve of disaster to seize upon the minds of men, as may be traced throughout history in almost every great national misadventure, had now set in, carrying with it the precautions, the hesitations, the dictates of good sense and common judgment.

Two other presentations of a similar kind to that at Auchterarder, Lethendy, and Marnoch, took place in succession with the same results. In both cases the

Presbytery, brought to pause by finding the appointment almost unanimously opposed by the respective parishes, were ordered by the Court of Session to proceed to the ordination of the repulsed presentees; and in one, that of Marnoch, they gave way to the unseemly and unjustifiable command, and carried out the orders of the law courts in disobedience to and defiance of their own spiritual authorities. This case had a peculiarity which made the confusion and chaos into which affairs were drifting especially remarkable. Marnoch was a Crown living, and the Government had signified to the representatives of the Church that it would not press any appointment made by it, against the will of the parish. The patron, therefore, was quite willing to reconsider the matter, and seek another candidate whom the people would accept. But the presentee, to whom neither the dislike and disapprobation of the parishioners (fatal circumstances for the efficiency of an after career), nor the danger of the Church, nor the risk of increasing that danger by the most exasperating circumstances, were evidently of any importance, pressed his legal warrant in despite even of those who gave it, and demanded his miserable pound of flesh in defiance of every generous argument. The blood of the spectator boils to think that it was for nothing that could be supposed to be an advantage to the public in any way, even a vindication of a principle, but solely for the aggrandizement of a few insignificant individuals that the enormous responsibility of breaking the Church asunder, and deeply injuring the country, should have thus been taken. How cheap a thing for Scotland to have bought up these paltry candidates and endowed them with income enough to have satisfied their wildest desires, rather than permit so great a catastrophe to have been brought about by their means! If the final result was one of the most remarkable and picturesque events of the century, and one, too, of which no patriotic Scotsman, however he may disapprove or even condemn, can help being proud, the first moving cause was contemptible beyond measure, and worth nothing but scorn and wonder on the part of all high-minded men.

The matter, however, was curiously enlarged and intensified, when an entire Presbytery (eight ministers in all, there being a minority who took no part in the proceedings) took a step so revolutionary, laying themselves open to the highest penalties of the Church, which, after some delay and many attempts to bring them to a sense of their dereliction from duty, were finally imposed upon them. They were solemnly deposed from their sacred offices by the General Assembly, which they had disobeyed and defied, in its session of 1841. By this time, however, the old Moderate party in the Church, "her Majesty's opposition," so to speak, which had hitherto agreed in maintaining more or less the Church's independence, and had taken no marked step to identify itself with any arbitrary and ecclesiastically illegal proceedings, was touched by the sense of party necessity and obligation, and by a protest against this act of the Assembly, placed itself formally on the other side, thus breaking the force of the stand made for the privileges of the Church, and making it apparent that even in the high places of that Church there were two sides to the question. The deposed Presbytery of Strathbogie, on the other hand, went back to their homes unaffected by the sentence passed upon them, in plain revolt to the sacred authority to which they had sworn obedience. They were able even to obtain an interdict from the Court of Session (also, it need not be said, disregarded) against any other clergyman who might be sent to preach or officiate in their parishes. Chaos had come again, and the internal government of the Church, helpless to prevent such a systematic rebellion, was brought to a standstill and thrown into complete disorganization. It was vain to speak of independence, of privilege, of Church government of any kind, while such an example of bold insubordination could not be put down. And to make matters worse, instead of helping to restore some appearance of constitutional deference, the Moderate party now publicly adopted the rebels, and went so far as to send an address to Government, desiring of the supreme authority that it would support the law, make no concession, but coerce the majority of the Church into submission to its fate.

During this time the most prolonged and endless negotiations had been going on with the Government of the day—first that of Lord Melbourne, afterwards that of which Sir Robert Peel was head—to obtain some measure by which the conflicting laws of Church and State might be re-established each in its proper sphere. The Government had hitherto been, if not favourable, yet by no means unfavourable, to the ruling party in the Scotch Church. The power and influence of Dr. Chalmers as a great power in the country had been perceived and acknowledged by both parties in politics, and his advice had been asked and his opinion taken on various subjects with the deference due to a great authority. To the framing of the Veto Act the Government had at least made no objection, if it did not yield a tacit approval. It had sanctioned the principle still more distinctly after the active troubles began, by more or less pledging itself in the case of Crown patronage to force no presentee upon an unwilling parish (an act condemned by the Scotch lawyers as unconstitutional). It was, therefore, with good hope of some action on the part of Government which should make the position more possible, that Chalmers, the acknowledged leader of the Church, and his colleagues approached the Ministry. Something must, it was evident, be done to meet the emergency. The Church could not go calmly on with a portion of its officers in full rebellion, and with the possibility of being met at every step, whether in the granting of holy orders, whether in the internal discipline of its own organization, by an interdict forbidding any action. So far had this already gone that a few guilty and disreputable ministers, one charged with theft and another with drunkenness, had already refused the jurisdiction of the Church, and resorted to the defence of the Court of Session to protect them against any inquiry into their conduct. The situation had thus become intolerable, and some outlet it was necessary to find. There could be, perhaps, no question more embarrassing for a Government fully occupied with other imperial concerns, very ignorant as to ecclesiastical questions, and with little leisure to devote to any such problems. They were glad to contribute so much as a conciliatory undertaking to yield to popular feeling so far as regarded any appointment of their own, an undertaking which no doubt would have been acquiesced in by a great number of patrons, nobody in reason desiring to exasperate or force into violent measures the authorities of the Church. But already the current of events had begun to acquire that velocity which no mild conciliatory measure could stop, and no Ministry was prepared to take a step universally discountenanced by every Government, and give to the Church a free hand, as against the stipulations and control of the State. To recognize that it was unfortunate and undesirable that a Scotch parish should be driven out of all comfort and self-command by the imposition upon it of a minister it hated, was one thing; but to support the *liberum arbitrium* of a Church Court against the right of the individual to secure a living which had been promised him, and of the courts of law to give him possession of his rights, was quite another matter. First one Minister and then another refused to move. Then there stepped into the breach Lord Aberdeen, a statesman of mild and peaceable views, who had the advantage of understanding the subject, though not as would appear of being able or willing to express himself so clearly as to be distinctly understood by the Church leaders, who at first put unlimited trust in him. We can enter into this subject in only the briefest way, at the risk of leaving but an imperfect impression on the mind of the reader. It is too complicated, too long, for full treatment in the space at our disposal, nor is it likely that the reader of to-day could enter into its complexities with anything like the keen and burning interest which even in Scotland has now dropped, but which once attended every detail of the controversy. It is enough to say that the negotiations were carried on from 1838, the year in which the Auchterarder case was settled, until 1843, when the Government rejected the Church's Claim of Rights, and the step to which the majority had by this time pledged themselves had to be taken. This step, at first mentioned in the discussion as a possibility which nobody seriously contemplated, a withdrawal from the support of the State, or a withdrawal by the State of that support, is mentioned for the first time in Chalmers' speech above quoted as a danger which every effort must be made to avert; but gradually, as the excitement grew and the conflict went on, the expression he had used became more and more a common word in men's mouths and a prospect in their minds. "The calamity of a disruption betwixt us," Chalmers said in the Assembly of 1839, meaning solely betwixt the Church and State, not between the two parties in the Church. By 1841, however, the sense of some great event impending had proceeded so far that there was a proposal made by several ministers, headed by Mr. Smith of Greenock, that a formal demand should be made by the Church either of complete independence or severance altogether from the State, a proposition with which Chalmers declared himself to be "quite in love," though anxious to wait a little before offering such a trenchant proposal to the consideration of either party. One cannot help feeling that such a demand could scarcely be thought of by those who believed it likely to be accepted, and that it was in fact more a threat than a proposal. Indeed, this feeling seems to underlie much of the discussion throughout. It would almost seem as if the Church could not realize or imagine it possible that the State could in the long run deny her claim, or risk the extraordinary catastrophe of her withdrawal from the long partnership. An attitude of this kind is not unknown in private difficulties, when one person proposes with a calmness born of a conviction of its impossibility, a tragic separation to which he is deeply persuaded the other will never consent, until suddenly, in the course of mutual exasperation, that other turns to bay and does consent, to the confusion, yet angry or solemn acquiescence of its original proposer. It is impossible not to perceive something of this in the attitude of the majority of the Church. The impassible State raised many hopes, gave many disappointments, yet could not, would not let the whole clergy of Scotland go, and must at the last yield to something that could be accepted as a standing-ground. On the other hand, the State, cynical as every Government is compelled to be, was equally convinced that the clergy of Scotland would *not* go, and that when a man's eyes were fully (and with greater force the eyes of a number of men) opened to the fact that all his interests hung in the balance, and that his daily bread was at stake, no theoretical "cause" would prove strong enough to make him take the decisive step. On both sides the conception of the other's purpose and power was mistaken: neither could comprehend the possibility of heroic and irredeemable action on the other part.

The compromise attempted by Lord Aberdeen proposed to enact that parishioners, discontented with a presentee, should have the power of presenting distinct objections against him to the Presbytery, upon the validity of which they should be permitted to judge, but that the mere fact that he was disliked or disapproved, without solid and definite warrant—his want of "acceptability" in short as a minister—should not be allowed as a reason for his rejection. The Duke of Argyle, on the other hand, originated a measure making the Veto Act, in even a form wider than the original, a part of the British Constitution. The latter of these proposals was impossible as an Act to be passed by Parliament; the former seemed to Chalmers and his followers to beg the whole question, putting aside that *liberum arbitrium* which was the chief point in their contention.

Throughout the whole discussion, which we have attempted to describe merely in its historical aspect, Chalmers was the leading figure. It was he who conducted every new advance, who led on from step to step. His opinion is asked and his advice taken almost with the vigilant watch upon every change of his countenance with which obedient ministers approach an absolute Sovereign. Lord Aberdeen puts this position very strongly and simply in the letters addressed by him to Chalmers on the construction of the proposed Bill. He has endeavoured, he says, to convince the deputation sent from Edinburgh to confer with him, and consisting of an eminent clergyman and equally well-known layman, of his "sincere desire to meet their views"; but he adds—

"After all, however, I am well aware that the success of this measure will mainly depend on the reception with which it may meet from yourself. I believe that the peace of the Church is at this moment in your hands; for although from the accident of birth and social position I have had the means of proposing this measure to the Legislature, it will depend upon you whether it is to receive life and efficacy."

In still more solemn tones in an after letter, Lord

Aberdeen writes again "to bring distinctly before you the state and prospects of the Church of Scotland so far as the Legislature is concerned, as well as respectfully to represent to you the awful responsibility under which you are about to be placed. I have now only to pray that by an effort of moral courage you may save the Establishment from the dangers by which it is threatened." Nor does the tone of the members of the Church and his fellow-leaders differ much from this assumption. It is to Chalmers when they return that their first report is made. It is he who furnishes detailed instructions for the guidance of the various embassies sent to London, for the Declaration of Rights to be presented to Government, and for every successive act in the struggle. Nor does he disclaim the overwhelming position attributed to him. "I feel the responsibility of my position," he says, in his reply to Lord Aberdeen. It will scarcely be necessary to point out to the reader who has seen, so far as we have been able to present it, the course of Chalmers' life, how this position was produced. After his short but splendid reign in Glasgow, which had made him the foremost figure in the Church, he had been seated (for fifteen years before the crisis came) at the very source and fountain-head of influence as Professor of Divinity in Edinburgh, the head-quarters of ecclesiastical interests. Many of the younger ministers of the Church had thus passed through his hands, and been subjected to his impetuous and overwhelming influence. He had himself asserted, as one of his chief reasons for leaving Glasgow, even when only the comparatively insignificant Chair of Moral Philosophy in St. Andrews was in question, that no individual charge in the Church could be so important as the office of training and educating the minds of its future clergy; and he had amply carried out his own prevision in this respect. On the other hand, he had been instrumental by his great movement for Church Extension, though only partially successful and much interrupted by the succeeding great controversy, in adding many new ministers to the number of the Church. We may add to this the charm which his strong sense and practical genius exercised over men of the world (to use the word in its best sense), the many devout and strong-headed men, not clerical, who are in Scotland scarcely less concerned in the management and development of the Church than the ministers. He was the pride both of the Church and the country, the greatest religious orator of the day, bringing, as Scotland loves, his fame to swell the national glory. Government and people alike recognized his moral predominance. Notwithstanding the Presbyterian parity, which is the rule of his Church, no Archbishop was ever more truly the Primate of the great province which he swayed.

But perhaps such a position—in the midst, not of a calm community pursuing its equal way, with so much routine to balance its enthusiasm that an occasional fiery impulse is a godsend: but of an agitated and eager population with a burning question flung into its midst—is too great a responsibility for any man, especially for one in whose character impetuosity had so great a place. He had never been a patient man in any of the circumstances of his life. He who had vindicated his own boyish claims to respect in his first small tutorship, and who had set St. Andrews by the ears in vehement justification of his injured dignity at the very beginning of his career—he who fulminated against the Glasgow dinner-parties, and found the crowds who attended his path intolerable, was not less impetuous in full maturity than in his fiery youth. If any derogation from his personal independence set him aflame, it may be imagined with how much stronger force the attack upon the independence of the Church, the ideal which he had so fondly cherished and so proudly proclaimed, would move him. Sagacious as he was, practical as he was, the art of compromise was unfamiliar and uncongenial to him. We may think now, looking back, that with such a measure as that of Lord Aberdeen, the Church in the exercise of prudence and patience, with use of all the means within its power to stave off unpopular presentations in the meantime, and in the future the hope of that entire abolition of patronage which has since been attained, might very well have made shift to live and hold her ground attending better things. The Church of England has been often content with a compromise much less in her favour. But the Scot, so canny in the conventional idea, so cautious in the common opinion, is by nature absolute and unaccommodating in all matters of mind and sentiment. He is more logical than his brother on the other side of the Tweed, less apt to find a *via media*, or to wish to find it, and more apt to act *en masse* with that momentum and accumulation of velocity which attends a great general impulse. The "unanimous hero nation," as Carlyle calls it, is apt to go too far, with too great a swing of united movement. In politics the same effect has been recently produced under our eyes. In religion the current is still stronger. A leader with power such as that of

Chalmers should have the faculty of holding back, of putting on the drag; but Chalmers was himself the most striking example of the national characteristic. When he delivered a great speech, it was not only his audience whom he worked up to fever heat, but himself. The foam flew from his mouth and the sparks from his eyes, which in repose were almost dull, wrapped in veils of abstraction and musing. At first some of his fraternal critics in his own party considered him too conservative, inventing the veto by way of saving patronage: but long ere the matter had reached its climax Chalmers had thrown aside the veto. "I am sickened to despair," he cried, with his accustomed vehemence, though in the stillness of a letter, "that we must foist in Non-Intrusion upon every occasion." He flung all these smaller details to the winds. "Anything short of an unfettered spiritual power in the Church would be fatal to its national establishment," he replies to Lord Aberdeen. "The integrity of our jurisdiction," not the details by which that is carried out, becomes his war-cry. "The cause of our spiritual independence, or which is tantamount to this, the sacred cause of the Headship of Christ." Thus his demand, the necessity which possessed him, swelled and rose. It is easy to say and to understand that to force upon an unwilling community as its religious instructor a man whom it disapproves and dislikes, is a reasonable grievance, and very prejudicial to the cause, not only of religion, but of the good conduct and orderly life which are of so much importance to the State—but "the sacred cause of the Headship of Christ," as manifested in the unfettered power of Presbyteries and Assemblies, was a very different matter, and it is scarcely wonderful that the Government paused astonished before this plea. It is the claim of Rome, one continually struggled against by all kings and parliaments, subsisting only by the force of the strongest and most prevailing of ancient institutions, and tempered by every limitation which the ingenuity of statesmen have been able to impose upon a power which asserts itself to hold the keys of eternal life and death. The Church of Scotland made no such assertion, claimed even no Divine authority for its special organization, admitted Christian expediency as one of the foundations for its distinctive peculiarities—yet made the same claim as Rome.

It would be perhaps too much to say that Chalmers in the position which circumstances and his own genius had procured him, as leader of the Church, lost his head, to use a common expression; yet it is very apparent that the whirl and impetus of a rising excitement swelled in him, making his demand not less but more comprehensive and absolute, and bringing the alternative—at first produced as a threat, then gradually settling into an ultimatum, to frighten the other side into compliance, again rising to the height of a necessity and pledge of honour—more and more into view. In the beginning of the year 1843 this alternative had become the nearest and most pressing of all things, a shadow that filled the whole landscape, and was in every man's thoughts—That Government should either grant the Church full independence, or sever altogether her connexion with the State. But this was an impossible way of putting it; for the last thing the State was likely to do—except grant that independence—was of its own accord to sever the bond between itself and the Church. The formula required to be put in another way—That the Church should either win complete independence, or give up the livings and privileges of the Establishment. In that form it became comprehensible and practical. If not free with bread to eat and a roof to shelter her, than free without either bread or roof, as she had been before, as she had chosen many times to be. The heroic way has always a charm, especially to simple minds and those more conversant with the high motives of religion than with the complications of the world: and the Scotch imagination has always thrilled to the idea of the Church in the wilderness, the worship on the hillside, which is one of its most cherished traditions. The blood of the Covenanters is in all our veins. There is an attraction even in the very idea of sacrifice—a sacrifice great enough to make the ears of all men tingle all over the world, to penetrate the very universe with a high beat and throb of emotion. It might be said, and was said, that for Chalmers and his colleagues—men of the highest influence and reputation, sure anywhere of a high place, and of undiminished popular support—it was an easy matter to give up their existing position and means; and no doubt there was a certain truth in the statement. The real battle was fought out in obscure country manses, where devout men of small gifts, the humble parish priests to whom no glow of eloquence or charm of influence had been given, able only to look after their little flocks and preach their modest sermons, saw before them a step into the darkness, a destitution of all things, something more doubtful still than the cave in the desert and the raven's cake of bread: for the prophet had no astonished group of little children hanging on his skirts, no wistful woman treading by his side the way through the wilderness. What discussions, what consultations must have arisen in the chill spring evenings in those country manses between the minister and his wife, the man and woman upon whom the anguish of this burden lay! He whom it did not become to relinquish his birthright, to sully his personal honour, to betray as he thought his Lord, by any going back; and she, as careful of all these high principles as he, but with a closer sense of all the details of renunciation, and with the thought of the children tugging at both their hearts. If the Government accepted the Claim of Rights, well: but if not—then— Upon what troubled and anxious scenes the early sunshine of May, beginning to linger out in the sweetness of the long northern evening, must have looked down.

On the other side there were jibes and jests and provocations. The spectators were uneasy, expectant, full of gathering excitement too. Who would go out? would any one go out? Would there be forty of them? would there be a dozen? The men in the clubs in Princes Street and the young Briefless in the Parliament House made bets upon the event. Would it end in a great fiasco, and Homeric roar of laughter over the collapse of so many heroics? Edinburgh at least could think of nothing else. The opposite party in the Church, uneasy and alarmed, tried to comfort itself with predictions, with calculations. Chalmers, of course, would go—unless indeed, in the boundless skill of his mathematical genius, he found out still at the last moment some exquisite reason to smooth the necessity away. It was worth while to live at such a moment, to feel the prick and thrill of that great question, the human problem of what a man will do in a pressing emergency, exposed to every curious looker-on, and to be solved before their eyes—the most entertaining, the most absorbing interest of humanity. That Government would reject the Claim of Rights everybody was assured—short of a miracle; but then there is in every soul the profound certainty that a miracle is always possible, whatever science may say. This question was settled just before the meeting of the General Assembly. The Government did reject the Claim of Rights, and the question became more exciting, more earnest than ever—What will they do?

The Assembly met on the 18th of May, 1843, in the midst of this atmosphere surcharged with the highest excitement. By four o'clock in the morning eager spectators had begun to fill the church in which its deliberations were held, and the streets were crowded with a surging mass of people. In the long hall of Holyrood, where the preposterous portraits of imaginary kings are still allowed to hang, the Lord High Commissioner was holding his usual *levée,* when a little accident took place; a noise, and the portrait of King William III. fell from the wall opposite to the spot where her Majesty's representative stood. "There goes the Revolution Settlement," cried a voice tingling over the crowd, which even there was full of the pervading excitement. The accident was indeed significant enough to be remarked. In St. Andrews Church all was expectation as the music of the approaching procession, escorting the Lord High Commissioner, was heard. That functionary came in, in his little state, and the church filled with the black-coated mass of the clergy, while the multitude outside thronged to the very steps impatient for the event. One can feel the rustle yet hush of that crowd when, after a few minutes of breathless expectation, occupied within by necessary formalities, a rustle of movement was heard, and the well-known white head and pale, impressive heavy countenance of Chalmers became suddenly visible, with the Moderator in his robes by his side, issuing from the door: and behind him an endless line, figure after figure, appearing like an army. The crowd held its breath, then breaking into tumultuous cheers, opened a narrow line in which three men could walk abreast, in the ever-lengthening line: and soon that dark and silent procession, a quarter of a mile long, wound on between these living walls, recognized, shouted over, cheered with the wild outcries of unrestrainable emotion along the whole course of the way. More than four hundred ministers walked in that line, leaving their all in this world—their incomes, their positions, their homes—behind them for ever.

> "Ah, Freedom is a noble thing!
> Freedom makes man to have liking.
> Freedom all solace to man gives,
> He lives at ease who freely lives.
> Grief, sickness, poortith, want, are all
> Summed up within the name of thrall."

This sentiment has always been dear to the mind of Scotland. It overwhelmed the country with one great sympathetic thrill, which carried every other interest away. To Lord Jeffrey, sitting quiet in his library, a sudden visitor broke in with the cry, "More than four hundred of them are out!" The little judge and critic, no clerical, but with a heart open to every noble and generous emotion, sprang to his feet with an answering shout, "I am proud of my country; there is not another country upon earth where such a deed could have been done."

Nobody has ever cared to inquire what went on in the deserted place from which that crowd (nearly a thousand altogether, for there were more than an equal number of elders in the procession) went forth, nor what was the sick sensation at the heart of the other men who stood looking on aghast to see the Church rent in two. There must have been many good and honest men on that other side, as is proved by the course of history, to whom the fact now accomplished, which so long they had hoped and believed to be impossible, must have conveyed the keenest pang. But they are left out in all the narratives. With the Scotch faculty of stamping a name upon a foe which is often highly felicitous and effective, the remaining portion of the Church were distinguished at once as "Residuaries," and thus consigned to a popular limbo of ridicule and jibe. The men who "went out" were the heroes of universal sympathy and fame.

We are glad, this event once over, of which we cannot but feel both the cause and the result to be full of matter for painful consideration, to find our Chalmers again in his most characteristic development. It is not to be supposed that such a born legislator and administrator suffered this great convulsion to happen without having made preparation for it—preparation in which he was in his element, the right man in the right place. He who in almost his first utterance in the new place of meeting warned the country that he had in no degree changed his mind on the subject of a National Church, and that though he had now to count upon voluntary help for the sustenance of the Church, he was in no way converted to the voluntary principle, had not waited till now to organize that voluntary help into a fund bearing all the character of a great endowment. The Sustentation Fund of the Free Church—the only thing which could have enabled this great band of ministers, 470 in all, to keep their order and organization and maintain the whole frame-work of an ecclesiastical establishment without a bank or purse, after having thus suddenly deprived them-selves of all their means of subsistence, their homes and places of worship—was Chalmers' last great work. The plan had been forming in his mind for some time before, taking the place of that great effort for Church Extension which he had entered into with so much enthusiasm, but had not been able to carry to the end he hoped. The plans which he had formed for that remained a ready machinery for the new and more pressing need. Before the new Free Church Assembly immediately formed in Canonmills' Hall, the place to which he led his four hundred when they left St. Andrews Church—had been in existence for many days, he was able to inform the excited and triumphant band —triumphant in their loss, with a conviction of having conquered and overcome, such as no material victory could have given—that already this new and great inheritance was provided for them. Six hundred and eighty-seven associations had been formed, extending over the whole country. The first-fruits of their con-tributions already amounted to £17,000, and he had, supposing no advance to be made on this beginning, the promise of a yearly revenue of £74,000. Nothing could better show the state of exultation and success, the sense of a great and unlimited future before them, than this speech.

"I doubt not," said Chalmers (addressing, not the vast assembly of people, but the band of the "fathers and brethren" who held the central place around him), "I doubt not there are a good many here who heard me predict such a result as that which I have this day laid before you; and I trust you will forgive me for saying, though I am not a professor of physiognomy, that when I chanced to lift my eyes from the paper to the countenances of those who were before me, I observed in them a good-natured leer of incredulity, mixed up no doubt with a benignant complacency, which they cast on the statements and high-coloured representations of a very sanguine Utopian. At the hazard of being regarded as a Utopian this second time, and at this new stage of our advance, I will make as confident an avowal now as I did then, that if we only make a proper use of the summer that is before us in stirring up—I do not say the people of Scotland, but that portion of them who are the friends of our protesting Church—if we do what we might and what we ought, we will not only be able to repair the whole Disruption, but will get landed in the great and glorious work of Church Extension. For you will recollect that though the application of the first portion of the funds goes towards, I will not say the support of the ejected ministers, but the upholding of the continuance of their services, yet, after that is secured, and after the maximum has been attained, the over and above sums will go, not to the augmentation of ministerial income, but to the augmentation of ministerial services—not to the increase of the salaries of the ministers, but to the increase of their numbers; and we shall not stop short, I trust, in our glorious enterprise till, in the language you have already heard, 'the light of the gospel be carried to every cottage door within the limits of the Scottish territory.'"

The principle of the great fund, called, as has been said, with the usual felicity of nomenclature which distinguished this agitation and conflict, the Sustentation Fund, was entirely that of an endowment. That a minister should be dependent upon the gifts of his special congregation, or in any respect their hired servant, was obnoxious to every feeling of the race and profession with which Chalmers had to deal, as well as with his own. In actual practice that system, we presume, works well enough without bearing too hardly upon the shoulders or the souls of Nonconformists dependent upon the voluntary principle; and yet in the smaller Dissenting congregations, among the uneducated and vulgar, it does, we are told, often bear hardly enough. The ministers of Scotland had no experience of any such thing; their means were often small, but their position and modest dignity were secure; and to the greater part of them no humiliation of poverty would have been so great as that which should have compelled them to gather painfully their own individual living from those who had hitherto been in the position of their pupils and charges, the flock which they were commissioned to feed. The fund instituted by Chalmers gave at once from a Central Board an allowance to each minister, "an equal dividend or stipend, not to exceed an amount to be fixed by way of maximum," and thus secured their independence. To each or any, his congregation might offer a supplementary fund, according to their sense of what was fit; but his daily bread came from an abstract source, the best substitute for a formal endowment which could have been invented—nay, an endowment in the best sense of the word. The maximum was not great. It was not, to begin with, much over £100 a year, though it rose afterwards to £150; but neither are Scotch endowments great, and so much as it was, it was at least independent, sure, and free from any caprice of popularity—an unspeakable advantage. The extraordinary success of the scheme was as great as its form was admirable. We quote from a little biography of Chalmers, written by Mr. James Dodds, a brief summary of this financial triumph, which was his latest work.

"The number of ministers that came out in 1843 was about 500: in 1868 the Free Church ministry was 950.

"Within the same period—twenty-five years—there have been erected 900 churches, 650 manses, 600 schools, three colleges, a noble assembly hall, and an extensive and valuable library has been instituted.

"The central and local building funds have together raised £1,605,000.

"The value of property and other assets belonging to the body is £2,000,000.

"The yearly revenue for all purposes, which in 1863 was £343,000, in 1868 was £421,000.

"The Sustentation Fund in particular, which in 1844 was £146,000, in 1868 was £265,600."

These numbers are amazing: they form a budget surpassing that of some States. "I doubt," says Dr. Robert Buchanan, one of its chief administrators, "if there is any other revenue in the kingdom, civil or ecclesiastical, which comes in with such reliable regularity as our Free Church Sustentation Fund." It has undergone changes, we believe, since Chalmers' day. But Chalmers' plan has never failed to insure the high advantage he conceived. It has established and endowed his Church. It is a precedent if any such painful necessity should occur again. Whatever may be said of his action before the event, whether we may blame his impetuosity, his rashness, his absolutism, his failure in patience and duty to that very ideal of a Church which he held so high, here his praise and fame are supreme. If he were in any way guilty of that great breach which has rent Scotland in two, he did at last take the burden manfully upon his shoulders, and do for those who trusted in him his very best.

And after—— ? This is a dreary question to ask after almost every great crisis in life. The enthusiasm, the zeal, the warmth of feeling roused by the unexampled event of the Disruption were beyond description. Perhaps everybody concerned was too conscious that it was an unexampled event; but this consciousness in itself of having done something greater than had ever been known before, of having borne the most conspicuous public testimony since the Reformation of trust and faith—even in the weakness of human character, of having left dismay and death behind—no doubt had a share in keeping up the courage of the ministers who had made that sacrifice, during at least the first troublous portion of their after career. But when the steady roll of events had gone on for a period of years, what was there found for the elevation of the country and the cure of all its evils in this step which cost so much? Little, very little, was fulfilled of that of which they had dreamed. After many a jibe and jest at the "Residuaries," whom they had left astonied and cast down like men who dream, on their triumphant exit, it became apparent that they had not emptied or ruined the old framework of the Kirk, which would have been the only entire justification of the step they had taken. Had they carried all with them, and left only a vacant sanctuary behind, the sight of a unanimous Church severing itself from the bonds of State control would have been satisfactory to every ideal, and made no schism. But this was what they did not do. The old National Church, after a pause indeed of consternation and weakness, slowly rose again from her ashes, proving her truth after all by a new form of that everlasting pledge that the gates of hell shall not prevail against the Church. These were no gates of hell: they were far more dangerous, they were the severed forces of true religion and devotion; but no more than the bands of evil did they prevail. And the issue has been no glorious revolution, but only the planting of another great Church by the side of the old, not for the conversion of the home-heathen or the spreading of Christian life among those alien to it, but, at least in the first place, for rivalship and contention, a struggle over the few sheep in the wilderness, an internecine warfare. That also by this time has quieted down, and the two Churches now exist side by side—the National Establishment strong as ever, the Free Church too, a majestic structure in its kind, full of power and influence. They hold the same doctrines, they use the same books, they sign the same creeds. The patronage which was the root of all dissensions has been swept away. No hateful summons of the State sounds at the one door more than at the other; the only distinction between has been extinguished. Why, then, do they stand still apart? It is a question difficult to answer. Because they have drifted into channels more apart than at the first, the National Church veering one way, the Free another, in impulse and heart, some people say. But every Church, like every human institution, has always had two sides, two tendencies, and neither has yet departed from the great standards round which both cling. "Though we quit the Establishment," said Chalmers, amid all the excitement of the Disruption, "we go out on the Establishment principle; we quit a vitiated Establishment, but would rejoice in returning to a pure one." His Church has never, so far as we know, contradicted his declaration. Why, then, do these two Churches stand apart?

It is a question full of solemn and most important meaning. We can only propound it as spectators of a great imperfection: we cannot answer nor even suggest a reply. The year now begun is the fiftieth year since these things were. What a thing would it be for Scotland, an act still more heroic because more liable to misconstruction, and less capable of the stimulus of high excitement and popular feeling, could the jubilee of the Free Church be celebrated by a reunion, and the deadly rent be healed!

CHAPTER VII.

THERE is no more sad or solemn thing in nature than to see how often the acknowledged hand of heaven, not only the award which is recognized as that of fate, will "keep the word of promise to the ear, and break it to the hope." Nothing can more clearly and over again testify to this than the end of the life of Chalmers. He was permitted to see churches rising over all the country, as he had dreamed and prayed to see: but they were not the churches of his dream, not the new homes to which a deserted and untaught people were to be seduced and drawn by every wile of Christian kindness and help. The churches were built, but they were built in competition with the existing churches to draw away from one to another the respectable bands of the Scotch bourgeoisie, the God-fearing peasant population, church-goers from their youth. If he recognized this at all in the quiet of his own thoughts, there is no word to say; certainly he did not appear to think of it in the public utterances of his enthusiasm, when his vehement spirit and impetuous nature flung themselves forth to meet the emergency which was great enough to occupy every faculty. Even at the moment he satisfied his visionary soul by a sweep forward into the time when, all immediate wants supplied, the new Church should rush forth, carrying all before her, into "the glorious field of Church Extension." That far glance into a future teeming with possibilities he permitted himself, and it would seem to have satisfied him. And fortunately he did not live long enough to realize the boundaries set hard and fast, as in the oldest of establishments, which formed themselves at once round the new organization of which he was the soul and chief.

He lived only four years after the great event which had filled with its controversies, its economics, and its triumphs the latter part of his life. When he had set the Sustentation Fund in full working order, he would seem to have withdrawn more or less from the agitations of business into the formation of the New College, of which he was at once appointed Principal. Not that his familar countenance was withdrawn from the high places of the Church, but a softened and subdued mood became apparent in all he said and did, a sort of gently stealing conviction that his work was over, and no more conflict or championship to be required of him. He had spoken before in his *Diary* of the seventh decade of life as of the Sabbath of man's days, the time of natural quietness and rest. This had begun for him in anything but rest; but when the immediate strain of the great crisis and catastrophe was over, as soon as circumstances permitted he seems to have sought the quietness which he had identified with this period of life. And never was life more full of honours, of popular recognition, of the homage of a world which had long been taught that it could make no mistake in any acknowledgment of the greatness of

Chalmers. So far as this was concerned, he had indeed nothing left to attain.

One new effort, however, remained for him to make. Besides the work of his classes, immediately reconstituted in a new Free Church College after his severance from the old, the one piece of work into which he threw himself with much of his old vehemence was the mission in the West Port, a very poor and degraded portion of Edinburgh, which he took in hand immediately after the Disruption, by way of resuming practically the work which he had begun in Glasgow, which he had meant to pursue on a large scale in his scheme of Church Extension, and to which we are glad to return as the dominant idea, in the midst of all interruptions and delays, of his entire public life. "I have determined," he wrote to a correspondent, "to assume a poor district of two thousand people and superintend it myself, though it be a work greatly too much for my declining strength and means. Yet such do I hold to be the efficiency of the method with the Divine blessing, that perhaps, as the concluding act of my public life, I shall make the effort to exemplify what as yet I have only expounded." He began the experiment with a delight and satisfaction which renewed many plans and visions of old. He found another name for the scheme, as he had already found so many striking and popular names. It was henceforth the Territorial Scheme, the local effort to be made from door to door, from street to street, to draw the careless people, who knew little of the gospel and nothing of the pious customs of religious life, to the church and school and helpful charities planted in their midst. He could not now, alas! as in the old masterful Glasgow way, take the poor and their provision upon his shoulders and beat down poor-houses and poor-laws and pauperism altogether out of the charmed parish, substituting brotherly help and Christian laws instead, with all the stern but kind restraints of constant supervision; but to Christianize after all was the great point, better even than to depauperize, and to his fervent mind the one always more or less included the other. It was the plan that had pleased his earliest thought. Intrusion and non-intrusion, veto and interdict, were hindrances in themselves hateful, though he had flung his whole soul into them when the struggle stood in the way of everything and had to be settled before anything else could be done. "Who cares about the Free Church," he cried indignantly, as soon as his hands were free, "compared with the Christian good of the people of Scotland?" It was not his now to organize that great and united assault upon the powers of darkness in their innermost dens, of which he had dreamed; but at least he could prove its possibility, as he had proved the possibility of that other devout imagination in Glasgow, and leave to all who came after him that best of lessons—that what men had done, men might again do. The district of which he took possession lay in absolute misery and depravity, cared for by no man. Its physical and moral condition were alike deplorable; one-fourth of the population were paupers on the poor-roll, and one-fourth were beggars, thieves, or unfortunate women. Drunkenness was almost universal, scarcely a third of the children were under any sort of instruction, and barring a few Roman Catholics, over whom the priests had still some hold, and a few stray intruders from better regions dwelling among these children of Heth against their will, the mass of the people were entirely beyond the reach of any religious influence. It was to this mass of human corruption that the great orator and legislator, sick of the commotion and the struggle, gladly turned his way. Once more his wonderful powers of organization were called into effect. He got up once more his "agency," humble citizens, chiefly of the poorer classes themselves. He divided the ground into "proportions," and began the work with all the enthusiasm of early days. Impatient and impetuous everywhere else, here he was patience itself, cheering his fellow-workers in every discouragement, bidding them never to despair.

This work was begun in 1843: four years after, in 1847, a church had been built, in which three hundred sittings were at once let to the surrounding families: and one hundred communicants from this once depraved and hopeless district assembled at the first Communion Service held a little later: the school was full, the parents paying the little school-fees cheerfully, and the whole face of the district changed. "I have got now the desire of my heart," Chalmers says, after that first communion. "The church is finished, the schools are flourishing, our ecclesiastical machinery is about complete, and all in good working order. God has indeed heard my prayer, and I would now lay down my head in peace and die." "I wish to communicate what to me is the most joyful event of my life," he wrote to one of his confidential correspondents. "I have been intent for thirty years on a territorial experiment, and I have now to bless God for the consummation of it." Five years after, when he had been long gone to his reward, the minister of the West

Port (Chalmers' Church, so called) had to report that the new congregation thus picked out of the waters of misery, was maintaining all its expenses by its own offerings, the income of the district for religious purposes amounting to nearly £250 a year, besides contributions amounting to £70 for other objects; that the church was filled to overflowing, and "it is not known that there is a single child of a family resident within the West Port who is not at school." This was the meaning and object of Thomas Chalmers' life. He was not permitted—what great visionary ever is?—to fulfil it grandly, his own way. Moses does not lead his bands over Jordan into the Land of Promise. Had the prophet been given that triumph, who can say what disappointments would have overwhelmed his great soul in the accomplishment of its hope? But he had his glimpse from the mountain heights of that fair land, and of that vague future which is always glorious to human eyes as long as it is unattained. And Chalmers, too, had his glimpse from Pisgah—his little savage West Port purified and taught and cleansed and made sacred to God; better, who could doubt, for him, than had he beheld his fresh and novel scheme settled down into the commonplace, battled over by combative philanthropists, lost in the rise and flow of other thoughts and other ambitions. But it is difficult to refrain from the thought—If he had been faithful to his first inspiration and resisted that charm of academic quiet which drew him away from Glasgow, but did not suit him after all when he tried it—if he had been so happy as to secure support for his grand scheme of Church Extension, when it filled all his veins with the divine delirium of eager zeal and enterprise—then there might have been no division, no breach, but a United Church, aggressive as he would have had it, assailing all the Powers of Darkness, beating out by cheerful force of multitudinous armies, Sin and Ignorance and Poverty and Discontent, the demons of his highest hatred! A devout imagination! yet surely one that some day will come true, all other means failing, by this one means, which the Happy Warrior, the Christian philosopher, thus proved and tried—leaving a warrant and an example for other men to tread in his steps.

But the ifs and thens are in a higher power—or rather, if we were to express our inmost thought, are never forced by that Divine Arbiter who has the issues of death in His hand: but who compels no man, and no body of men, to do well against their own will and meaning and desire.

It is almost amusing, if we dare apply such a word to a good man's prayers, to find in the record of his private devotions a prayer to understand the will of God "in regard to the right place and performances of a female agency," betraying thus a perplexity which must have been one time and another strongly developed in the minds of many clergymen; and on the other hand, to find him bursting forth in indignation as to the reluctance of some of the ministers to encourage his beloved "territorial" work, lest it should carry off some members from their own churches. "For the sake of the paltry few that would drop from this or that man's congregation," he cries, "am I to let the masses live in dirt and die in darkness?" He was impatient as of old with this and every petty thought, but never impatient of the hesitations or stupidities of the poor, always willing to wait, to foster every beginning, to break no bruised reed.

It is not much short of fifty years since Chalmers died, and his generation has departed too, carrying with them the personal impress of his aspect and character which was so strong upon all with whom he came in contact: and the materials for forming any new and independent views are wanting: yet we trust some impression of the inner man, with his weaknesses as well as his greatness, with the formality of the old middle-class Scotsman, and the vehemence of ardent genius, curiously supplementing, inspiring, and clothing each other, with his accent and flavour of intense nationality, and his big and generous soul, have been at least indicated in this summary of his great and busy life. It was not in his nature, nor was it happily the custom of his time and nation, to unfold his domestic life to the public, or open all the secret places of his being to the inquisition of men. His private journals, his prayers and meditations, were indeed published after his death: but there is in these private musings, sacred as they are, so much that is abstract, so little that is individual, that, as in all the similar records of that period and manners, very little is to be gleaned either of the character of the thinker or indeed of his personal way of contemplating the Divine subjects, of which they are full. We do not pretend to know whether the records of spiritual experience in our own day will be found more individual or more interesting when the next generation has them to know us by. But there will probably be not so many of them, nor will the pious soul seek to find pasture so consistently as was done fifty years ago among these often arid wastes. The letters of spiritual communion—which for a whole lifetime continue to call upon the reader to take the very first step in the Christian life as if no advance upon that were possible, and which after thirty or forty years of full acceptance of the mystery of faith still exhort both writer and reader to "Believe in the Lord Jesus Christ," as if they had not been devoutly doing so, as if that had not been the secret of their lives all the time—are, it seems to us, singularly unprofitable writings, notwithstanding that they have been so largely received by the devout as the language of religion. We have no profane meaning in saying so. It seems to us that a man who had lived by that faith, and in the light of constant communion with the Father of Spirits, should have a thousand things to tell us of that sacred intimacy, so real and all-pervading. But perhaps the very sacredness of the intercourse which makes the soul shy of its own deepest feelings, leads a man to take refuge in a mode of expression, constantly repeated and accepted by so many as the only language for such experiences, which is indeed conventional beyond description, and as little life-giving as any commonplace utterance could be. On his last day on earth, Chalmers, musing in his garden, softly walking like Isaac among the flowers in evening quiet, was heard murmuring to himself, "Father, my Heavenly Father." There is more to ourselves in this murmur than in the many pages of abstract piety which in the form of journals and letters fill so great a part of the volumes which contain the record of his life.

His domestic habits and tenor of existence are kept also in much unintentional abstractness. He had an excellent wife, congenial to him in every way, a woman who kept his path smooth and entered into his plans and thoughts: and that is all we know of her—everything, it is true, that is necessary, but yet nothing at all. His family consisted entirely of daughters, for whom he had a preference (as is said) over sons—but neither do we know anything of them. A glimpse of a grandchild, bearing in his life the part that "Hugh Little John" took in that of Scott, affords us a more pleasant prospect of that always beautiful communion, the intercourse between an old man and a child. And yet Chalmers scarcely lived to be, according to that extension which in theory at least we now make of life, an old man at all. He died at sixty-seven, not even reaching that ancient limit of existence which we now see so many overpass while retaining all their vigour: yet he had recognized himself for many years before as an old man, though there are no signs that his eyes were dim or his natural force abated. Towards the end of his life, however, we find a few details, specially in his last visit to his native home at Anstruther, which may be worth quoting. He wandered about there in his old haunts, recalling everything, reminding some of his old school-fellows, friends of fifty years or more, humble villagers that had never left their native boundaries, of ancient incidents of the far-away past. "You were the first man that ever gave me a notion of the form of the earth," he said to one. "I thought it was round like a shilling till you told me it was round like a marble." Another, who like himself was marked with small-pox, he congratulated on their mutual advantage over "folks with finer faces." "Theirs have been aye getting the waur, but ours have been aye getting the better of the wear." But the prettiest incident of all is one of a sentimental kind, also not unlike an incident in Sir Walter's life. Tom Chalmers, in his schooldays, a big, uncouth boy, had been much smitten in his boyish chaotic soul by the daily apparition of a little maiden riding in on her pony from her father's house in the country to homely Anster for lessons. Whether the bashful schoolboy ever reached so far as to speak to this vision of youth and loveliness we are not told. We presume that she was a Miss Ramsay of Barnsmuir, and therefore above the level of John Chalmers' son, but her road would lie past his house daily. The young lady grew up and married, and there is no sign that they ever met. But when he was an old and a great man, sixty-five, and one of the most notable personages in the country, he had a meeting with a younger sister of this little lady of his dreams. She herself was by this time dead; but he asked to hear everything about her, both her life and dying. At last he inquired whether there was any portrait of her in the house. The lady took him to a room in which a little profile, one of those black silhouettes so common in those days, hung upon the wall, when the following exceedingly quaint incident, full of clumsy but touching tenderness, took place—

"He placed himself before it, gazed on it with intense earnestness, took down the picture, took out his card, and by two wafers fixed it firmly on the back of the portrait, exactly opposite to the face. Having replaced the likeness, he stood before it and burst into a flood of tears, accompanied by the warmest expressions of attachment. After leaving the house he sauntered in silence round the garden, buried in old recollections, heaving a sigh occasionally and muttering to himself, 'More than forty years ago.'"

What was the queer meaning in the old man's mind, of that card placed behind the little dark shadow of his little love's face, who can tell? A kind of visionary appropriation of her and her youthful image amid the wilderness before and after of the unknown?

His son-in-law supplies, as if unwillingly, some little touches of his personal appearance and habits towards the end. After his early studies in the morning, which he kept up, spending some hours every day in writing, "he came forth beaming and buoyant with a step springing as that of childhood, and a spirit overflowing with benignity. If his grandson or any of the younger members of the family were alone in the breakfast-room, a broad and hearty 'Hurro! Hurro!' ringing through the hall announced his coming, and carried to them his morning greeting." He never gave up the native Scots, which had always hung upon his tongue in accent and expression in the midst of his most brilliant successes. Here is a statement, virtually the same as that which has been so much commented on as spoken by Carlyle, a congenial spirit. "Eh, man" (it was his Tommy who was addressed), "if a' the gowks in the world were brought together, they would fill a great muckle house." The bitterness goes out of the sentiment as thus expressed, if there was any bitterness in it. His remark on Carlyle, by the way, is worth preserving in its sagacious simplicity. They had met in London, and recognized each other at once, as like draws to like. "It is a most interesting phenomenon to me, Carlyle's state of mind. The lad" (this was in 1845) "looking with a most graphic and intelligent eye on the peculiarities of Calvinism, having a sort of regard for them too, and yet——" His opinion of other great persons further back in the world's history is highly characteristic too. "I like Isaac," he said, "there was a great mildness about him; it is very picturesque, his going forth to meditate in the evening. Jacob's early life is most distasteful to me; he was the sneck-drawer and Esau was the snool about the pottage. But how impressive his interview with Pharaoh and his closing scene! There was great chivalry no doubt in David's pouring out the water before the Lord, the chivalry of the middle ages in the antique Jewish way of it. I cannot say I altogether sympathize with it. I would e'en hae ta'en a willy waucht of the water. I like everything that marks the identity of human nature. I am sure that judgment of Solomon's would make a great stir among the women: tongues would not be idle in Jerusalem."

Chalmers returned from a course of visits in England on a Friday in May, 1847. The Assembly was sitting, and he was to read a report, not then finished, on the Monday, before that body. He was tired next day and did not get up, but saw and talked to his friends, holding with one of them a remarkable conversation, which from the lips of a Calvinist, a Predestinarian, and Necessitarian—dreadful names in our days, and supposed to mean dreadful things—may be a revelation to some readers. Chalmers breathed neither fire nor flame on these subjects. He would not have any limitation of the Atonement. He thought that when Scripture said that Christ died for the world, it was most likely that it meant that and nothing else. He "did not like the explanation," that what it meant was Gentiles as well as Jews. "There is one text that puts that explanation entirely aside," he said; "God commandeth all men everywhere to repent." "In the offer of the gospel we must put no limitation whatever," and he ended one of the last of his religious utterances on earth with these striking words—

"Human beings," continued Dr. Chalmers, "have the most strange way of keeping their accounts; they have one way of keeping their accounts with the world, and another way of keeping their accounts with heaven. In relation to the world you will find men often open, generous, and unsuspicious; but then they keep their accounts with heaven in the most suspicious and niggardly manner—in a manner with which I can have no sympathy, continually striving against and fighting with the goodness and sincerity of God, and will not take God at His word."

The next day he was unusually well and full of brightness. "I am fond," he said, "of the Sabbath. Hail, sacred Sabbath morn!" and, as has been said, he was heard murmuring "Father!" to himself as he took his meditative walk about the garden before the evening fell. He had gone to church in the afternoon, and ailed nothing, body or mind. Immediately after evening prayers he withdrew, bidding his family remember that they must be early to-morrow, and waved his hand saying, "A general good-night." Next morning a note came early for him, but no answer was received when his servant knocked at his door. He was thought to be asleep, and was left in quiet till another communication arrived of a more urgent character. Then some one went into the room, spoke without receiving any reply, and finally opened the shutters to admit the light. "He sat there half-erect, his head reclining quietly on the pillow—the expression of his countenance that of fixed and majestic repose. He had been dead for hours."

Thus peacefully, nobly, and quietly this great servant of God, with all his impetuosities calmed into rest, was released from the life burden. A more beautiful ending no man could desire. The chariots of Israel had already been waiting when he spoke with his Heavenly Father in the garden ; and for him there had been no further need for trial or for pain.

THE END.

Richard Clay & Sons, Limited,
London & Bungay.

A CATALOGUE OF BOOKS AND ANNOUNCEMENTS OF METHUEN AND COMPANY PUBLISHERS : LONDON 36 ESSEX STREET W.C.

CONTENTS

FEBRUARY 1903

FEBRUARY 1903

MESSRS. METHUEN'S ANNOUNCEMENTS

BY COMMAND OF THE KING

THE CORONATION OF EDWARD VII. By J. E. C. BODLEY, Author of 'France.' *Demy 8vo.*

This important book is the official history of the Coronation, and has been written by the distinguished author of 'France,' by command of the King himself. The Coronation is the central subject, and of it a detailed account is given. But the book is in no sense an occasional volume, and the Ceremony is treated, not as an isolated incident, but as an event belonging to European and Imperial history. At the end of the work there will be an appendix containing official list of all the persons invited to the Abbey, and also lists drawn up with some historical detail of the Colonial and Indian troops who assisted at the Ceremony. It will therefore be an historical document of permanent value and interest.

THE COMPLETE WORKS OF CHARLES LAMB. Edited by E. V. LUCAS. With numerous Illustrations. *In Seven Volumes. Demy 8vo. 7s. 6d. each.*

This new edition of the works of Charles and Mary Lamb, in five volumes (to be followed by two volumes containing the Letters), will be found to contain a large quantity of new matter both in prose and verse—several thousand words in all. Mr. E. V. Lucas, the editor, has attempted in the notes, not only to relate Lamb's writings to his life, but to account for all his quotations and allusions—an ideal of thoroughness far superior to any that previous editors have set before themselves. A Life of Lamb by Mr. Lucas will follow in the autumn.

THE LIFE AND LETTERS OF OLIVER CROMWELL. By THOMAS CARLYLE. With an Introduction by C. H. FIRTH, M.A., and Notes and Appendices by Mrs. S. C. LOMAS. *Three Volumes. 6s. each.* [*Methuen's Standard Library.*

This edition is brought up to the standard of modern scholarship by the addition of numerous new letters of Cromwell, and by the correction of many errors which recent research has discovered.

CRITICAL AND HISTORICAL ESSAYS. By LORD MACAULAY Edited by F. C. MONTAGUE, M.A. *Three Volumes. Crown 8vo. 6s. each.* [*Methuen's Standard Library.*

The only edition of this book completely annotated.

A SHORT HISTORY OF FLORENCE. By F. A. HYETT. *Demy 8vo. 7s. 6d.*

This work is intended to occupy a middle position between the Guides and Histories of Florence. It tells the story of the rise and fall of the Republic consecutively, but more succinctly than the works of Napier, Trollope, or Villari, while it treats of Florentine Art and Letters parenthetically but more systematically than has been done by either of these writers.

DAVID COPPERFIELD. With Introduction by GEORGE GISSING, Notes by F. G. KITTON, and Illustrations by E. H. NEW. *Two Volumes. Crown 8vo.* 3s. 6d. *each.*
[*The Rochester Dickens.*

THIRTY YEARS IN AUSTRALIA. By Mrs. CROSS (ADA CAMBRIDGE). *Demy 8vo.* 7s. 6d.

A highly interesting account of a generation in Australia by a distinguished writer. Mrs. Cross's style is picturesque, and the book is more attractive than many novels. The early difficulties of Australian settlers, life in the towns and life on the farms are vividly described.

LETTERS FROM A SELF-MADE MERCHANT TO HIS SON. By GEORGE HORACE LORIMER. *Crown 8vo.* 6s.

This book is a masterpiece of humour and sound sense. It purports to be a collection of letters written by J. Graham, head of a great packing company in Chicago, to his son Pierrepont, and it describes in a racy and interesting form the secrets of success in business and in life.

WHEN I WAS A CHILD. By AN OLD POTTER BOY. *Crown 8vo.* 6s.

A BOOK OF THE COUNTRY AND THE GARDEN. By H. M. BATSON. Illustrated by F. CARRUTHERS GOULD and A. C. GOULD. *Demy 8vo.* 10s. 6d.

SHAKESPEARE'S GARDEN. By the Rev. J. H. BLOOM. With Illustrations. *Fcap. 8vo.* 3s. 6d.; *leather*, 3s. 6d. *net.*

A CONCISE HANDBOOK OF HERBACEOUS PLANTS. By H. M. BATSON. *Fcap. 8vo.* 3s. 6d.

A very complete and concise guide in alphabetical order.

THE LAND OF THE BLACK MOUNTAIN. Being a description of Montenegro. By R. WYON and G. PRANCE. With 40 Illustrations. *Crown 8vo.* 6s.

A BOOK OF EXMOOR. By F. J. SNELL. Illustrated. *Crown 8vo.* 6s.

This book deals with a variety of topics, embracing legend, folklore, dialect, sport, biography, history, and natural history, and renders accessible to the public a mass of particulars hitherto attainable only in expensive monographs or in scattered periodicals. The author has been at immense pains to consult every known source of information, both printed and oral; and his aim has been to produce, not so much a guide-book, but something more satisfying and substantial, viz. an exhaustive account of the matters in question. There are numerous illustrations.

THE DEVOTIONS OF BISHOP ANDREWES. By F. E. BRIGHTMAN, M.A., of Pusey House, Oxford. *Crown 8vo.* 6s.

This elaborate work has been in preparation for many years, and is the most complete edition that has ever been published of the famous devotions. It contains a long Introduction, with numerous Notes and References.

THE SPIRIT AND ORIGIN OF CHRISTIAN MONASTICISM. By JAMES O. HANNAY, M.A. *Crown 8vo.* 6s.

THE SATIRES OF JUVENAL. Translated by S. G. OWEN. *Crown 8vo.* 2s. 6d. [*Classical Translations.*

THE ENGLISH SUNDAY. By E. R. BERNARD, M.A., Canon of Salisbury. *Fcap. 8vo.* 1s. 6d.

The Little Library

Pott 8vo, cloth, 1s. 6d. net; leather, 2s. 6d. net each volume.

ROMANY RYE. By GEORGE BORROW. With Notes and an Introduction by JOHN SAMPSON.

ESMOND. By W. M. THACKERAY. Edited by STEPHEN GWYNN.

CHRISTMAS BOOKS. By W. M. THACKERAY. Edited by STEPHEN GWYNN.

CHRISTMAS BOOKS. By CHARLES DICKENS. Edited by STEPHEN GWYNN. *Two Volumes.*

A LITTLE BOOK OF ENGLISH SONNETS. Edited by J. B. B. NICHOLS.

THE SCARLET LETTER. By NATHANIEL HAWTHORNE.

The Arden Shakespeare

General Editor—W. J. CRAIG.

OTHELLO. Edited by H. C. HART. *Demy 8vo.* 3*s.* 6*d.*

CYMBELINE. Edited by EDWARD DOWDEN. *Demy 8vo.* 3*s.* 6*d.*

Little Biographies

Cloth, 3s. 6d.; leather, 4s. net.

THE YOUNG PRETENDER. By C. S. TERRY. With 12 Illustrations.

ROBERT BURNS. By T. F. HENDERSON. With 12 Illustrations.

CHATHAM. By A. S. M'DOWALL. With 12 Illustrations.

TENNYSON. By A. C. BENSON, M.A. With 12 Illustrations. *Fcap. 8vo.*

The Little Guides

Pott 8vo, cloth, 3s.; leather, 3s. 6d. net.

CORNWALL. By A. L. SALMON. Illustrated by B. C. BOULTER.

KENT. By G. CLINCH. Illustrated by F. D. BEDFORD.

HERTFORDSHIRE. By H. W. TOMPKINS, F.R.H.S. Illustrated by E. H. NEW.

ROME. By C. G. ELLABY. Illustrated by B. C. BOULTER.

The Library of Devotion

Pott 8vo, cloth, 2s.; leather, 2s. 6d. net.

GRACE ABOUNDING. By JOHN BUNYAN. Edited by S. C. FREER, M.A.

BISHOP WILSON'S SACRA PRIVATA. Edited by A. E BURN, B.D.

THE DEVOTIONS OF ST. ANSELM. Edited by C. C. J. WEBB, M.A.

LYRA SACRA: A Book of Sacred Verse. Selected and edited by H. C. BEECHING, M.A., Canon of Westminster.

Educational Books

AN INTRODUCTION TO THE STUDY OF TEXTILE FABRICS AND TEXTILE DESIGN. By ALDRED F. BARKER, Author of 'Pattern Analysis,' etc. With numerous Diagrams and Illustrations. *Demy 8vo.*

AGRICULTURAL GEOLOGY. By J. E. MARR, F.R.S. With numerous Illustrations. *Crown 8vo.*

MENSURATION. By C. T. MILLIS, M.I.M.E., Principal of the Borough Polytechnic College. With Diagrams. *Crown 8vo.*

THE ACTS OF THE APOSTLES. Edited by A. E. RUBIE, M.A., Headmaster Royal Naval School, Eltham. *Crown 8vo.* 2*s.* [*Methuen's Junior School Books.*

A JUNIOR FRENCH GRAMMAR. By L. A. SORNET and M. J. ACATOS, Modern Language Masters at King Edward's School, Birmingham. [*Methuen's Junior School Books.*

THE STUDENTS' PRAYER BOOK. PART I. MORNING AND EVENING PRAYER AND LITANY. Edited by W. H. FLECKER, M.A., D.C.L., Headmaster of the Dean Close School, Cheltenham. *Crown 8vo.* 2*s.* 6*d.*

Fiction

LORD LEONARD THE LUCKLESS. By W. E. NORRIS. *Crown 8vo.* 6*s.*

THE BETTER SORT. By HENRY JAMES. *Crown 8vo.* 6*s.*

ANTHEA'S WAY. By ADELINE SERGEANT. *Crown 8vo.* 6*s.*

OUTSIDE AND OVERSEAS. By G. MAKGILL. *Crown 8vo.* 6*s.*

THE SQUIREEN. By SHAN. F. BULLOCK. *Crown 8vo.* 6*s.*

AUNT BETHIA'S BUTTON. By J. RANDAL. *Crown 8vo.* 6*s.*

LOVE IN A LIFE. By ALLAN MONKHOUSE. *Crown 8vo.* 6*s.*

A MIXED MARRIAGE. By Mrs. F. E. PENNY. *Crown 8vo.* 6*s.*

THE SWORD OF AZRAEL, a Chronicle of the Great Mutiny. By R. E. FORREST. *Crown 8vo.* 6*s.*

A FREE LANCE OF TO-DAY. By HUGH CLIFFORD. *Crown 8vo.* 6*s.*

A STRETCH OFF THE LAND. By C. STEWART BOWLES. *Crown 8vo.* 6*s.*

THE KNIGHT PUNCTILIOUS. By ARTHUR MOORE. *Crown 8vo.* 6*s.*

THE POET'S CHILD. By EMMA BROOKE. *Crown 8vo.* 6*s.*

THE DIVERTED VILLAGE. By GRACE RHYS and ANOTHER. With Illustrations by DOROTHY GWYN JEFFRIES. *Crown 8vo.* 6*s.*

THE RED HOUSE. By Mrs. E. BLAND (E. NESBIT). Illustrated. *Crown 8vo.* 6*s.*

WORLD'S PEOPLE. By JULIEN GORDON. *Crown 8vo.* 6*s.*

THE CYNIC AND THE SYREN. By J. W. MAYALL. *Crown 8vo.* 6*s.*

A BRANDED NAME. By J. BLOUNDELLE BURTON. *Crown 8vo.* 6*s.*

SILENT DOMINION. By Mrs. E. W. TRAFFORD-TAUNTON. *Crown 8vo.* 6*s.*

THE MACHINATIONS OF THE MYO-OK. By CECIL LOWIS. *Crown 8vo.* 6*s.*

ABRAHAM'S SACRIFICE. By GUSTAF JANSON. *Crown 8vo.* 6*s.*

PLAIN AND VELDT. By J. H. M. ABBOT, Author of 'Tommy Cornstalk.' *Crown 8vo.* 6*s.*

BY A FINNISH LAKE. By PAUL WAINEMAN. *Crown 8vo.* 6*s.*

A LOST ESTATE. By M. E. MANN. A New Edition. *Crown 8vo.* 6*s.*

THE PARISH OF HILBY. By M. E. MANN. A New Edition. *Crown 8vo.* 6*s.*

LITTLE TU'PENNY. By S. BARING-GOULD. A New Edition *Crown 8vo.* 6*d.*

FOUR NOVELS TRANSFERRED

New Editions. Crown 8vo. 3s. 6d. each.

TALES OF SPACE AND TIME. By H. G. WELLS.

WHEN THE SLEEPER WAKES. By H. G. WELLS.

LOVE AND MR. LEWISHAM. By H. G. WELLS.

THE INVISIBLE MAN. By H. G. WELLS.

The Novelist

Messrs. METHUEN are issuing under the above general title a Monthly Series of Novels by popular authors at the price of Sixpence. Each Number is as long as the average Six Shilling Novel.

Jan. DRIFT. By L. T. MEADE.

Feb. THE MASTER OF BEECHWOOD. By ADELINE SERGEANT.

March. CLEMENTINA. By A. E. W. MASON.

April. THE ALIEN. By F. F. MONTRESOR.

May. THE BROOM SQUIRE. By S. BARING-GOULD.

June. HONEY. By HELEN MATHERS.

July. THE FOOTSTEPS OF A THRONE. By MAX PEMBERTON.

Additional Volumes and Reprints

III. THE INCA'S TREASURE. By ERNEST GLANVILLE. *Reprint.*

IX. A FLASH OF SUMMER. By Mrs. W. K. CLIFFORD, *in place of* 'The Adventure of Princess Sylvia.'

Methuen's Sixpenny Library

New Volumes 1903.

Jan. A STATE SECRET. By B. M. CROKER.

Feb. SAM'S SWEETHEART. By HELEN MATHERS.

March. HANDLEY CROSS. By R. S. SURTEES.

April. ANNE MAULEVERER. By Mrs. CAFFYN.

May. THE ADVENTURERS. By H. B. MARRIOT WATSON.

THE CEDAR STAR. By M. E. MANN.

June. MASTER OF MEN. By E. P. OPPENHEIM.

July. THE TRAIL OF THE SWORD. By GILBERT PARKER.

A CATALOGUE OF

MESSRS. METHUEN'S PUBLICATIONS

PART I.—GENERAL LITERATURE

Jacob Abbot. THE BEECHNUT BOOK. Edited by E. V. LUCAS. Illustrated. *Square Fcap 8vo.* 2s. 6d. [Little Blue Books.

W. F. Adeney, M.A. See Bennett and Adeney.

Æschylus. AGAMEMNON, CHOEPHOROE, EUMENIDES. Translated by LEWIS CAMPBELL, LL.D., late Professor of Greek at St. Andrews. 5s. [Classical Translations.

G. A. Aitken. See Swift.

William Alexander, D.D., Archbishop of Armagh. THOUGHTS AND COUNSELS OF MANY YEARS. Selected from the writings of Archbishop ALEXANDER. *Square Pott 8vo.* 2s. 6d.

Aristophanes. THE FROGS. Translated into English by E. W. HUNTINGFORD, M.A., Professor of Classics in Trinity College, Toronto. *Crown 8vo.* 2s. 6d.

Aristotle. THE NICOMACHEAN ETHICS. Edited, with an Introduction and Notes, by JOHN BURNET, M.A., Professor of Greek at St. Andrews. *Demy 8vo.* 15s. *net.*

'We have seldom, if ever, seen an edition of any classical author in which what is held in common with other commentators is so clearly put, and what is original is of such value and interest.'—*Pilot.*

J. B. Atkins. THE RELIEF OF LADYSMITH. With 16 Plans and Illustrations. *Third Edition. Crown 8vo.* 6s.

J. B. Atlay. See R. H. Barham.

St. Augustine, THE CONFESSIONS OF. Newly Translated, with an Introduction and Notes, by C. BIGG, D.D., late Student of Christ Church. *Third Edition. Pott 8vo. Cloth,* 2s; *leather,* 2s. 6d. *net.* [Library of Devotion.

'The translation is an excellent piece of English, and the introduction is a masterly exposition. We augur well of a series which begins so satisfactorily.'—*Times.*

Jane Austen. PRIDE AND PREJUDICE. Edited by E. V. LUCAS. *Two Volumes. Pott 8vo. Each volume, cloth,* 1s. 6d.; *leather,* 2s. 6d. *net.* [Little Library.

NORTHANGER ABBEY. Edited by E. V. LUCAS. *Pott 8vo. Cloth,* 1s. 6d.; *leather,* 2s. 6d. *net.* [Little Library.

Constance Bache. BROTHER MUSICIANS. Reminiscences of Edward and Walter Bache. With 16 Illustrations. *Crown 8vo.* 6s. *net.*

R. S. S. Baden-Powell, Major-General. THE DOWNFALL OF PREMPEH. A Diary of Life in Ashanti, 1895. With 21 Illustrations and a Map. *Third Edition. Large Crown 8vo.* 6s.

THE MATABELE CAMPAIGN, 1896. With nearly 100 Illustrations. *Fourth and Cheaper Edition. Large Crown 8vo.* 6s.

Graham Balfour. THE LIFE OF ROBERT LOUIS STEVENSON. *Second Edition. Two Volumes. Demy 8vo.* 25s. net.

'Mr. Balfour has done his work extremely well—done it, in fact, as Stevenson himself would have wished it done, with care and skill and affectionate appreciation.'—*Westminster Gazette.*

S. E. Bally. A FRENCH COMMERCIAL READER. With Vocabulary. *Second Edition. Crown 8vo.* 2s. [Commercial Series.

FRENCH COMMERCIAL CORRESPONDENCE. With Vocabulary. *Third Edition. Crown 8vo.* 2s. [Commercial Series.

A GERMAN COMMERCIAL READER. With Vocabulary. *Crown 8vo.* 2s. [Commercial Series.

GERMAN COMMERCIAL CORRESPONDENCE. With Vocabulary. *Crown 8vo.* 2s. 6d. [Commercial Series.

Elizabeth L. Banks. THE AUTOBIOGRAPHY OF A 'NEWSPAPER

GIRL.' With Portrait of the Author and her Dog. *Crown 8vo.* 6*s.*

'A picture of a strenuous and busy life, perhaps the truest and most faithful representation of the ups and downs of a lady journalist's career ever given to the public. A very lively and interesting book.'—*Daily Telegraph.*

'A very amusing, cheery, good-natured account of a young lady's journalistic struggle in America and London.'—*Times.*

R. H. Barham. THE INGOLDSBY LEGENDS. Edited by J. B. Atlay. *Two Volumes. Pott 8vo. Each volume, cloth,* 1*s.* 6*d. net; leather,* 2*s.* 6*d. net.*
[The Little Library.

S. Baring-Gould, Author of 'Mehalah,' etc. THE LIFE OF NAPOLEON BONAPARTE. With over 450 Illustrations in the Text, and 12 Photogravure Plates. *Gilt top. Large quarto.* 36*s.*

'The main feature of this gorgeous volume is its great wealth of beautiful photogravures and finely-executed wood engravings, constituting a complete pictorial chronicle of Napoleon I.'s personal history.'—*Daily Telegraph.*

THE TRAGEDY OF THE CÆSARS. With numerous Illustrations from Busts, Gems, Cameos, etc. *Fifth Edition. Royal 8vo.* 15*s.*

'A most splendid and fascinating book on a subject of undying interest. It is brilliantly written, and the illustrations are supplied on a scale of profuse magnificence.'—*Daily Chronicle.*

A BOOK OF FAIRY TALES. With numerous Illustrations and Initial Letters by ARTHUR J. GASKIN. *Second Edition. Crown 8vo. Buckram.* 6*s.*

OLD ENGLISH FAIRY TALES. With numerous Illustrations by F. D. BEDFORD. *Second Edition. Cr. 8vo. Buckram.* 6*s.*

'A charming volume.'—*Guardian.*

THE CROCK OF GOLD. Fairy Stories. *Crown 8vo.* 6*s.*

'Twelve delightful fairy tales.'—*Punch.*

THE VICAR OF MORWENSTOW: A Biography. A new and Revised Edition. With Portrait. *Crown 8vo.* 3*s.* 6*d.*

A completely new edition of the well-known biography of R. S. Hawker.

DARTMOOR: A Descriptive and Historical Sketch. With Plans and numerous Illustrations. *Crown 8vo.* 6*s.*

'A most delightful guide, companion and instructor.'—*Scotsman.*

THE BOOK OF THE WEST. With numerous Illustrations. *Two volumes.* Vol. I. Devon. *Second Edition.* Vol. II. Cornwall. *Second Edition. Crown 8vo.* 6*s. each.*

'Bracing as the air of Dartmoor, the legend weird as twilight over Dozmare Pool, they give us a very good idea of this enchanting and beautiful district.'—*Guardian.*

A BOOK OF BRITTANY. With numerous Illustrations. *Crown 8vo.* 6*s.*

Uniform in scope and size with Mr. Baring-Gould's well-known books on Devon, Cornwall, and Dartmoor.

BRITTANY. Illustrated by Miss J. WYLIE. *Pott 8vo. Cloth,* 3*s.*; *leather,* 3*s.* 6*d. net.*
[The Little Guides.

'A dainty representative of "The Little Guides."'—*Times.*

'An excellent little guide-book.'—*Daily News.*

OLD COUNTRY LIFE. With 67 Illustrations. *Fifth Edition. Large Cr. 8vo.* 6*s.*

AN OLD ENGLISH HOME. With numerous Plans and Illustrations. *Cr. 8vo.* 6*s.*

HISTORIC ODDITIES AND STRANGE EVENTS. *Fifth Edition. Cr. 8vo.* 6*s.*

YORKSHIRE ODDITIES AND STRANGE EVENTS. *Fifth Edition. Crown 8vo.* 6*s.*

STRANGE SURVIVALS AND SUPERSTITIONS. *Second Edition. Cr. 8vo.* 6*s.*

A GARLAND OF COUNTRY SONG: English Folk Songs with their Traditional Melodies. Collected and arranged by S. BARING-GOULD and H. F. SHEPPARD. *Demy 4to.* 6*s.*

SONGS OF THE WEST: Traditional Ballads and Songs of the West of England, with their Melodies. Collected by S. BARING-GOULD, M.A., and H. F. SHEPPARD, M.A. In 4 Parts. *Parts I., II., III.,* 3*s. each. Part IV.,* 5*s. In One Volume, French Morocco,* 15*s.*

'A rich collection of humour, pathos, grace, and poetic fancy.'—*Saturday Review.*

W. E. Barnes, D.D. ISAIAH. *Two Volumes. Fcap. 8vo.* 2*s. net each.* Vol. I. With Map. [Churchman's Bible.

Mrs. P. A. Barnett. A LITTLE BOOK OF ENGLISH PROSE. *Pott 8vo. Cloth,* 1*s.* 6*d. net; leather,* 2*s.* 6*d. net.*
[Little Library.

R. R. N Baron, M.A. FRENCH PROSE COMPOSITION. *Crown 8vo.* 2*s.* 6*d.* *Key,* 3*s. net.*

H. M. Barron, M.A., Wadham College, Oxford. TEXTS FOR SERMONS. With a Preface by Canon SCOTT HOLLAND. *Crown 8vo.* 3*s.* 6*d*

C. F. Bastable, M.A., Professor of Economics at Trinity College, Dublin. THE COMMERCE OF NATIONS. *Second Edition. Crown 8vo* 2*s.* 6*d.*
[Social Questions Series.

H. M. Batson. See Edward FitzGerald.

A Hulme Beaman. PONS ASINORUM; OR, A GUIDE TO BRIDGE. *Second Edition. Fcap.* 8*vo.* 2*s.*

W. S. Beard, Headmaster Modern School, Fareham. JUNIOR ARITHMETIC EXAMINATION PAPERS. *Fcap.* 8*vo.* 1*s.* [Junior Examination Series.

Peter Beckford. THOUGHTS ON HUNTING. Edited by J. OTHO PAGET, and Illustrated by G. H. JALLAND. *Demy* 8*vo.* 10*s.* 6*d.*

William Beckford. THE HISTORY OF THE CALIPH VATHEK. Edited by E. DENISON ROSS. *Pott* 8*vo. Cloth,* 1*s.* 6*d. net; leather,* 2*s* 6*d. net.* [Little Library.

F. D. Bedford. See E. V. Lucas.

H. C. Beeching, M.A. See Tennyson.

Jacob Behmen. THE SUPERSENSUAL LIFE. Edited by BERNARD HOLLAND. *Fcap.* 8*vo.* 3*s.* 6*d.*

Hilaire Belloc. PARIS. With Maps and Illustrations. *Crown* 8*vo.* 6*s.*

H. H. L. Bellot, M.A. THE INNER AND MIDDLE TEMPLE. With numerous Illustrations. *Crown* 8*vo.* 6*s. net.*

'A vast store of entertaining material.'—*Liverpool Mercury.*

'A delightful and excellently illustrated book; a real encyclopædia of Temple history.'—*Pilot.*

W. H. Bennett, M.A.. A PRIMER OF THE BIBLE. *Second Edition. Crown* 8*vo.* 2*s.* 6*d.*

'The work of an honest, fearless, and sound critic, and an excellent guide in a small compass to the books of the Bible.' —*Manchester Guardian.*

W. H. Bennett and W. F. Adeney. A BIBLICAL INTRODUCTION. *Crown* 8*vo.* 7*s.* 6*d.*

'It makes available to the ordinary reader the best scholarship of the day in the field of Biblical introduction. We know of no book which comes into competition with it.' —*Manchester Guardian.*

A. C. Benson, M.A. THE LIFE OF LORD TENNYSON. With 12 Illustrations. *Fcap.* 8*vo. Cloth,* 3*s.* 6*d.*; *Leather,* 4*s. net.* [Little Biographies.

R. M. Benson. THE WAY OF HOLINESS: a Devotional Commentary on the 119th Psalm. *Crown* 8*vo.* 5*s.*

M. Bidez. See Parmentier.

C. Bigg, D.D. See St. Augustine, À Kempis, and William Law.

C. R. D. Biggs, B.D. THE EPISTLE TO THE PHILIPPIANS. Edited by. *Fcap.* 8*vo.* 1*s.* 6*d. net.* [Churchman's Bible.

'Mr. Biggs' work is very thorough, and he has managed to compress a good deal of information into a limited space.' —*Guardian.*

T. Herbert Bindley, B.D. THE OECUMENICAL DOCUMENTS OF THE FAITH. With Introductions and Notes. *Crown* 8*vo.* 6*s.*

A historical account of the Creeds.

William Blake. See Little Library.

B. Blaxland, M.A. THE SONG OF SONGS. Being Selections from ST. BERNARD. *Pott* 8*vo. Cloth,* 2*s.*; *leather,* 2*s.* 6*d. net.* [Library of Devotion.

George Body, D.D. THE SOUL'S PILGRIMAGE: Devotional Readings from his published and unpublished writings. Selected and arranged by J. H. BURN, B.D. *Pott* 8*vo.* 2*s.* 6*d.*

Cardinal Bona. A GUIDE TO ETERNITY. Edited with an Introduction and Notes, by J. W. STANBRIDGE, B.D., late Fellow of St. John's College, Oxford. *Pott* 8*vo. Cloth,* 2*s.*; *leather,* 2*s.* 6*d. net.* [Library of Devotion.

F. C. Boon, B.A. A COMMERCIAL GEOGRAPHY OF FOREIGN NATIONS. *Crown* 8*vo.* 2*s.* Commercial Series.

George Borrow. LAVENGRO. Edited by F. HINDES GROOME. *Two Volumes. Pott* 8*vo. Each volume, cloth,* 1*s.* 6*d. net; leather,* 2*s.* 6*d. net.* [Little Library.

J. Ritzema Bos. AGRICULTURAL ZOOLOGY. Translated by J. R. AINSWORTH DAVIS, M.A. With an Introduction by ELEANOR A. ORMEROD, F.E.S. With 155 Illustrations. *Cr.* 8*vo.* 3*s.* 6*d.*

C. G. Botting, B.A. JUNIOR LATIN EXAMINATION PAPERS. *Fcap.* 8*vo.* 1*s.* [Junior Examination Series.

EASY GREEK EXERCISES. *Cr.* 8*vo.* 2*s.*

E. M. Bowden. THE EXAMPLE OF BUDDHA: Being Quotations from Buddhist Literature for each Day in the Year. *Third Edition.* 16*mo.* 2*s.* 6*d.*

E. Bowmaker. THE HOUSING OF THE WORKING CLASSES. *Crown* 8*vo.* 2*s.* 6*d.* [Social Questions Series.

F. G. Brabant, M.A. SUSSEX. Illustrated by E. H. NEW. *Pott* 8*vo. Cloth,* 3*s.*; *leather,* 3*s.* 6*d. net.* [Little Guides.

'A charming little book; as full of sound information as it is practical in conception.' —*Athenæum.*

THE ENGLISH LAKES. Illustrated by E. H. NEW. *Pott* 8*vo. Cloth,* 4*s.*; *leather,* 4*s.* 6*d. net.* [The Little Guides.

Miss M. Brodrick and Miss Anderson Morton. A CONCISE HANDBOOK OF EGYPTIAN ARCHÆOLOGY. With many Illustrations. *Crown* 8*vo.* 3*s.* 6*d.*

E. W. Brooks. See F. J. Hamilton.

C. L. Brownell. THE HEART OF JAPAN. Illustrated. *Crown* 8*vo.* 6*s.*

'These lively pages are full of portraits from the life.'—*Morning Post.*

'It is the work of one who has lived in Japan among the people.'—*Athenæum.*

'A more readable and interesting book about Japan has not been written.' —*Scotsman.*

Robert Browning. SELECTIONS FROM THE EARLY POEMS OF. With Introduction and Notes by W. HALL GRIFFIN. *Pott 8vo.* 1s. 6d. *net.*; *leather,* 2s. 6d. *net.* [Little Library.

O. Browning, M.A. A SHORT HISTORY OF MEDIÆVAL ITALY, A.D. 1250-1530. *In Two Volumes. Crown 8vo.* 5s. *each.*

VOL. I. 1250-1409.—Guelphs and Ghibellines.

VOL. II. 1409-1530.—The Age of the Condottieri.

J. Buchan. See Isaak Walton.

Miss Bulley. See Lady Dilke.

John Bunyan. THE PILGRIM'S PROGRESS. Edited, with an Introduction, by C. H. FIRTH, M.A. With 39 Illustrations by R. ANNING BELL. *Cr. 8vo.* 6s.

'The best "Pilgrim's Progress."'—*Educational Times.*

G. J. Burch, M.A., F.R.S. A MANUAL OF ELECTRICAL SCIENCE. With numerous Illustrations. *Crown 8vo.* 3s. [University Extension Series.

Gelett Burgess. GOOPS AND HOW TO BE THEM. With numerous Illustrations. *Small 4to.* 6s.

A. E. Burn, B.D., Examining Chaplain to the Bishop of Lichfield. AN INTRODUCTION TO THE HISTORY OF THE CREEDS. *Demy 8vo.* 10s. 6d. [Handbooks of Theology.

'This book may be expected to hold its place as an authority on its subject.'—*Spectator.*

J. H. Burn, B.D., F.R.S.E. A MANUAL OF CONSOLATION FROM THE SAINTS AND FATHERS. *Pott 8vo. Cloth,* 2s.; *leather,* 2s. 6d. *net.* [Library of Devotion.

Robert Burns. THE POEMS OF ROBERT BURNS. Edited by ANDREW LANG and W. A. CRAIGIE. With Portrait. *Second Edition. Demy 8vo, gilt top.* 6s.

J. B. Bury, LL.D. See Gibbon.

Alfred Caldecott, D.D. THE PHILOSOPHY OF RELIGION IN ENGLAND AND AMERICA. *Demy 8vo.* 10s. 6d. [Handbooks of Theology.

'A lucid and informative account, which certainly deserves a place in every philosophical library.'—*Scotsman.*

D. S. Calderwood, Headmaster of the Normal School, Edinburgh. TEST CARDS IN EUCLID AND ALGEBRA. In three packets of 40, with Answers. 1s. each. Or in three Books, price 2*d.*, 2*d.*, and 3*d.*

E. F. H. Capey. THE LIFE OF ERASMUS. With 12 Illustrations. *Cloth,* 3s. 6d. *net*; *leather,* 4s. *net.* [Little Biographies.

Thomas Carlyle. THE FRENCH REVOLUTION. Edited by C. R. L. FLETCHER, Fellow of Magdalen College, Oxford. *Three Volumes. Crown 8vo.* 6s. each. [Methuen's Standard Library.

'This last edition, or annotation, may be said to be final. It will be impossible to produce any other in which the notes shall be more thorough, in which every point will be more accurately noted, or in which the correctness of date, locality, and every other detail will be better preserved. The work has been done once for all, it cannot be done again.'—*Speaker.*

R. M. and A. J. Carlyle, M.A. BISHOP LATIMER. With Portrait. *Crown 8vo.* 3s. 6d. [Leaders of Religion.

C. C. Channer and M. E. Roberts. LACE-MAKING IN THE MIDLANDS, PAST AND PRESENT. With 16 full-page Illustrations. *Crown 8vo.* 2s. 6d.

'An interesting book, illustrated by fascinating photographs.'—*Speaker.*

Lord Chesterfield, THE LETTERS OF, TO HIS SON. Edited, with an Introduction, by C. STRACHEY, and Notes by A. CALTHROP. *Two Volumes. Crown 8vo.* 6s. *each.* [Methuen's Standard Library.

F. W. Christian. THE CAROLINE ISLANDS. With many Illustrations and Maps. *Demy 8vo.* 12s. 6d. *net.*

Cicero. DE ORATORE I. Translated by E. N. P. MOOR, M.A. *Crown 8vo.* 3s. 6d. [Classical Translations.

SELECT ORATIONS (Pro Milone, Pro Murena, Philippic II., In Catilinam). Translated by H. E. D. BLAKISTON, M.A., Fellow and Tutor of Trinity College, Oxford. *Crown 8vo.* 5s. [Classical Translations.

DE NATURA DEORUM. Translated by F. BROOKS, M.A., late Scholar of Balliol College, Oxford. *Crown 8vo.* 3s. 6d. [Classical Translations.

DE OFFICIIS. Translated by G. B. GARDINER, M.A. *Crown 8vo.* 2s. 6d. [Classical Translations.

F. A. Clarke, M.A. BISHOP KEN. With Portrait. *Crown 8vo.* 3s. 6d. [Leaders of Religion.

E. H. Colbeck, M.D. DISEASES OF THE HEART. With numerous Illustrations. *Demy 8vo.* 12s.

W. G. Collingwood, M.A. THE LIFE OF JOHN RUSKIN. With Portraits. *Cheap Edition. Crown 8vo.* 6s.

J. C. Collins, M.A. See Tennyson.

W. E. Collins, M.A. THE BEGINNINGS OF ENGLISH CHRISTIANITY. With Map. *Crown 8vo.* 3s. 6d. [Churchman's Library.

A. M. Cook, M.A. See E. C. Marchant.

R. W. Cooke-Taylor. THE FACTORY SYSTEM. *Crown* 8*vo.* 2*s.* 6*d.* [Social Questions Series.

Marie Corelli. THE PASSING OF THE GREAT QUEEN : A Tribute to the Noble Life of Victoria Regina. *Small* 4*to.* 1*s.*

A CHRISTMAS GREETING. *Sm.* 4*to.* 1*s.*

Rosemary Cotes. DANTE'S GARDEN. With a Frontispiece. *Second Edition. Fcap.* 8*vo. cloth* 2*s.* 6*d.*; *leather*, 3*s.* 6*d. net.*

Harold Cox, B.A. LAND NATIONALIZATION. *Crown* 8*vo.* 2*s.* 6*d.* [Social Questions Series.

W. J. Craig. See Shakespeare.

W. A. Craigie. A PRIMER OF BURNS. *Crown* 8*vo.* 2*s.* 6*d.*

Mrs. Craik. JOHN HALIFAX, GENTLEMAN. Edited by ANNIE MATHESON. *Two Volumes. Pott* 8*vo. Each Volume, Cloth,* 1*s.* 6*d. net*; *leather*, 2*s.* 6*d. net.* [Little Library.

Richard Crashaw, THE ENGLISH POEMS OF. Edited by EDWARD HUTTON. *Pott* 8*vo. Cloth,* 1*s.* 6*d. net*; *leather*, 2*s.* 6*d. net.* [Little Library.

F. G. Crawford. See Mary C. Danson.

C. G. Crump, M.A. See Thomas Ellwood.

F. H. E. Cunliffe, Fellow of All Souls' College, Oxford. THE HISTORY OF THE BOER WAR. With many Illustrations, Plans, and Portraits. *In* 2 *vols. Vol. I.*, 15*s.*

E. L. Cutts, D.D. AUGUSTINE OF CANTERBURY. With Portrait. *Crown* 8*vo.* 3*s.* 6*d.* [Leaders of Religion.

The Brothers Dalziel. A RECORD OF FIFTY YEARS' WORK. With 150 Illustrations. *Large* 4*to.* 21*s. net.*

The record of the work of the celebrated Engravers, containing a Gallery of beautiful Pictures by F. Walker, Sir J. Millais, Lord Leighton, and other great Artists. The book is a history of the finest black-and-white work of the nineteenth century.

G. W. Daniell, M.A. BISHOP WILBERFORCE. With Portrait. *Crown* 8*vo.* 3*s.* 6*d.* [Leaders of Religion.

Mary C. Danson and F. G. Crawford. FATHERS IN THE FAITH. *Small* 8*vo.* 1*s.* 6*d.*

Dante Alighieri. LA COMMEDIA DI DANTE. The Italian Text edited by PAGET TOYNBEE, Litt.D., M.A. *Demy* 8*vo. Gilt top.* 8*s.* 6*d.* *Also, Crown* 8*vo.* 6*s.* [Methuen's Standard Library.

THE INFERNO OF DANTE. Translated by H. F. CARY. Edited by PAGET TOYNBEE, Litt.D., M.A. *Pott* 8*vo. Cloth,* 1*s.* 6*d. net*; *leather* 2*s.* 6*d. net.* [Little Library.

THE PURGATORIO OF DANTE. Translated by H. F. CARY. Edited by PAGET TOYNBEE, Litt.D., M.A. *Pott* 8*vo. Cloth,* 1*s.* 6*d. net*; *leather*, 2*s.* 6*d. net.* [Little Library.

THE PARADISO OF DANTE. Translated by H. F. CARY. Edited by PAGET TOYNBEE, Litt.D., M.A. *Post* 8*vo. Cloth,* 1*s.* 6*d. net*; *leather*, 2*s.* 6*d. net.* [Little Library.

See also Paget Toynbee.

A. C. Deane. Edited by. A LITTLE BOOK OF LIGHT VERSE. *Pott* 8*vo. Cloth,* 1*s.* 6*d. net*; *leather*, 2*s.* 6*d. net.* [Little Library.

Percy Dearmer. See N. Hawthorne.

Leon Delbos. THE METRIC SYSTEM. *Crown* 8*vo.* 2*s.*

A theoretical and practical guide, for use in schools and by the general reader.

Demosthenes: THE OLYNTHIACS AND PHILIPPICS. Translated upon a new principle by OTHO HOLLAND. *Crown* 8*vo.* 2*s.* 6*d.*

Demosthenes. AGAINST CONON AND CALLICLES. Edited with Notes and Vocabulary, by F. DARWIN SWIFT, M.A. *Fcap.* 8*vo.* 2*s.*

Charles Dickens.

THE ROCHESTER EDITION. *Crown* 8*vo. Each Volume, cloth,* 3*s.* 6*d.* With Introductions by GEORGE GISSING, Notes by F. G. KITTON, and Topographical Illustrations.

THE PICKWICK PAPERS. With Illustrations by E. H. NEW. *Two Volumes.*

NICHOLAS NICKLEBY. With Illustrations by R. J. WILLIAMS. *Two Volumes.*

BLEAK HOUSE. With Illustrations by BEATRICE ALCOCK. *Two Volumes.*

OLIVER TWIST. With Illustrations by E. H. NEW.

THE OLD CURIOSITY SHOP. With Illustrations by G. M. BRIMELOW. *Two Volumes.*

BARNABY RUDGE. With Illustrations by BEATRICE ALCOCK. *Two Volumes.*

G. L. Dickinson, M.A., Fellow of King's College, Cambridge. THE GREEK VIEW OF LIFE. *Second Edition. Crown* 8*vo.* 2*s.* 6*d.* [University Extension Series.

H. N. Dickson, F.R.S.E., F.R.Met. Soc. METEOROLOGY. The Elements of Weather and Climate. Illustrated. *Crown* 8*vo.* 2*s.* 6*d.* [University Extension Series.

Lady Dilke, Miss Bulley, and **Miss Whitley.** WOMEN'S WORK. *Crown* 8*vo.* 2*s.* 6*d.* [Social Questions Series.

P. H. Ditchfield, M.A., F.S.A. ENGLISH VILLAGES. Illustrated. *Crown* 8*vo.* 6*s.*

'A book which for its instructive and pictorial value should find a place in every village library.'—*Scotsman.*

THE STORY OF OUR ENGLISH TOWNS. With Introduction by AUGUSTUS JESSOP, D.D. *Second Edition. Crown 8vo.* 6s.

OLD ENGLISH CUSTOMS: Extant at the Present Time. An Account of Local Observances, Festival Customs, and Ancient Ceremonies yet Surviving in Great Britain. *Crown 8vo.* 6s.

W. M. Dixon, M.A. A PRIMER OF TENNYSON. *Second Edition. Crown 8vo.* 2s. 6d.

'Much sound and well-expressed criticism. The bibliography is a boon.'—*Speaker.*

ENGLISH POETRY FROM BLAKE TO BROWNING. *Second Edition. Crown 8vo.* 2s. 6d. [University Extension Series.

E. Dowden, Litt.D. See Shakespeare.

J. Dowden, D.D., Lord Bishop of Edinburgh. THE WORKMANSHIP OF THE PRAYER BOOK: Its Literary and Liturgical Aspects. *Second Edition. Crown 8vo.* 3s. 6d. [Churchman's Library.

S. R. Driver., D.D., Canon of Christ Church, Regius Professor of Hebrew in the University of Oxford. SERMONS ON SUBJECTS CONNECTED WITH THE OLD TESTAMENT. *Crown 8vo.* 6s.

'A welcome companion to the author's famous "Introduction."'—*Guardian.*

S. J. Duncan (Mrs. COTES), Author of 'A Voyage of Consolation.' ON THE OTHER SIDE OF THE LATCH. *Second Edition. Crown 8vo.* 6s.

J. T. Dunn, D.Sc., **and V. A. Mundella.** GENERAL ELEMENTARY SCIENCE. With 114 Illustrations. *Crown 8vo.* 3s. 6d. [Methuen's Science Primers.

The Earl of Durham. A REPORT ON CANADA. With an Introductory Note. *Demy 8vo.* 7s. 6d. *net.*

A reprint of the celebrated Report which Lord Durham made to the British Government on the state of British North America in 1839. It is probably the most important utterance on British colonial policy ever published.

W. A. Dutt. NORFOLK. Illustrated by B. C. BOULTER. *Pott 8vo. Cloth,* 3s.; *leather,* 3s. 6d. *net.* [Little Guides.

Clement Edwards. RAILWAY NATIONALIZATION. *Crown 8vo.* 2s. 6d. [Social Questions Series

W. Douglas Edwards. COMMERCIAL LAW. *Crown 8vo.* 2s. [Commercial Series.

H. E. Egerton, M.A. A HISTORY OF BRITISH COLONIAL POLICY. *Demy 8vo.* 12s. 6d.

'It is a good book, distinguished by accuracy in detail, clear arrangement of facts, and a broad grasp of principles.'—*Manchester Guardian.*

Thomas Ellwood, THE HISTORY OF THE LIFE OF. Edited by C. G. CRUMP, M.A. *Crown 8vo.* 6s. [Methuen's Standard Library.

This edition is the only one which contains the complete book as originally published. It has a long Introduction and many Footnotes.

E. Engel. A HISTORY OF ENGLISH LITERATURE: From its Beginning to Tennyson. Translated from the German. *Demy 8vo.* 7s. 6d. *net.*

W. H. Fairbrother, M.A. THE PHILOSOPHY OF T. H. GREEN. *Second Edition. Crown 8vo.* 3s. 6d.

Dean Farrar. See A Kempis.

Susan Ferrier. MARRIAGE. Edited by Miss GOODRICH FREER and Lord IDDESLEIGH. *Two Volumes. Pott 8vo. Each volume, cloth,* 1s. 6d. *net; leather,* 2s. 6d. *net.* [Little Library.

THE INHERITANCE. *Two Volumes. Pott 8vo. Each Volume, cloth,* 1s. 6d. *net.; leather,* 2s. 6d. *net.* [The Little Library.

C. H. Firth, M.A. CROMWELL'S ARMY: A History of the English Soldier during the Civil Wars, the Commonwealth, and the Protectorate. *Crown 8vo.* 7s. 6d.

An elaborate study and description of Cromwell's army by which the victory of the Parliament was secured. The 'New Model' is described in minute detail.

G. W. Fisher, M.A. ANNALS OF SHREWSBURY SCHOOL. With numerous Illustrations. *Demy 8vo.* 10s. 6d.

Edward FitzGerald. THE RUBAIYAT OF OMAR KHAYYAM. With a Commentary by H. M. BATSON, and a Biography of Omar by E. D. ROSS. *Crown 8vo.* 6s.

E. A. FitzGerald. THE HIGHEST ANDES. With 2 Maps, 51 Illustrations, 13 of which are in Photogravure, and a Panorama. *Royal 8vo.* 30s. *net.*

C. R. L. Fletcher. See Thomas Carlyle.

W. Warde Fowler. M.A. See Gilbert White.

J. F. Fraser. ROUND THE WORLD ON A WHEEL. With 100 Illustrations. *Fourth Edition Crown 8vo.* 6s.

'A classic of cycling, graphic and witty.' —*Yorkshire Post.*

J. H. Freese. See Plautus.

W. French, M.A., Principal of the Storey Institute, Lancaster. PRACTICAL CHEMISTRY. Part I. With numerous Diagrams. *Crown 8vo.* 1s. 6d. [Textbooks of Technology.

'An excellent and eminently practical little book.'—*Schoolmaster.*

Ed. von Freudenreich. DAIRY BACTERIOLOGY. A Short Manual for the Use of Students. Translated by J. R. AINSWORTH DAVIS, M.A. *Second Edition. Revised. Crown 8vo.* 2s. 6d.

H. W. Fulford, M.A. THE EPISTLE OF ST. JAMES. Edited by. *Fcap.* 8*vo.* 1*s.* 6*d. net.* [Churchman's Bible.

Mrs. Gaskell. CRANFORD. Edited by E. V. LUCAS. *Pott* 8*vo. Cloth,* 1*s.* 6*d. net; leather,* 2*s.* 6*d. net.* [Little Library.

H. B. George, M.A., Fellow of New College, Oxford. BATTLES OF ENGLISH HISTORY. With numerous Plans. *Third Edition. Crown* 8*vo.* 6*s.*

'Mr. George has undertaken a very useful task—that of making military affairs intelligible and instructive to non-military readers—and has executed it with a large measure of success.'—*Times.*

H. de B. Gibbins, Litt.D., M.A. INDUSTRY IN ENGLAND: HISTORICAL OUTLINES. With 5 Maps. *Second Edition. Demy* 8*vo.* 10*s.* 6*d.*

A COMPANION GERMAN GRAMMAR. *Crown* 8*vo.* 1*s.* 6*d.*

THE INDUSTRIAL HISTORY OF ENGLAND. *Eighth Edition.* Revised. With Maps and Plans. *Crown* 8*vo.* 3*s.* [University Extension Series.

THE ECONOMICS OF COMMERCE. *Crown* 8*vo.* 1*s.* 6*d.* [Commercial Series.

COMMERCIAL EXAMINATION PAPERS. *Crown* 8*vo.* 1*s.* 6*d.* [Commercial Series.

BRITISH COMMERCE AND COLONIES FROM ELIZABETH TO VICTORIA. *Third Edition. Crown* 8*vo.* 2*s.* [Commercial Series.

ENGLISH SOCIAL REFORMERS. *Second Edition. Crown* 8*vo.* 2*s.* 6*d.* [University Extension Series.

H. de B. Gibbins, Litt.D., M.A., and **R. A. Hadfield,** of the Hecla Works, Sheffield. A SHORTER WORKING DAY. *Crown* 8*vo.* 2*s.* 6*d.* [Social Questions Series.

Edward Gibbon. THE DECLINE AND FALL OF THE ROMAN EMPIRE. A New Edition, edited with Notes, Appendices, and Maps, by J. B. BURY, LL.D., Fellow of Trinity College, Dublin. *In Seven Volumes. Demy* 8*vo. Gilt top,* 8*s.* 6*d. each. Also, Crown* 8*vo.* 6*s. each.*

'At last there is an adequate modern edition of Gibbon. . . . The best edition the nineteenth century could produce.'—*Manchester Guardian.*

'A great piece of editing.'—*Academy.*

MEMOIRS OF MY LIFE AND WRITINGS. Edited, with an Introduction and Notes, by G. BIRKBECK HILL, LL.D. *Crown* 8*vo.* 6*s.*

'An admirable edition of one of the most interesting personal records of a literary life. Its notes and its numerous appendices are a repertory of almost all that can be known about Gibbon.'—*Manchester Guardian.*

E. C. S. Gibson, D.D., Vicar of Leeds. THE BOOK OF JOB. With Introduction and Notes. *Demy* 8*vo.* 6*s.* [Westminster Commentaries.

'Dr. Gibson's work is worthy of a high degree of appreciation. To the busy worker and the intelligent student the commentary will be a real boon; and it will, if we are not mistaken, be much in demand. The Introduction is almost a model of concise, straightforward, prefatory remarks on the subject treated.'—*Athenæum.*

THE XXXIX. ARTICLES OF THE CHURCH OF ENGLAND. With an Introduction. *Third and Cheaper Edition in One Volume. Demy* 8*vo.* 12*s.* 6*d.* [Handbooks of Theology.

'We welcome with the utmost satisfaction a new, cheaper, and more convenient edition of Dr. Gibson's book. It was greatly wanted. Dr. Gibson has given theological students just what they want, and we should like to think that it was in the hands of every candidate for orders.'—*Guardian.*

THE LIFE OF JOHN HOWARD. With 12 Illustrations. *Pott* 8*vo. Cloth,* 3*s.; leather,* 3*s.* 6*d. net.* [Little Biographies.

See also George Herbert.

George Gissing. See Dickens.

A. D. Godley, M.A., Fellow of Magdalen College, Oxford. LYRA FRIVOLA. *Third Edition. Fcap.* 8*vo.* 2*s.* 6*d.*

VERSES TO ORDER. *Cr.* 8*vo.* 2*s.* 6*d. net.*

SECOND STRINGS. *Fcap.* 8*vo.* 2*s.* 6d.

A new volume of humorous verse uniform with *Lyra Frivola.*

'Neat, brisk, ingenious.'—*Manchester Guardian.*

'The verse is facile, the wit is ready.' *Daily Mail.*

'Excellent and amusing.'—*St. James's Gazette.*

Miss Goodrich-Freer. See Susan Ferrier.

P. Anderson Graham. THE RURAL EXODUS. *Crown* 8*vo.* 2*s.* 6*d.* [Social Questions Series.

F. S. Granger, M.A., Litt.D. PSYCHOLOGY. *Second Edition. Crown* 8*vo.* 2*s.* 6*d.* [University Extension Series.

THE SOUL OF A CHRISTIAN. *Crown* 8*vo.* 6*s.*

A book dealing with the evolution of the religious life and experiences.

E. M'Queen Gray. GERMAN PASSAGES FOR UNSEEN TRANSLATION. *Crown* 8*vo.* 2*s.* 6*d.*

P. L. Gray, B.Sc., formerly Lecturer in Physics in Mason University College, Birmingham. THE PRINCIPLES OF MAGNETISM AND ELECTRICITY: an Elementary Text-Book. With 181 Diagrams. *Crown* 8*vo.* 3*s.* 6*d.*

G. Buckland Green, M.A., Assistant Master at Edinburgh Academy, late Fellow of St. John's College, Oxon. NOTES ON GREEK AND LATIN SYNTAX. *Crown 8vo.* 3*s.* 6*d.*
Notes and explanations on the chief difficulties of Greek and Latin Syntax, with numerous passages for exercise.

E. T. Green, M.A. THE CHURCH OF CHRIST. *Crown 8vo.* 6*s.*
[Churchman's Library.

R. A. Gregory. THE VAULT OF HEAVEN. A Popular Introduction to Astronomy. With numerous Illustrations. *Crown 8vo.* 2*s.* 6*d.*
[University Extension Series.

W. Hall Griffin, M.A. See Robert Browning.

C. H. Grinling. A HISTORY OF THE GREAT NORTHERN RAILWAY, 1845-95. With Illustrations. *Demy 8vo.* 10*s.* 6*d.*

F. Hindes Groome. See George Borrow.

M. L. Gwynn. A BIRTHDAY BOOK. *Royal 8vo.* 12*s.*
This is a birthday-book of exceptional dignity, and the extracts have been chosen with particular care.

Stephen Gywnn. See Thackeray.

John Hackett, B.D. A HISTORY OF THE ORTHODOX CHURCH OF CYPRUS. With Maps and Illustrations. *Demy 8vo.* 15*s. net.*

A. C. Haddon, Sc.D., F.R.S. HEAD-HUNTERS, BLACK, WHITE, AND BROWN. With many Illustrations and a Map. *Demy 8vo.* 15*s.*
A narrative of adventure and exploration in Northern Borneo. It contains much matter of the highest scientific interest.

R. A. Hadfield. See H. de B. Gibbins.

R. N. Hall and W. G. Neal. THE ANCIENT RUINS OF RHODESIA. With numerous Illustrations. *Demy 8vo.* 21*s. net.*

F. J. Hamilton, D.D., **and E. W. Brooks.** ZACHARIAH OF MITYLENE. Translated into English. *Demy 8vo.* 12*s.* 6*d. net.*
[Byzantine Texts.

D. Hannay. A SHORT HISTORY OF THE ROYAL NAVY, FROM EARLY TIMES TO THE PRESENT DAY. Illustrated. *Two Volumes. Demy 8vo.* 7*s.* 6*d. each.* Vol. I. 1200-1688.

A. T. Hare, M.A. THE CONSTRUCTION OF LARGE INDUCTION COILS. With numerous Diagrams. *Demy 8vo.* 6*s.*

Clifford Harrison. READING AND READERS. *Fcap. 8vo.* 2*s.* 6*d.*
'An extremely sensible little book.'—*Manchester Guardian.*

Nathaniel Hawthorne. THE SCARLET LETTER. Edited by PERCY DEARMER. *Pott 8vo. Cloth,* 1*s.* 6*d. net; leather,* 2*s.* 6*d. net.*
[Little Library.

Sven Hedin, Gold Medallist of the Royal Geographical Society. THROUGH ASIA. With 300 Illustrations from Sketches and Photographs by the Author, and Maps. *Two Volumes. Royal 8vo.* 36*s. net.*

T. F. Henderson. A LITTLE BOOK OF SCOTTISH VERSE. *Pott 8vo. Cloth,* 1*s.* 6*d. net; leather,* 2*s.* 6*d. net.*
[Little Library.
See also D. M. Moir.

W. E. Henley. ENGLISH LYRICS. *Crown 8vo. Gilt top.* 3*s.* 6*d.*

W. E. Henley and C. Whibley. A BOOK OF ENGLISH PROSE. *Crown 8vo. Buckram, gilt top.* 6*s.*

H. H. Henson, M.A., Fellow of All Souls', Oxford, Canon of Westminster. APOSTOLIC CHRISTIANITY: As Illustrated by the Epistles of St. Paul to the Corinthians. *Crown 8vo.* 6*s.*
LIGHT AND LEAVEN: HISTORICAL AND SOCIAL SERMONS. *Crown 8vo.* 6*s.*
DISCIPLINE AND LAW. *Fcap. 8vo.* 2*s.* 6*d.*

George Herbert. THE TEMPLE. Edited, with an Introduction and Notes, by E. C. S. GIBSON, D.D., Vicar of Leeds. *Pott 8vo. Cloth,* 2*s.*; *leather,* 2*s.* 6*d. net.*
[Library of Devotion.
This edition contains Walton's Life of Herbert, and the text is that of the first edition.

Herodotus: EASY SELECTIONS. With Vocabulary. By A. C. LIDDELL, M.A. *Fcap. 8vo.* 1*s.* 6*d.*

W. A. S. Hewins, B.A. ENGLISH TRADE AND FINANCE IN THE SEVENTEENTH CENTURY. *Crown 8vo.*
[University Extension Series.

T. Hilbert. THE AIR GUN: or, How the Mastermans and Dobson Major nearly lost their Holidays. Illustrated. *Square Fcap. 8vo.* 2*s.* 6*d.* [Little Blue Books.

Clare Hill, Registered Teacher to the City and Guilds of London Institute. MILLINERY, THEORETICAL, AND PRACTICAL. With numerous Diagrams. *Crown 8vo.* 2*s.*
[Textbooks of Technology.

Henry Hill, B.A., Headmaster of the Boy's High School, Worcester, Cape Colony. A SOUTH AFRICAN ARITHMETIC. *Crown 8vo.* 3*s.* 6*d.*
This book has been specially written for use in South African schools.

G. Birkbeck Hill, LL.D. See Gibbon.

Howard C. Hillegas. WITH THE BOER FORCES. With 24 Illustrations. *Second Edition. Crown 8vo.* 6*s.*

Emily Hobhouse. THE BRUNT OF THE WAR. With Map and Illustrations. *Crown 8vo.* 6s.

L. T. Hobhouse, Fellow of C.C.C., Oxford. THE THEORY OF KNOWLEDGE. *Demy 8vo.* 21s.

J. A. Hobson, M.A. PROBLEMS OF POVERTY: An Inquiry into the Industrial Condition of the Poor. *Fourth Edition. Crown 8vo.* 2s. 6d.
[Social Questions Series and University Extension Series.

THE PROBLEM OF THE UNEMPLOYED. *Crown 8vo.* 2s. 6d.
[Social Questions Series.

T. Hodgkin, D.C.L. GEORGE FOX, THE QUAKER. With Portrait. *Crown 8vo.* 3s. 6d. [Leaders of Religion.

Chester Holcombe. THE REAL CHINESE QUESTION. *Crown 8vo.* 6s.
'It is an important addition to the materials before the public for forming an opinion on a most difficult and pressing problem.'—*Times.*

Sir T. H. Holdich, K.C.I.E. THE INDIAN BORDERLAND: being a Personal Record of Twenty Years. Illustrated. *Demy 8vo.* 15s. *net.*
'Interesting and inspiriting from cover to cover, it will assuredly take its place as the classical work on the history of the Indian frontier.'—*Pilot.*

Canon Scott Holland. LYRA APOSTOLICA. With an Introduction. Notes by H. C. BEECHING, M.A. *Pott 8vo. Cloth,* 2s.; *leather,* 2s. 6d. *net.*
[Library of Devotion.

G. J. Holyoake. THE CO-OPERATIVE MOVEMENT TO-DAY. *Third Edition. Crown 8vo.* 2s. 6d.
[Social Questions Series.

Horace: THE ODES AND EPODES. Translated by A. GODLEY, M.A., Fellow of Magdalen College, Oxford. *Crown 8vo.* 2s. [Classical Translations.

E. L. S. Horsburgh, M.A. WATERLOO: A Narrative and Criticism. With Plans. *Second Edition. Crown 8vo.* 5s.
'A brilliant essay—simple, sound, and thorough.'—*Daily Chronicle.*

THE LIFE OF SAVONAROLA. With Portraits and Illustrations. *Fcap. 8vo. Cloth,* 3s. 6d.; *leather,* 4s. *net.*
[Little Biographies.

R. F. Horton, D.D. JOHN HOWE. With Portrait. *Crown 8vo.* 3s. 6d.
[Leaders of Religion.

Alexander Hosie. MANCHURIA. With Illustrations and a Map. *Demy 8vo.* 10s. 6d. *net.*

G. Howell. TRADE UNIONISM—NEW AND OLD. *Third Edition. Crown 8vo.* 2s. 6d. [Social Questions Series.

A. W. Hutton, M.A. CARDINAL MANNING. With Portrait. *Crown 8vo.* 3s. 6d. [Leaders of Religion.
See also TAULER.

Edward Hutton. See Richard Crashaw.

R. H. Hutton. CARDINAL NEWMAN. With Portrait. *Crown 8vo.* 3s. 6d.
[Leaders of Religion.

W. H. Hutton, M.A. THE LIFE OF SIR THOMAS MORE. With Portraits. *Second Edition. Crown 8vo.* 5s.

WILLIAM LAUD. With Portrait. *Second Edition. Crown 8vo.* 3s. 6d.
[Leaders of Religion.

Henrik Ibsen. BRAND. A Drama. Translated by WILLIAM WILSON. *Third Edition. Crown 8vo.* 3s. 6d.

Lord Iddesleigh. See Susan Ferrier.

W. R. Inge, M.A., Fellow and Tutor of Hertford College, Oxford. CHRISTIAN MYSTICISM. The Bampton Lectures for 1899. *Demy 8vo.* 12s. 6d. *net.*
'It is fully worthy of the best traditions connected with the Bampton Lectureship.'—*Record.*

A. D. Innes, M.A. A HISTORY OF THE BRITISH IN INDIA. With Maps and Plans. *Crown 8vo.* 7s. 6d.
'Written in a vigorous and effective style . . . a thoughtful and impartial account.'—*Spectator.*

S. Jackson, M.A. A PRIMER OF BUSINESS. *Third Edition. Crown 8vo.* 1s. 6d. [Commercial Series.

F. Jacob, M.A. JUNIOR FRENCH EXAMINATION PAPERS. *Fcap. 8vo.* 1s. [Junior Examination Series.

J. Stephen Jeans. TRUSTS, POOLS, AND CORNERS. *Crown 8vo.* 2s. 6d.
[Social Questions Series.

E. Jenks, M.A., Professor of Law at University College, Liverpool. ENGLISH LOCAL GOVERNMENT. *Crown 8vo.* 2s. 6d. [University Extension Series.

C. S. Jerram, M.A. See Pascal.

Augustus Jessopp, D.D. JOHN DONNE. With Portrait. *Crown 8vo.* 3s. 6d.
[Leaders of Religion.

F. B. Jevons, M.A., Litt.D., Principal of Hatfield Hall, Durham. EVOLUTION. *Crown 8vo.* 3s. 6d. [Churchman's Library.

AN INTRODUCTION TO THE HISTORY OF RELIGION. *Second Edition. Demy 8vo.* 10s. 6d.
[Handbooks of Theology.
'The merit of this book lies in the penetration, the singular acuteness and force of the author's judgment. He is at once critical and luminous, at once just and suggestive. A comprehensive and thorough book.'—*Birmingham Post.*

Sir H. H. Johnston, K.C.B. BRITISH CENTRAL AFRICA. With nearly 200 Illustrations and Six Maps. *Second Edition. Crown 4to.* 18*s. net.*

H. Jones. A GUIDE TO PROFESSIONS AND BUSINESS. *Crown* 8*vo.* 1*s.* 6*d.* [Commercial Series.

Lady Julian of Norwich. REVELATIONS OF DIVINE LOVE. Edited by GRACE WARRACK. *Crown* 8*vo.* 3*s.* 6*d.*

A partially modernised version, from the MS. in the British Museum of a book which Mr. Inge in his Bampton Lectures calls 'The beautiful but little known *Revelations*.'

M. Kaufmann. SOCIALISM AND MODERN THOUGHT. *Crown* 8*vo.* 2*s.* 6*d.* [Social Questions Series.

J. F. Keating, D.D. THE AGAPE AND THE EUCHARIST. *Crown* 8*vo.* 3*s.* 6*d.*

John Keble. THE CHRISTIAN YEAR. With an Introduction and Notes by W. LOCK, D.D., Warden of Keble College. Illustrated by R. ANNING BELL. *Second Edition. Fcap.* 8*vo.* 3*s.* 6*d*; *padded morocco*, 5*s.*

THE CHRISTIAN YEAR. With Introduction and Notes by WALTER LOCK, D.D., Warden of Keble College. *Second Edition. Pott* 8*vo. Cloth*, 2*s.*; *leather*, 2*s.* 6*d. net.* [Library of Devotion.

LYRA INNOCENTIUM. Edited, with Introduction and Notes, by WALTER LOCK, D.D., Warden of Keble College, Oxford. *Pott* 8*vo. Cloth*, 2*s.*; *leather*, 2*s.* 6*d. net.* [Library of Devotion.

'This sweet and fragrant book has never been published more attractively.'—*Academy.*

Thomas À Kempis. THE IMITATION OF CHRIST. With an Introduction by DEAN FARRAR. Illustrated by C. M. GERE. *Second Edition. Fcap.* 8*vo.* 3*s.* 6*d. net*; *padded morocco*, 5*s.*

THE IMITATION OF CHRIST. A Revised Translation, with an Introduction by C. BIGG, D.D., late Student of Christ Church. *Third Edition. Pott* 8*vo. Cloth*, 2*s.*; *leather*, 2*s.* 6*d. net.* [Library of Devotion.

A practically new translation of this book which the reader has, almost for the first time, exactly in the shape in which it left the hands of the author.

THE SAME EDITION IN LARGE TYPE. *Crown* 8*vo.* 3*s.* 6*d.*

James Houghton Kennedy, D.D., Assistant Lecturer in Divinity in the University of Dublin. ST. PAUL'S SECOND AND THIRD EPISTLES TO THE CORINTHIANS. With Introduction, Dissertations and Notes. *Crown* 8*vo.* 6*s.*

J. D. Kestell. THROUGH SHOT AND FLAME: Being the Adventures and Experiences of J. D. KESTELL, Chaplain to General Christian de Wet. *Crown* 8*vo.* 6*s.*

C. W. Kimmins, M.A. THE CHEMISTRY OF LIFE AND HEALTH. Illustrated. *Crown* 8*vo.* 2*s.* 6*d.* [University Extension Series.

A. W. Kinglake. EOTHEN. With an Introduction and Notes. *Pott* 8*vo. Cloth*, 1*s.* 6*d. net*; *leather*, 2*s.* 6*d. net.* [Little Library.

Rudyard Kipling. BARRACK-ROOM BALLADS. 73*rd Thousand. Crown* 8*vo.* 6*s.*; *leather*, 6*s. net.*

'Mr. Kipling's verse is strong, vivid, full of character. . . . Unmistakable genius rings in every line.'—*Times.*

'The ballads teem with imagination, they palpitate with emotion. We read them with laughter and tears: the metres throb in our pulses, the cunningly ordered words tingle with life; and if this be not poetry, what is?'—*Pall Mall Gazette.*

THE SEVEN SEAS. 62*nd Thousand. Crown* 8*vo. Buckram, gilt top*, 6*s.*; *leather*, 6*s. net.*

'The Empire has found a singer; it is no depreciation of the songs to say that statesmen may have, one way or other, to take account of them.'—*Manchester Guardian.*

F. G. Kitton. See Dickens.

W. J. Knox Little. See St. Francis de Sales.

Charles Lamb, THE ESSAYS OF ELIA. With over 100 Illustrations by A. GARTH JONES, and an Introduction by E. V. LUCAS. *Demy* 8*vo.* 10*s.* 6*d.*

'This edition is in many respects of peculiar beauty.'—*Daily Chronicle.*

ELIA, AND THE LAST ESSAYS OF ELIA. Edited by E. V. LUCAS. *Pott* 8*vo. Cloth*, 1*s.* 6*d. net*; *leather*, 2*s.* 6*d. net.* [Little Library.

THE KING AND QUEEN OF HEARTS: An 1805 Book for Children. Illustrated by WILLIAM MULREADY. A new edition, in facsimile, edited by E. V. LUCAS. 1*s.* 6*d.*

This little book is a literary curiosity, and has been discovered and identified as the work of Charles Lamb by E. V. Lucas. It is an exact facsimile of the original edition, which was illustrated by Mulready.

Professor Lambros. ECTHESIS CHRONICA. Edited by. *Demy* 8*vo.* 7*s.* 6*d. net.* [Byzantine Texts.

Stanley Lane-Poole. THE LIFE OF SIR HARRY PARKES. *A New and Cheaper Edition. Crown* 8*vo.* 6*s.*

A HISTORY OF EGYPT IN THE MIDDLE AGES. Fully Illustrated. *Crown* 8*vo.* 6*s.*

F. Langbridge, M.A. BALLADS OF THE BRAVE: Poems of Chivalry, Enterprise, Courage, and Constancy. *Second Edition. Crown 8vo.* 2s. 6d.

'The book is full of splendid things.'—*World.*

William Law. A SERIOUS CALL TO A DEVOUT AND HOLY LIFE. Edited, with an Introduction, by C. BIGG, D.D., late Student of Christ Church. *Pott 8vo. Cloth,* 2s.; *leather,* 2s. 6d. *net.* [Library of Devotion.

This is a reprint, word for word and line for line, of the *Editio Princeps.*

G. S. Layard. THE LIFE OF MRS. LYNN LINTON. Illustrated. *Demy 8vo.* 12s. 6d.

Captain Melville Lee. A HISTORY OF POLICE IN ENGLAND. *Crown 8vo.* 7s. 6d.

'A learned book, comprising many curious details to interest the general reader as well as the student who will consult it for exact information.'—*Daily News.*

V. B. Lewes, M.A. AIR AND WATER. Illustrated. *Crown 8vo.* 2s. 6d. [University Extension Series.

W. M. Lindsay. See Plautus.

Walter Lock, D.D., Warden of Keble College. ST. PAUL, THE MASTER-BUILDER. *Crown 8vo.* 3s. 6d.

See also Keble and New Commentaries.

JOHN KEBLE. With Portrait. *Crown 8vo.* 3s. 6d. [Leaders of Religion.

E. V. Lucas. THE VISIT TO LONDON. Described in Verse, with Coloured Pictures by F. D. BEDFORD. *Small 4to.* 6s.

This charming book describes the introduction of a country child to the delights and sights of London. It is the result of a well-known partnership between author and artist.

'A beautiful children's book.' *Black and White.*

'The most inimitable verses and interesting pictures.'—*Daily Chronicle.*

'Of quite unusual charm.' *Daily Telegraph.*

See also Jane Austen and Mrs. Gaskell and Charles Lamb.

Lucian. SIX DIALOGUES (Nigrinus, Icaro-Menippus, The Cock, The Ship, The Parasite, The Lover of Falsehood). Translated by S. T. Irwin, M.A., Assistant Master at Clifton; late Scholar of Exeter College, Oxford. *Crown 8vo.* 3s. 6d. [Classical Translations.

L. W. Lyde, M.A. A COMMERCIAL GEOGRAPHY OF THE BRITISH EMPIRE. *Third Edition. Crown 8vo.* 2s. [Commercial Series.

Hon. Mrs. Lyttelton. WOMEN AND THEIR WORK. *Crown 8vo.* 2s. 6d.

'Thoughtful, interesting, practical.'—*Guardian.*

'The book is full of sound precept given with sympathy and wit.'—*Pilot.*

Lord Macaulay. CRITICAL AND HISTORICAL ESSAYS. Edited by F. C. MONTAGUE, M.A. *Three Volumes. Cr. 8vo.* 6s. *each.* [Methuen's Standard Library.

The only edition of this book completely annotated.

J. E. B. M'Allen, M.A. THE PRINCIPLES OF BOOKKEEPING BY DOUBLE ENTRY. *Crown 8vo.* 2s. [Commercial Series.

J. A. MacCulloch. COMPARATIVE THEOLOGY. *Crown 8vo.* 6s. [The Churchman's Library.

'Most carefully executed, readable and informing.'—*Scotsman.*

F. MacCunn. JOHN KNOX. With Portrait. *Crown 8vo.* 3s. 6d. [Leaders of Religion.

A. M. Mackay. THE CHURCHMAN'S INTRODUCTION TO THE OLD TESTAMENT. *Crown 8vo.* 3s. 6d. [Churchman's Library.

'The book throughout is frank and courageous.'—*Glasgow Herald.*

Laurie Magnus, M.A. A PRIMER OF WORDSWORTH. *Crown 8vo.* 2s. 6d.

J. P. Mahaffy, Litt.D. A HISTORY OF THE EGYPT OF THE PTOLEMIES. Fully Illustrated. *Crown 8vo.* 6s.

F. W. Maitland, LL.D., Downing Professor of the Laws of England in the University of Cambridge. CANON LAW IN ENGLAND. *Royal 8vo.* 7s. 6d.

H. E. Malden, M.A. ENGLISH RECORDS. A Companion to the History of England. *Crown 8vo.* 3s. 6d.

THE ENGLISH CITIZEN: HIS RIGHTS AND DUTIES. *Crown 8vo.* 1s. 6d.

E. C. Marchant, M.A., Fellow of Peterhouse, Cambridge, and Assistant Master at St. Paul's School. A GREEK ANTHOLOGY. *Crown 8vo.* 3s. 6d.

E. C. Marchant, M.A., and **A. M. Cook,** M.A. PASSAGES FOR UNSEEN TRANSLATION. *Second Edition. Crown 8vo.* 3s. 6d.

'We know no book of this class better fitted for use in the higher forms of schools.' —*Guardian.*

J. E. Marr, F.R.S., Fellow of St. John's College, Cambridge. THE SCIENTIFIC STUDY OF SCENERY. *Second Edition.* Illustrated. *Crown 8vo.* 6s.

'A volume, moderate in size and readable in style, which will be acceptable alike to the student of geology and geography and to the tourist.'—*Athenæum.*

. J. Mason. THOMAS CRANMER. With Portrait. *Crown* 8*vo.* 3*s.* 6*d.* [Leaders of Religion.

eorge Massee. THE EVOLUTION OF PLANT LIFE: Lower Forms. With Illustrations. *Crown* 8*vo.* 2*s.* 6*d.* [University Extension Series.

. F. G. Masterman, M.A. TENNYSON AS A RELIGIOUS TEACHER. *Crown* 8*vo.* 6*s.*

'A thoughtful and penetrating appreciation, full of interest and suggestion.'—*World.*

nnie Matheson. See Mrs. Craik.

mma S. Mellows. A SHORT STORY OF ENGLISH LITERATURE. *Crown* 8*vo.* 3*s.* 6*d.*

'A lucid and well-arranged account of the growth of English literature.'—*Pall Mall Gazette.*

. C. Miall, F.R.S. See Gilbert White.

. B. Michell. THE ART AND PRACTICE OF HAWKING. With 3 Photogravures by G. E. LODGE, and other Illustrations. *Demy* 8*vo.* 10*s.* 6*d.*

. G. Millais. THE LIFE AND LETTERS OF SIR JOHN EVERETT MILLAIS, President of the Royal Academy. With 319 Illustrations, of which 9 are Photogravure. 2 *vols. Royal* 8*vo.* 20*s. net.*

'This splendid work.'—*World.*

'Of such absorbing interest is it, of such completeness in scope and beauty. Special tribute must be paid to the extraordinary completeness of the illustrations.'—*Graphic.*

. G. Milne, M.A. A HISTORY OF ROMAN EGYPT. Fully Illustrated. *Crown* 8*vo.* 6*s.*

. Chalmers Mitchell, M.A. OUTLINES OF BIOLOGY. Illustrated. *Second Edition. Crown* 8*vo.* 6*s.*

A text-book designed to cover the Schedule issued by the Royal College of Physicians and Surgeons.

. M. Moir. MANSIE WAUCH. Edited by T. F. HENDERSON. *Pott* 8*vo. Cloth,* 1*s.* 6*d. net; leather,* 2*s.* 6*d. net.* [Little Library.

. C. Montague, M.A. See Macaulay.

. E. Moore. BACK TO THE LAND: An Inquiry into the cure for Rural Depopulation. *Crown* 8*vo.* 2*s.* 6*d.* [Social Questions Series.

. R. Morfill, Oriel College, Oxford. A HISTORY OF RUSSIA FROM PETER THE GREAT TO ALEXANDER II. With Maps and Plans. *Crown* 8*vo.* 7*s.* 6*d.*

This history, is founded on a study of original documents, and though necessarily brief, is the most comprehensive narrative in existence. Considerable attention has been paid to the social and literary development of the country, and the recent expansion of Russia in Asia.

R. J. Morich, late of Clifton College. GERMAN EXAMINATION PAPERS IN MISCELLANEOUS GRAMMAR AND IDIOMS. *Sixth Edition. Crown* 8*vo.* 2*s.* 6*d.* [School Examination Series.

A KEY, issued to Tutors and Private Students only, to be had on application to the Publishers. *Second Edition. Crown* 8*vo.* 6*s. net.*

Miss Anderson Morton. See Miss Brodrick.

H C. G. Moule, D D., Lord Bishop of Durham. CHARLES SIMEON. With Portrait. *Crown* 8*vo.* 3*s.* 6*d.* [Leaders of Religion.

M. M. Pattison Muir, M.A. THE CHEMISTRY OF FIRE. The Elementary Principles of Chemistry. Illustrated. *Crown* 8*vo.* 2*s.* 6*d.* [University Extension Series.

V. A. Mundella, M.A. See J. T. Dunn.

W. G. Neal. See R. N. Hall.

H. W. Nevinson. LADYSMITH: The Diary of a Siege. With 16 Illustrations and a Plan. *Second Edition. Crown* 8*vo.* 6*s.*

J. B. B. Nichols. A LITTLE BOOK OF ENGLISH SONNETS. *Pott* 8*vo. Cloth,* 1*s.* 6*d. net; leather,* 2*s.* 6*d. net.* [The Little Library.

James Northcote, R.A., THE CONVERSATIONS OF, WITH JAMES WARD. Edited by ERNEST FLETCHER. With many Portraits. *Demy* 8*vo.* 10*s.* 6*d.*

A. H. Norway, Author of 'Highways and Byways in Devon and Cornwall.' NAPLES: PAST AND PRESENT. With 40 Illustrations by A. G. FERARD. *Crown* 8*vo.* 6*s.*

Mrs. Oliphant. THOMAS CHALMERS. With Portrait. *Crown* 8*vo.* 3*s.* 6*d.* [Leaders of Religion.

C. W. Oman, M.A., Fellow of All Souls', Oxford. A HISTORY OF THE ART OF WAR. Vol. II.: The Middle Ages, from the Fourth to the Fourteenth Century. Illustrated. *Demy* 8*vo.* 21*s.*

'The whole art of war in its historic evolution has never been treated on such an ample and comprehensive scale, and we question if any recent contribution to the exact history of the world has possessed more enduring value.'—*Daily Chronicle.*

Prince Henri of Orleans. FROM TONKIN TO INDIA. Translated by HAMLEY BENT, M.A. With 100 Illustrations and a Map. *Crown* 4*to, gilt top.* 25*s.*

R. L. Ottley, M.A., late Fellow of Magdalen College, Oxon., and Principal of Pusey House. THE DOCTRINE OF THE INCARNATION. *Second and cheaper Edition. Demy* 8*vo.* 12*s.* 6*d.* [Handbooks of Theology.

'A clear and remarkably full account of the main currents of speculation. Scholarly precision . . . genuine tolerance . . . intense interest in his subject—are Mr. Ottley's merits.'—*Guardian.*

LANCELOT ANDREWES. With Portrait. *Crown 8vo.* 3*s.* 6*d.*
[Leaders of Religion.

J. H. Overton, M.A. JOHN WESLEY. With Portrait. *Crown 8vo.* 3*s.* 6*d.*
[Leaders of Religion.

M. N. Oxford, of Guy's Hospital. A HANDBOOK OF NURSING. *Crown 8vo.* 3*s.* 6*d.*

'The most useful work of the kind that we have seen. A most valuable and practical manual.'—*Manchester Guardian.*

W. C. C. Pakes. THE SCIENCE OF HYGIENE. With numerous Illustrations. *Demy 8vo.* 15*s.*

'A thoroughgoing working text-book of its subject, practical and well-stocked.'—*Scotsman.*

Prof. Léon Parmentier and M. Bidez. EVAGRIUS. Edited by. *Demy 8vo.* 10*s.* 6*d. net.* [Byzantine Texts.

Pascal, THE THOUGHTS OF. With Introduction and Notes by C. S. JERRAM. *Pott 8vo.* 2*s.*; *leather*, 2*s.* 6*d. net.*
[Library of Devotion.

George Paston. SIDELIGHTS ON THE GEORGIAN PERIOD. With many Illustrations. *Demy 8vo.* 10*s* 6*d.*

'Touched with lightness and sympathy. We recommend this book to all who are tired with the trash of novels.'—*Spectator.*

'This book is the highly diverting product of research and compilation. It is a magazine of instructive and amusing information.'—*Academy.*

H. W. Paul. See Laurence Sterne.

E. H. Pearce, M.A. THE ANNALS OF CHRIST'S HOSPITAL. With many Illustrations. *Demy 8vo.* 7*s.* 6*d.*

'A well-written, copious, authentic history.'—*Times.*

R. E. Peary, Gold Medallist of the Royal Geographical Society. NORTHWARD OVER THE GREAT ICE. With over 800 Illustrations. 2 *vols. Royal 8vo.* 32*s. net.*

'His book will take its place among the permanent literature of Arctic exploration.'—*Times.*

Sidney Peel, late Fellow of Trinity College, Oxford, and Secretary to the Royal Commission on the Licensing Laws. PRACTICAL LICENSING REFORM. *Second Edition. Crown 8vo.* 1*s.* 6*d.*

M. Perugini. SELECTIONS FROM WILLIAM BLAKE. *Pott 8vo. Cloth*, 1*s.* 6*d. net*; *leather*, 2*s.* 6*d. net.*
[Little Library.

J. P. Peters, D.D. THE OLD TESTAMENT AND THE NEW SCHOLARSHIP. *Crown 8vo.* 6*s.*
[Churchman's Library.

'Every page reveals wide reading, used with sound and scholarly judgment.'
—*Manchester Guardian.*

W. M. Flinders Petrie, D.C.L., LL.D., Professor of Egyptology at University College. A HISTORY OF EGYPT, FROM THE EARLIEST TIMES TO THE PRESENT DAY. Fully Illustrated. *In six volumes. Crown 8vo.* 6*s. each.*

'A history written in the spirit of scientific precision so worthily represented by Dr. Petrie and his school cannot but promote sound and accurate study, and supply a vacant place in the English literature of Egyptology.'—*Times.*

VOL. I. PREHISTORIC TIMES TO XVITH DYNASTY. *Fifth Edition.*

VOL. II. THE XVIITH AND XVIIITH DYNASTIES. *Third Edition.*

VOL. IV. THE EGYPT OF THE PTOLEMIES. J. P. MAHAFFY, Litt.D.

VOL. V. ROMAN EGYPT. J. G. MILNE, M.A.

VOL. VI. EGYPT IN THE MIDDLE AGES. STANLEY LANE-POOLE, M.A.

RELIGION AND CONSCIENCE IN ANCIENT EGYPT. Fully Illustrated. *Crown 8vo.* 2*s.* 6*d.*

SYRIA AND EGYPT, FROM THE TELL EL AMARNA TABLETS. *Crown 8vo.* 2*s.* 6*d.*

EGYPTIAN TALES. Illustrated by TRISTRAM ELLIS. *In Two Volumes. Crown 8vo.* 3*s.* 6*d. each.*

EGYPTIAN DECORATIVE ART. With 120 Illustrations. *Crown 8vo.* 3*s.* 6*d.*

'In these lectures he displays rare skill in elucidating the development of decorative art in Egypt.'—*Times.*

Philip Pienaar. WITH STEYN AND DE WET. *Second Edition. Crown 8vo.* 3*s.* 6*d.*

A narrative of the adventures of a Boer telegraphist of the Orange Free State during the war.

Plautus. THE CAPTIVI. Edited, with an Introduction, Textual Notes, and a Commentary, by W. M. LINDSAY, Fellow of Jesus College, Oxford. *Demy 8vo.* 10*s.* 6*d. net.*

For this edition all the important MSS. have been re-collated. An appendix deals with the accentual element in early Latin verse. The Commentary is very full.

THE CAPTIVI. Adapted for Lower Forms, by J. H. FREESE, M.A., late Fellow of St. John's, Cambridge. 1*s.* 6*d.*

J. T. Plowden-Wardlaw, B.A., King's College, Cambridge. EXAMINATION PAPERS IN ENGLISH HISTORY. *Crown 8vo.* 2*s.* 6*d.*
[School Examination Series.

'rank Podmore. MODERN SPIRITUALISM. *Two Volumes. Demy 8vo.* 21*s. net.*

A History and a Criticism.

'A complete guide to a very complex subject.'—*Academy.*

'Of great scientific value and considerable popular interest.'—*Scotsman.*

'A masterpiece of scientific analysis and exposition. There is no doubt it will hold the field for a long time.'—*Star.*

'The entire book is characterised by the greatest candour and fairness, and affords pleasant reading upon an entrancing theme.' —*Public Opinion.*

. W. Pollard. OLD PICTURE BOOKS. With many Illustrations. *Demy 8vo.* 7*s.* 6*d. net.*

I. C. Potter, M.A., F.L.S. A TEXT-BOOK OF AGRICULTURAL BOTANY. Illustrated. *2nd Edition. Crown 8vo.* 4*s.* 6*d.* [University Extension Series.

. Pradeau. A KEY TO THE TIME ALLUSIONS IN THE DIVINE COMEDY. With a Dial. *Small quarto.* 3*s.* 6*d.*

. L. Price, M.A., Fellow of Oriel College, Oxon. A HISTORY OF ENGLISH POLITICAL ECONOMY. *Fourth Edition. Crown 8vo.* 2*s.* 6*d.*
[University Extension Series.

'Q." THE GOLDEN POMP. A Procession of English Lyrics. Arranged by A. T. QUILLER COUCH. *Crown 8vo. Buckram.* 6*s.*

. B. Rackham, M.A. THE ACTS OF THE APOSTLES. With Introduction and Notes. *Demy 8vo.* 12*s.* 6*d.*
[Westminster Commentaries.

'A really helpful book. Both introduction and commentary are marked by common sense and adequate knowledge.'—*Guardian.*

. W. Randolph, D.D., Principal of the Theological College, Ely. THE PSALMS OF DAVID. With an Introduction and Notes. *Pott 8vo. Cloth,* 2*s.*; *leather,* 2*s.* 6*d. net.* Library of Devotion.

A devotional and practical edition of the Prayer Book version of the Psalms.

Iastings Rashdall, M.A., Fellow and Tutor of New College, Oxford. DOCTRINE AND DEVELOPMENT. *Crown 8vo.* 6*s.*

V. Reason, M.A. UNIVERSITY AND SOCIAL SETTLEMENTS. *Crown 8vo.* 2*s.* 6*d.* [Social Questions Series.

Charles Richardson. THE ENGLISH TURF. With numerous Illustrations and Plans. *Demy 8vo.* 15*s.*

I. E. Roberts. See C. C. Channer.

A. Robertson, D.D., Principal of King's College, London. REGNUM DEI. The Bampton Lectures of 1901. *Demy 8vo.* 12*s.* 6*d. net.*

'A notable volume. Its chief value and interest is in its historic treatment of its great theme.'—*Daily News.*

'It is altogether a solid piece of work and a valuable contribution to the history of Christian thought.'—*Scotsman.*

Sir G. S. Robertson, K.C.S.I. CHITRAL: The Story of a Minor Siege. With numerous Illustrations, Map and Plans. *Second Edition. Demy 8vo.* 10*s.* 6*d.*

'A book which the Elizabethans would have thought wonderful. More thrilling, more piquant, and more human than any novel.'—*Newcastle Chronicle.*

J. W. Robertson-Scott. THE PEOPLE OF CHINA. With a Map. *Crown 8vo.* 3*s.* 6*d.*

A. W. Robinson, M.A. THE EPISTLE TO THE GALATIANS. Explained. *Fcap. 8vo.* 1*s.* 6*d. net.* [Churchman's Bible.

'The most attractive, sensible, and instructive manual for people at large, which we have ever seen.'—*Church Gazette.*

Cecilia Robinson. THE MINISTRY OF DEACONESSES. With an Introduction by the Lord Bishop of Winchester. *Crown 8vo.* 3*s.* 6*d.*

G. Rodwell, B.A. NEW TESTAMENT GREEK. A Course for Beginners. With a Preface by WALTER LOCK, D.D., Warden of Keble College. *Fcap. 8vo.* 3*s.* 6*d.*

Fred Roe. ANCIENT COFFERS AND CUPBOARDS: Their History and Description. With many Illustrations. *Quarto.* £3, 3*s. net.*

E. S. Roscoe. ROBERT HARLEY, EARL OF OXFORD. Illustrated. *Demy 8vo.* 7*s.* 6*d.*

This is the only life of Harley in existence.

Edward Rose. THE ROSE READER. With numerous Illustrations. *Crown 8vo.* 2*s.* 6*d. Also in 4 Parts. Parts I. and II.* 6*d. each; Part III.* 8*d.*; *Part IV.* 10*d.*

A reader on a new and original plan.

The distinctive feature of this book is the entire avoidance of irregularly-spelt words until the pupil has thoroughly mastered the principle of reading, and learned its enjoyment. The reading of connected sentences begins from the first page, before the entire alphabet is introduced.

E. Denison Ross, M.A. See W. Beckford

A. E. Rubie, M.A., Head Master of the Royal Naval School, Eltham. THE GOSPEL ACCORDING TO ST. MARK. Edited by. With three Maps. *Crown 8vo.* 1*s.* 6*d.* [Methuen's Junior School Books.

W. Clark Russell. THE LIFE OF ADMIRAL LORD COLLINGWOOD. With Illustrations by F. BRANGWYN. *Fourth Edition. Crown 8vo.* 6*s*.

'A book which we should like to see in the hands of every boy in the country.'—*St. James's Gazette.*

St. Anselm, THE DEVOTIONS OF. Edited by C. C. J. WEBB, M.A. *Pott 8vo. Cloth,* 2*s.*; *leather,* 2*s.* 6*d. net.* [Library of Devotion.

Viscount St. Cyres. THE LIFE OF FRANÇOIS DE FENELON. Illustrated. *Demy 8vo.* 10*s.* 6*d.*

'We have in this admirable volume a most valuable addition to our historical portrait gallery.'—*Daily News.*

St. Francis de Sales. ON THE LOVE OF GOD. Edited by W. J. KNOX-LITTLE, M.A. *Pott 8vo. Cloth,* 2*s.*; *leather,* 2*s.* 6*d. net.* [Library of Devotion.

A. L. Salmon. CORNWALL. Illustrated by B. C. BOULTER. *Pott 8vo. Cloth,* 3*s.*; *leather,* 3*s.* 6*d. net.* [The Little Guides.

J. Sargeaunt, M.A. ANNALS OF WESTMINSTER SCHOOL. With numerous Illustrations. *Demy 8vo.* 7*s.* 6*d.*

C. Sathas. THE HISTORY OF PSELLUS. *Demy 8vo.* 15*s. net.* [Byzantine Texts.

H. G. Seeley, F.R.S. DRAGONS OF THE AIR. With many Illustrations. *Crown 8vo.* 6*s.*

A popular history of the most remarkable flying animals which ever lived. Their relations to mammals, birds, and reptiles, living and extinct, are shown by an original series of illustrations.

V. P. Sells, M.A. THE MECHANICS OF DAILY LIFE. Illustrated. *Crown 8vo.* 2*s.* 6*d.* [University Extension Series.

Edmund Selous. TOMMY SMITH'S ANIMALS. Illustrated by G. W. ORD. *Second Edition. Fcap. 8vo.* 2*s.* 6*d.*

'A quaint, fascinating little book: a nursery classic.'—*Athenæum.*

William Shakespeare.

THE ARDEN EDITION.

Demy 8vo. 3*s.* 6*d. each volume.* General Editor, W. J. CRAIG. An Edition of Shakespeare in single Plays. Edited with a full Introduction, Textual Notes, and a Commentary at the foot of the page.

'No edition of Shakespeare is likely to prove more attractive and satisfactory than this one. It is beautifully printed and paged and handsomely and simply bound.'—*St. James's Gazette.*

HAMLET. Edited by EDWARD DOWDEN, Litt.D.

ROMEO AND JULIET. Edited by EDWARD DOWDEN, Litt.D.

KING LEAR. Edited by W. J. CRAIG.

JULIUS CAESAR. Edited by M. MACMILLAN, M.A.

THE TEMPEST. Edited by MORTON LUCE.

A. Sharp. VICTORIAN POETS. *Crown 8vo.* 2*s.* 6*d.* [University Extension Series.

J. S. Shedlock. THE PIANOFORTE SONATA: Its Origin and Development. *Crown 8vo.* 5*s.*

Arthur Sherwell, M.A. LIFE IN WEST LONDON *Third Edition. Crown 8vo.* 2*s.* 6*d.* [Social Questions Series.

Evan Small, M.A. THE EARTH. An Introduction to Physiography. Illustrated. *Crown 8vo.* 2*s.* 6*d.* [University Extension Series.

Nowell C. Smith, Fellow of New College, Oxford. SELECTIONS FROM WORDSWORTH. *Pott 8vo. Cloth,* 1*s.* 6*d. net*; *leather,* 2*s.* 6*d. net.* [Little Library.

Sophocles. ELECTRA AND AJAX. Translated by E. D. A. MORSHEAD, M.A., Assistant Master at Winchester. 2*s.* 6*d.* [Classical Translations.

R. Southey. ENGLISH SEAMEN (Howard, Clifford, Hawkins, Drake, Cavendish). Edited, with an Introduction, by DAVID HANNAY. *Second Edition. Crown 8vo.* 6*s.*

'A brave, inspiriting book.'—*Black and White.*

C. H. Spence, M.A., Clifton College. HISTORY AND GEOGRAPHY EXAMINATION PAPERS. *Second Edition. Crown 8vo.* 2*s.* 6*d.* [School Examination Series.

W. A. Spooner, M.A., Fellow of New College, Oxford. BISHOP BUTLER. With Portrait. *Crown 8vo.* 3*s.* 6*d.* [Leaders of Religion.

J. W. Stanbridge, B.D., Rector of Bainton, Canon of York, and sometime Fellow of St. John's College, Oxford. A BOOK OF DEVOTIONS. *Pott 8vo. Cloth,* 2*s.*; *leather,* 2*s.* 6*d. net.* [Library of Devotion.

'It is probably the best book of its kind. It deserves high commendation.'—*Church Gazette.*

See also Cardinal Bona.

'Stancliffe.' GOLF DO'S AND DONT'S. *Second Edition. Fcap. 8vo.* 1*s.*

A. M. M. Stedman, M.A.

INITIA LATINA: Easy Lessons on Elementary Accidence. *Sixth Edition. Fcap. 8vo.* 1*s.*

FIRST LATIN LESSONS. *Sixth Edition. Crown 8vo.* 2*s.*

FIRST LATIN READER. With Notes adapted to the Shorter Latin Primer and

Vocabulary. *Sixth Edition revised.* 18*mo.* 1*s.* 6*d.*

:ASY SELECTIONS FROM CÆSAR. The Helvetian War. *Second Edition.* 18*mo.* 1*s.*

:ASY SELECTIONS FROM LIVY. Part I. The Kings of Rome. 18*mo.* *Second Edition.* 1*s.* 6*d.*

:ASY LATIN PASSAGES FOR UNSEEN TRANSLATION. *Eighth Edition.* *Fcap.* 8*vo.* 1*s.* 6*d.*

XEMPLA LATINA. First Lessons in Latin Accidence. With Vocabulary. *Crown* 8*vo.* 1*s.*

ASY LATIN EXERCISES ON THE SYNTAX OF THE SHORTER AND REVISED LATIN PRIMER. With Vocabulary. *Ninth and Cheaper Edition, re-written.* *Crown* 8*vo.* 1*s.* 6*d.* KEY, 3*s.* *net.* *Original Edition.* 2*s.* 6*d.*

HE LATIN COMPOUND SENTENCE: Rules and Exercises. *Second Edition.* *Crown* 8*vo.* 1*s.* 6*d.* With Vocabulary. 2*s.*

'OTANDA QUAEDAM: Miscellaneous Latin Exercises on Common Rules and Idioms. *Fourth Edition.* *Fcap.* 8*vo.* 1*s.* 6*d.* With Vocabulary. 2*s.* Key, 2*s.* *net.*

ATIN VOCABULARIES FOR REPETITION: Arranged according to Subjects. *Eleventh Edition.* *Fcap.* 8*vo.* 1*s.* 6*d.*

VOCABULARY OF LATIN IDIOMS. 18*mo.* *Second Edition.* 1*s.*

TEPS TO GREEK. *Second Edition, revised.* 18*mo.* 1*s.*

SHORTER GREEK PRIMER. *Crown* 8*vo.* 1*s.* 6*d.*

ASY GREEK PASSAGES FOR UNSEEN TRANSLATION. *Third Edition, revised.* *Fcap.* 8*vo.* 1*s.* 6*d.*

REEK VOCABULARIES FOR REPETITION. Arranged according to Subjects. *Third Edition.* *Fcap.* 8*vo.* 1*s.* 6*d.*

REEK TESTAMENT SELECTIONS. For the use of Schools. With Introduction, Notes, and Vocabulary. *Third Edition.* *Fcap.* 8*vo.* 2*s.* 6*d.*

TEPS TO FRENCH. *Sixth Edition.* 18*mo.* 8*d.*

RST FRENCH LESSONS. *Sixth Edition, revised.* *Crown* 8*vo.* 1*s.*

ASY FRENCH PASSAGES FOR UNSEEN TRANSLATION. *Fifth Edition, revised.* *Fcap.* 8*vo.* 1*s.* 6*d.*

ASY FRENCH EXERCISES ON ELEMENTARY SYNTAX. With Vocabulary. *Second Edition.* *Crown* 8*vo.* 2*s.* 6*d.* KEY. 3*s.* *net.*

RENCH VOCABULARIES FOR REPETITION: Arranged according to Subjects. *Tenth Edition.* *Fcap.* 8*vo.* 1*s.*

FRENCH EXAMINATION PAPERS IN MISCELLANEOUS GRAMMAR AND IDIOMS. *Twelfth Edition.* *Crown* 8*vo.* 2*s.* 6*d.* [School Examination Series.

A KEY, issued to Tutors and Private Students only, to be had on application to the Publishers. *Fifth Edition.* *Crown* 8*vo.* 6*s.* *net.*

GENERAL KNOWLEDGE EXAMINATION PAPERS. *Fourth Edition.* *Crown* 8*vo.* 2*s.* 6*d.* [School Examination Series.

KEY (*Second Edition*) issued as above. 7*s.* *net.*

GREEK EXAMINATION PAPERS IN MISCELLANEOUS GRAMMAR AND IDIOMS. *Sixth Edition.* *Crown* 8*vo.* 2*s.* 6*d.* [School Examination Series.

KEY (*Third Edition*) issued as above. 6*s.* *net.*

LATIN EXAMINATION PAPERS IN MISCELLANEOUS GRAMMAR AND IDIOMS. *Eleventh Edition.* *Crown* 8*vo.* 2*s.* 6*d.* [School Examination Series.

KEY (*Fourth Edition*) issued as above. 6*s.* *net.*

R. Elliott Steel, M.A., F.C.S. THE WORLD OF SCIENCE. Including Chemistry, Heat, Light, Sound, Magnetism, Electricity, Botany, Zoology, Physiology, Astronomy, and Geology. 147 Illustrations. *Second Edition.* *Crown* 8*vo.* 2*s.* 6*d.*

PHYSICS EXAMINATION PAPERS. *Crown* 8*vo.* 2*s.* 6*d.* [School Examination Series.

C. Stephenson, of the Technical College, Bradford, and **F. Suddards,** of the Yorkshire College, Leeds. ORNAMENTAL DESIGN FOR WOVEN FABRICS. *Demy* 8*vo.* *Second Edition.* 7*s.* 6*d.*

J. Stephenson, M.A. THE CHIEF TRUTHS OF THE CHRISTIAN FAITH. *Crown* 8*vo.* 3*s.* 6*d.*

An attempt to present in clear and popular form the main truths of the Faith. The book is intended for lay workers in the Church, for educated parents and for teachers generally.

Laurence Sterne. A SENTIMENTAL JOURNEY. Edited by H. W. PAUL. *Pott* 8*vo.* *Cloth,* 1*s.* 6*d.* *net;* *leather,* 2*s.* 6*d.* *net.* [Little Library.

W. Sterry, M.A. ANNALS OF ETON COLLEGE. With numerous Illustrations. *Demy* 8*vo.* 7*s.* 6*d.*

Katherine Steuart. BY ALLAN WATER. *Second Edition.* *Crown* 8*vo.* 6*s.*

'A delightful mixture of fiction and fact, tradition and history. There is not a page which is not informing and not entertaining.'—*Spectator.*

'A charming book.'—*Glasgow Herald.*

'Has a unique charm.'—*Pilot.*
'A unique series of historical pictures.'—*Manchester Guardian.*

R. L. Stevenson. THE LETTERS OF ROBERT LOUIS STEVENSON TO HIS FAMILY AND FRIENDS. Selected and Edited, with Notes and Introductions, by SIDNEY COLVIN. *Sixth and Cheaper Edition. Crown* 8*vo.* 12*s.*

LIBRARY EDITION. *Demy* 8*vo.* 2 *vols.* 25*s. net.*

'Irresistible in their raciness, their variety, their animation . . . of extraordinary fascination. A delightful inheritance, the truest record of a "richly compounded spirit" that the literature of our time has preserved.'—*Times.*

VAILIMA LETTERS. With an Etched Portrait by WILLIAM STRANG. *Third Edition. Crown* 8*vo. Buckram.* 6*s.*

THE LIFE OF R. L. STEVENSON. See G. Balfour.

E. D. Stone, M.A., late Assistant Master at Eton. SELECTIONS FROM THE ODYSSEY. *Fcap.* 8*vo.* 1*s.* 6*d.*

Charles Strachey. See Chesterfield.

A. W. Streane, D.D. ECCLESIASTES. Explained. *Fcap.* 8*vo.* 1*s.* 6*d. net.* [Churchman's Bible.

'Scholarly, suggestive, and particularly interesting.'—*Bookman.*

Clement E. Stretton. A HISTORY OF THE MIDLAND RAILWAY. With numerous Illustrations. *Demy* 8*vo.* 12*s.* 6*d.*

H. Stroud, D.Sc., M.A., Professor of Physics in the Durham College of Science, Newcastle-on-Tyne. PRACTICAL PHYSICS. Fully Illustrated. *Crown* 8*vo.* 3*s.* 6*d.* [Textbooks of Technology.

Capt. Donald Stuart. THE STRUGGLE FOR PERSIA. With a Map. *Crown* 8*vo.* 6*s.*

'Is indispensable to any student of international politics in the Middle East.'—*Daily Chronicle.*

F. Suddards. See C. Stephenson.

Jonathan Swift. THE JOURNAL TO STELLA. Edited by G. A. AITKEN. *Crown* 8*vo.* 6*s.* [Methuen's Standard Library.

J. E. Symes, M.A. THE FRENCH REVOLUTION. *Crown* 8*vo.* 2*s.* 6*d.* [University Extension Series.

Tacitus. AGRICOLA. With Introduction, Notes, Map, etc. By R. F. DAVIS, M.A., late Assistant Master at Weymouth College. *Crown* 8*vo.* 2*s.*

GERMANIA. By the same Editor. *Crown* 8*vo.* 2*s.*

AGRICOLA AND GERMANIA. Translated by R. B. TOWNSHEND, late Scholar of Trinity College, Cambridge. *Crown* 8*v* 2*s.* 6*d.* [Classical Translation

J. Tauler. THE INNER WAY. Bei Thirty-six Sermons for Festivals by JO TAULER. Edited, with an Introductio By A. W. HUTTON, M.A. *Pott* 8*vo. Clot* 2*s.*; *leather,* 2*s.* 6*d. net.* [Library of Devotio

E. L. Taunton. A HISTORY OF TH JESUITS IN ENGLAND. With Illu trations. *Demy* 8*vo.* 21*s. net.*

'A history of permanent value, whi covers ground never properly investigat before, and is replete with the results original research. A most interesting a careful book.'—*Literature.*

F. G. Taylor, M.A. COMMERCIA ARITHMETIC. *Third Edition. Crow* 8*vo.* 1*s.* 6*d.* [Commercial Seri

Miss J. A. Taylor. SIR WALTE RALEIGH. With 12 Illustrations. *Fca* 8*vo. Cloth,* 3*s.* 6*d.*; *leather* 4*s. net.* [Little Biographie

T. M. Taylor, M.A., Fellow of Gonville a Caius College, Cambridge. A CONST TUTIONAL AND POLITICAL HI TORY OF ROME. *Crown* 8*vo.* 7*s.* 6*d*

'We fully recognise the value of th carefully written work, and admire especial the fairness and sobriety of his judgment a the human interest with which he has i spired his subject.'—*Athenæum.*

Alfred, Lord Tennyson. THE EARL POEMS OF. Edited, with Notes and a Introduction, by J. CHURTON COLLIN M.A. *Crown* 8*vo.* 6*s.* [Methuen's Standard Librar

Also with 10 Illustrations in Photogravu by W. E. F. BRITTEN. *Demy* 8*vo.* 10*s.* 6

An elaborate edition of the celebrate volume which was published in its final a definitive form in 1853.

IN MEMORIAM, MAUD, AND TH PRINCESS. Edited by J. CHURTC COLLINS, M.A. *Crown* 8*vo.* 6*s.* [Methuen's Standard Librar

MAUD. Edited by ELIZABETH WORD WORTH. *Pott* 8*vo. Cloth,* 1*s.* 6*d. ne leather,* 2*s.* 6*d. net.* [Little Librar

IN MEMORIAM. Edited, with an Intr duction and Notes, by H. C. BEECHIN M.A. *Pott* 8*vo. Cloth,* 1*s.* 6*d. ne leather,* 2*s.* 6*d. net.* [Little Librar

THE EARLY POEMS OF. Edited by C. COLLINS, M.A. *Pott* 8*vo. Cloth,* 1*s.* 6 *net*; *leather,* 2*s.* 6*d. net.* [Little Librar

THE PRINCESS. Edited by ELIZABET WORDSWORTH. *Pott* 8*vo. Cloth,* 1*s.* 6 *net*; *leather,* 2*s.* 6*d. net.* [Little Librar

Alice Terton. LIGHTS AND SHADOW IN A HOSPITAL. *Crown* 8*vo.* 3*s.* 6*d.*

W. M. Thackeray. VANITY FAI With an Introduction by S. GWYNN. *Thr*

Volumes. Pott 8vo. Each volume, cloth, 1s. 6d. *net; leather,* 2s. 6d. *net.* [Little Library.

PENDENNIS. Edited by S. GWYNN. *Three Volumes. Pott 8vo. Each volume, cloth,* 1s. 6d. *net* • *leather,* 2s. 6d. *net.* [Little Library.

ESMOND. Edited by STEPHEN GWYNN. *Two volumes. Pott 8vo. Each Volume, cloth,* 1s. 6d. *net; leather,* 2s. 6d. *net.* [Little Library.

F. W. Theobald, M.A. INSECT LIFE. Illustrated. *Crown 8vo.* 2s. 6d. [University Extension Series.

A. H. Thompson. CAMBRIDGE AND ITS COLLEGES. Illustrated by E. H. NEW. *Pott 8vo. Cloth,* 3s.; *leather,* 3s. 6d. *net.* [Little Guides.

'It is brightly written and learned, and is just such a book as a cultured visitor needs.'—*Scotsman.*

Paget Toynbee, Litt.D., M.A. See Dante. DANTE STUDIES AND RESEARCHES. *Demy 8vo.* 10s. 6d. *net.*

THE LIFE OF DANTE ALIGHIERI. With 12 Illustrations. *Second Edition. Fcap. 8vo. Cloth,* 3s. 6d.; *leather,* 4s. *net.* [Little Biographies.

Herbert Trench. DEIRDRE WED: and Other Poems. *Crown 8vo.* 5s.

G. E. Troutbeck. WESTMINSTER ABBEY. Illustrated by F. D. BEDFORD. *Pott 8vo. Cloth,* 3s.; *leather,* 3s. 6d. *net.* [Little Guides.

'In comeliness, and perhaps in completeness, this work must take the first place.'—*Academy.*

'A really first-rate guide-book.'—*Literature.*

Gertrude Tuckwell. THE STATE AND ITS CHILDREN. *Crown 8vo.* 2s. 6d. [Social Questions Series.

Louisa Twining. WORKHOUSES AND PAUPERISM. *Crown 8vo.* 2s. 6d. [Social Questions Series.

E. A. Tyler. A JUNIOR CHEMISTRY. With 73 Illustrations. *Crown 8vo.* 2s. 6d. [Methuen's Junior School Books.

G. W. Wade, D.D. OLD TESTAMENT HISTORY. With Maps. *Second Edition. Crown 8vo.* 6s.

'Careful, scholarly, embodying the best results of modern criticism, and written with great lucidity.'—*Examiner.*

Izaak Walton. THE LIVES OF DONNE, WOTTON, HOOKER, HERBERT AND SANDERSON. With an Introduction by VERNON BLACKBURN, and a Portrait. 3s. 6d.

THE COMPLEAT ANGLER. Edited by J. BUCHAN. *Pott 8vo. Cloth.* 1s. 6d. *net; leather,* 2s. 6d. *net.* [Little Library.

D. S. Van Warmelo. ON COMMANDO. With Portrait. *Crown 8vo.* 3s. 6d.

'A fighting Boer's simple, straightforward story of his life on commando. . . . Full of entertaining incidents.'—*Pall Mall Gazette.*

Grace Warrack. See Lady Julian of Norwich.

Mrs. Alfred Waterhouse. A LITTLE BOOK OF LIFE AND DEATH. Edited by. *Second Edition. Pott 8vo. Cloth,* 1s. 6d. *net; leather,* 2s. 6d. *net.* [Little Library.

C. C. J. Webb, M.A. See St. Anselm.

F. C. Webber. CARPENTRY AND JOINERY. With many Illustrations. *Third Edition. Crown 8vo.* 3s. 6d.

'An admirable elementary text-book on the subject.'—*Builder.*

Sidney H. Wells. PRACTICAL MECHANICS. With 75 Illustrations and Diagrams. *Second Edition. Crown 8vo.* 3s. 6d. [Textbooks of Technology.

J. Wells, M.A., Fellow and Tutor of Wadham College. OXFORD AND OXFORD LIFE. By Members of the University. *Third Edition Crown 8vo.* 3s. 6d.

A SHORT HISTORY OF ROME. *Fourth Edition.* With 3 Maps. *Cr. 8vo.* 3s. 6d.

This book is intended for the Middle and Upper Forms of Public Schools and for Pass Students at the Universities. It contains copious Tables, etc.

'An original work written on an original plan, and with uncommon freshness and vigour.'—*Speaker.*

OXFORD AND ITS COLLEGES. Illustrated by E. H. New. *Fifth Edition. Pott 8vo. Cloth,* 3s.; *leather,* 3s. 6d. *net.* [Little Guides.

'An admirable and accurate little treatise, attractively illustrated.'—*World.*

Helen C. Wetmore. THE LAST OF THE GREAT SCOUTS ('Buffalo Bill'). With Illustrations. *Second Edition. Demy 8vo.* 6s.

'A narrative of one of the most attractive figures in the public eye.'—*Daily Chronicle.*

C. Whibley. See Henley and Whibley.

L. Whibley, M.A., Fellow of Pembroke College, Cambridge. GREEK OLIGARCHIES: THEIR ORGANISATION AND CHARACTER. *Crown 8vo.* 6s.

G. H. Whitaker, M.A. THE EPISTLE OF ST. PAUL THE APOSTLE TO THE EPHESIANS. Edited by. *Fcap. 8vo.* 1s. 6d. *net.* [Churchman's Bible.

Gilbert White. THE NATURAL HISTORY OF SELBORNE. Edited by L. C. MIALL, F.R.S., assisted by W. WARDE FOWLER, M.A. *Crown 8vo.* 6s. [Methuen's Standard Library.

E. E. Whitfield. PRECIS WRITING AND OFFICE CORRESPONDENCE. *Second Edition. Crown 8vo.* 2s. [Commercial Series.

COMMERCIAL EDUCATION IN THEORY AND PRACTICE. *Crown 8vo.* 5s.

An introduction to Methuen's Commercial Series treating the question of Commercial Education fully from both the point of view of the teacher and of the parent. [Commercial Series.

Miss Whitley. See Lady Dilke.

W. H. Wilkins, B.A. THE ALIEN INVASION. *Crown 8vo.* 2s. 6d. [Social Questions Series.

W. Williamson. THE BRITISH GARDENER. Illustrated. *Demy 8vo.* 10s. 6d.

W. Williamson, B.A. JUNIOR ENGLISH EXAMINATION PAPERS. *Fcap. 8vo.* 1s. [Junior Examination Series.

A JUNIOR ENGLISH GRAMMAR. With numerous passages for parsing and analysis, and a chapter on Essay Writing. *Crown 8vo.* 2s. [Methuen's Junior School Books.

A CLASS-BOOK OF DICTATION PASSAGES. *Seventh Edition. Crown 8vo.* 1s. 6d. [Methuen's Junior School Books.

EASY DICTATION AND SPELLING. *Second Edition. Fcap. 8vo.* 1s.

E. M. Wilmot-Buxton. THE MAKERS OF EUROPE. *Crown 8vo.* 3s. 6d.

A Text-book of European History for Middle Forms.

'A book which will be found extremely useful.'—*Secondary Education.*

Beckles Willson. LORD STRATHCONA: the Story of his Life. Illustrated. *Demy 8vo.* 7s. 6d.

'An admirable biography, telling in the happiest manner the wonderful career of this giant of empire.'—*Black and White.*

'We should be glad to see this work taken as a model for imitation. He has given us an excellent and quite adequate account of the life of the distinguished Scotsman.'—*World.*

Richard Wilton, M.A., Canon of York. LYRA PASTORALIS: Songs of Nature, Church, and Home. *Pott 8vo.* 2s. 6d.

A volume of devotional poems.

S. E. Winbolt, M.A., Assistant Master in Christ's Hospital. EXERCISES IN LATIN ACCIDENCE. *Crown 8vo.* 1s. 6d.

An elementary book adapted for Lower Forms to accompany the Shorter Latin Primer.

B. C. A. Windle, F.R.S., D.Sc. SHAKESPEARE'S COUNTRY. Illustrated by E. H. NEW. *Second Edition. Pott 8vo. Cloth,* 3s.; *leather,* 3s. 6d. *net.* [Little Guides.

'One of the most charming guide books. Both for the library and as a travelling companion the book is equally choice and serviceable.'—*Academy.*

THE MALVERN COUNTRY. Illustrated by E. H. NEW. *Pott 8vo. Cloth,* 3s.; *leather,* 3s. 6d. *net.* [Little Guides.

Canon Winterbotham, M.A., B.Sc., LL.B. THE KINGDOM OF HEAVEN HERE AND HEREAFTER. *Crown 8vo.* 3s. 6d. [Churchman's Library.

J. A. E. Wood. HOW TO MAKE A DRESS. Illustrated. *Second Edition. Crown 8vo.* 1s. 6d. [Text Books of Technology.

Elizabeth Wordsworth. See Tennyson.

Arthur Wright, M.A., Fellow of Queen's College, Cambridge. SOME NEW TESTAMENT PROBLEMS. *Crown 8vo.* 6s. [Churchman's Library.

Sophie Wright. GERMAN VOCABULARIES FOR REPETITION. *Fcap. 8vo.* 1s. 6d.

A. B. Wylde. MODERN ABYSSINIA. With a Map and a Portrait. *Demy 8vo.* 15s. *net.*

G. Wyndham, M.P. THE POEMS OF WILLIAM SHAKESPEARE. With an Introduction and Notes. *Demy 8vo. Buckram, gilt top.* 10s. 6d.

'We have no hesitation in describing Mr. George Wyndham's introduction as a masterly piece of criticism, and all who love our Elizabethan literature will find a very garden of delight in it.'—*Spectator.*

W. B. Yeats. AN ANTHOLOGY OF IRISH VERSE. *Revised and Enlarged Edition. Crown 8vo.* 3s. 6d.

T. M. Young. THE AMERICAN COTTON INDUSTRY: A Study of Work and Workers. With an Introduction by ELIJAH HELM, Secretary to the Manchester Chamber of Commerce. *Crown 8vo. Cloth,* 2s. 6d.; *paper boards,* 1s. 6d.

'Thorough, comprehensive, disconcerting.'—*St. James's Gazette.*

'Able and interesting; a really excellent contribution.'—*Pilot.*

Methuen's Standard Library

Crown 8vo. 6s. each Volume.

'A series which, by the beauty and excellence of production as well as by the qualifications of its editors, is one of the best things now to be found in the book market.'—*Manchester Guardian.*

MEMOIRS OF MY LIFE AND WRITINGS. By Edward Gibbon. Edited by G. Birkbeck Hill, LL.D.

THE DECLINE AND FALL OF THE ROMAN EMPIRE. By Edward Gibbon. Edited by J. B. Bury, LL.D. *In Seven Volumes. Also, Demy 8vo. Gilt top.* 8s. 6d. *each.*

THE NATURAL HISTORY OF SELBORNE. By Gilbert White. Edited by L. C. Miall, F.R.S., Assisted by W. Warde Fowler, M.A.

THE HISTORY OF THE LIFE OF THOMAS ELLWOOD. Edited by C. G. Crump, M.A.

LA COMMEDIA DI DANTE ALIGHIERI. The Italian Text. Edited by Paget Toynbee, Litt.D., M.A. *Also, Demy 8vo. Gilt top.* 8s. 6d.

THE EARLY POEMS OF ALFRED, LORD TENNYSON. Edited by J. Churton Collins, M.A.

IN MEMORIAM, MAUD, AND THE PRINCESS. By Alfred, Lord Tennyson. Edited by J. Churton Collins, M.A.

THE JOURNAL TO STELLA. By Jonathan Swift. Edited by G. A. Aitken, M.A.

THE LETTERS OF LORD CHESTERFIELD TO HIS SON. Edited by C. Strachey, and Notes by A. Calthrop. *Two Volumes.*

CRITICAL AND HISTORICAL ESSAYS. By Lord Macaulay. Edited by F. C. Montague, M.A. *Three Volumes.*

THE FRENCH REVOLUTION. By Thomas Carlyle. Edited by C. R. L. Fletcher, Fellow of Magdalen College, Oxford. *Three Volumes.*

Byzantine Texts.

Edited by J. B. BURY, M.A., Litt.D.

ACHARIAH OF MITYLENE. Translated by F. J. Hamilton, D.D., and E. W. Brooks. *Demy 8vo.* *12s. 6d. net.*

VAGRIUS. Edited by Léon Parmentier and M. Bidez. *Demy 8vo.* *10s. 6d. net.*

THE HISTORY OF PSELLUS. Edited by C. Sathas. *Demy 8vo.* *15s. net.*

ECTHESIS CHRONICA. Edited by Professor Lambros. *Demy 8vo.* *7s. 6d. net.*

The Little Library

With Introductions, Notes, and Photogravure Frontispieces.

Pott 8vo. Each Volume, cloth, 1s. 6d. net; leather, 2s. 6d. net.

'Altogether good to look upon, and to handle.'—*Outlook.*
'A perfect series.'—*Pilot.*
'It is difficult to conceive more attractive volumes.'—*St. James's Gazette.*
'Very delicious little books.'—*Literature.*

ANITY FAIR. By W. M. Thackeray. Edited by S. Gwynn. *Three Volumes.*

ENDENNIS. By W. M. Thackeray. Edited by S. Gwynn. *Three Volumes.*

SMOND. By W. M. Thackeray. Edited by Stephen Gwynn. *Two Volumes.*

OHN HALIFAX, GENTLEMAN. By Mrs. Craik. Edited by Annie Matheson. *Two Volumes.*

RIDE AND PREJUDICE. By Jane Austen. Edited by E. V. Lucas. *Two Volumes.*

ORTHANGER ABBEY. By Jane Austen. Edited by E. V. Lucas.

HE PRINCESS. By Alfred, Lord Tennyson. Edited by Elizabeth Wordsworth.

AUD. By Alfred, Lord Tennyson. Edited by Elizabeth Wordsworth.

N MEMORIAM. By Alfred, Lord Tennyson. Edited by H. C. Beeching, M.A.

HE EARLY POEMS OF ALFRED, LORD TENNYSON. Edited by J. C. Collins, M.A.

LITTLE BOOK OF ENGLISH LYRICS. With Notes.

HE INFERNO OF DANTE. Translated by H. F. Cary. Edited by Paget Toynbee, Litt.D., M.A.

HE PURGATORIO OF DANTE. Translated by H. F. Cary. Edited by Paget Toynbee, Litt.D., M.A.

HE PARADISO OF DANTE. Translated by H. F. Cary. Edited by Paget Toynbee, Litt.D., M.A.

LITTLE BOOK OF SCOTTISH VERSE. Edited by T. F. Henderson.

LITTLE BOOK OF LIGHT VERSE. Edited by A. C. Deane.

LITTLE BOOK OF ENGLISH SONNETS. Edited by J. B. B. Nichols.

ELECTIONS FROM WORDSWORTH. Edited by Nowell C. Smith.

SELECTIONS FROM THE EARLY POEMS OF ROBERT BROWNING. Edited by W. Hall Griffin, M.A.

THE ENGLISH POEMS OF RICHARD CRASHAW. Edited by Edward Hutton.

SELECTIONS FROM WILLIAM BLAKE. Edited by M. Perugini.

A LITTLE BOOK OF LIFE AND DEATH. Edited by Mrs. Alfred Waterhouse.

A LITTLE BOOK OF ENGLISH PROSE. Edited by Mrs. P. A. Barnett.

EOTHEN. By A. W. Kinglake. With an Introduction and Notes.

CRANFORD. By Mrs. Gaskell. Edited by E. V. Lucas.

LAVENGRO. By George Borrow. Edited by F. Hindes Groome. *Two Volumes.*

THE HISTORY OF THE CALIPH VATHEK. By William Beckford. Edited by E. Denison Ross.

THE COMPLEAT ANGLER. By Izaak Walton. Edited by J. Buchan.

MARRIAGE. By Susan Ferrier. Edited by Miss Goodrich-Freer and Lord Iddesleigh. *Two Volumes.*

THE INHERITANCE. By Susan Ferrier. Edited by Miss Goodrich-Freer and Lord Iddesleigh. *Two Volumes.*

ELIA, AND THE LAST ESSAYS OF ELIA. By Charles Lamb. Edited by E. V. Lucas.

A SENTIMENTAL JOURNEY. By Laurence Sterne. Edited by H. W. Paul.

MANSIE WAUCH. By D. M. Moir. Edited by T. F. Henderson.

THE INGOLDSBY LEGENDS. By R. H. Barham. Edited by J. B. Atlay. *Two Volumes.*

THE SCARLET LETTER. By Nathaniel Hawthorne.

The Little Guides

Pott 8vo, cloth, 3s.; leather, 3s. 6d. net.

XFORD AND ITS COLLEGES. By J. Wells, M.A. Illustrated by E. H. New. *Fourth Edition.*

AMBRIDGE AND ITS COLLEGES. By A. Hamilton Thompson. Illustrated by E. H. New.

HE MALVERN COUNTRY. By B. C. A. Windle, D.Sc., F.R.S. Illustrated by E. H. New.

HAKESPEARE'S COUNTRY. By B. C. A. Windle, D.Sc., F.R.S. Illustrated by E. H. New. *Second Edition.*

USSEX. By F. G. Brabant, M.A. Illustrated by E. H. New.

WESTMINSTER ABBEY. By G. E. Troutbeck. Illustrated by F. D. Bedford.

NORFOLK. By W. A. Dutt. Illustrated by B. C. Boulter.

CORNWALL. By A. L. Salmon. Illustrated by B. C. Boulter.

BRITTANY. By S. Baring-Gould. Illustrated by J. Wylie.

THE ENGLISH LAKES. By F. G. Brabant, M.A. Illustrated by E. H. New. *4s.; leather, 4s. 6d. net.*

Little Biographies

Fcap. 8vo. Each volume, cloth, 3s. 6d.; leather, 4s. net.

DANTE ALIGHIERI. By Paget Toynbee, Litt.D., M.A. With 12 Illustrations. *Second Edition.*

SAVONAROLA. By E. L. S. Horsburgh, M.A. With Portraits and Illustrations.

JOHN HOWARD. By E. C. S. Gibson, D.D., Vicar of Leeds. With 12 Illustrations.

TENNYSON. By A. C. Benson, M.A. With 12 Illustrations.

WALTER RALEIGH By Miss J. A. Taylor. With 12 Illustrations.

ERASMUS. By E. F. H. CAPEY. With Illustrations.

The Little Blue Books

General Editor, E. V. LUCAS.

Illustrated. Square Fcap. 8vo. 2s. 6d.

'Very elegant and very interesting volumes.'—*Glasgow Herald.*
'A delightful series of diminutive volumes.'—*World.*
'The series should be a favourite among juveniles.'—*Observer.*

1. THE CASTAWAYS OF MEADOWBANK. By T. COBB.
2. THE BEECHNUT BOOK. By JACOB ABBOTT. Edited by E. V. LUCAS.
3. THE AIR GUN. By T. HILBERT.
4. A SCHOOL YEAR. By NETTA SYRETT.
5. THE PEELES AT THE CAPITAL. By T. HILBERT.
6. THE TREASURE OF PRINCEGATE PRIORY. By T. COBB.

The Library of Devotion

With Introductions and (where necessary) Notes.

Pott 8vo, cloth, 2s.; leather, 2s. 6d. net.

'This series is excellent.'—THE LATE BISHOP OF LONDON.
'Well worth the attention of the Clergy.'—THE BISHOP OF LICHFIELD.
'The new "Library of Devotion" is excellent.'—THE BISHOP OF PETERBOROUGH.
'Charming.'—*Record.* 'Delightful.'—*Church Bells.*

THE CONFESSIONS OF ST. AUGUSTINE. Edited by C. Bigg, D.D. *Third Edition.*

THE CHRISTIAN YEAR. Edited by Walter Lock, D.D. *Second Edition.*

THE IMITATION OF CHRIST. Edited by C. Bigg, D.D. *Second Edition.*

A BOOK OF DEVOTIONS. Edited by J. W. Stanbridge, B.D.

LYRA INNOCENTIUM. Edited by Walter Lock, D.D.

A SERIOUS CALL TO A DEVOUT AND HOLY LIFE. Edited by C. Bigg, D.D. *Second Edition.*

THE TEMPLE. Edited by E. C. S. Gibson, D.D.

A GUIDE TO ETERNITY. Edited by J. W. Stanbridge, B.D.

THE PSALMS OF DAVID. Edited by B. W. Ra[ndolph], D.D.

LYRA APOSTOLICA. Edited by Canon Scott Holla[nd] and H. C. Beeching, M.A.

THE INNER WAY. Edited by A. W. Hutton, M.A.

THE THOUGHTS OF PASCAL. Edited by C. Jerram, M.A.

ON THE LOVE OF GOD. Edited by W. J. Kn[ox] Little, M.A.

A MANUAL OF CONSOLATION FROM THE SAIN[TS] AND FATHERS. Edited by J. H. Burn, B.D.

THE SONG OF SONGS. Edited by B. Blaxland, M.

THE DEVOTIONS OF ST. ANSELM. Edited by C. J. Webb, M.A.

The Westminster Commentaries

General Editor, WALTER LOCK, D.D., Warden of Keble College, Dean Ireland's Professor of Exegesis in the University of Oxford.

THE BOOK OF JOB. Edited by E. C. S. Gibson, D.D. *Demy 8vo. 6s.*

THE ACTS OF THE APOSTLES. Edited by R. Rackham, M.A. *Demy 8vo. 12s. 6d.*

Handbooks of Theology

General Editor, A. ROBERTSON, D.D., Principal of King's College, London.

THE XXXIX. ARTICLES OF THE CHURCH OF ENGLAND. Edited by E. C. S. Gibson, D.D. *Third and Cheaper Edition in One Volume. Demy 8vo. 12s. 6d.*

AN INTRODUCTION TO THE HISTORY OF RELIGION. By F. B. Jevons, M.A., Litt.D. *Second Edition. Demy 8vo. 10s. 6d.*

THE DOCTRINE OF THE INCARNATION. By R. Ottley, M.A. *Second and Cheaper Edition. Dem[y] 8vo. 12s. 6d.*

AN INTRODUCTION TO THE HISTORY OF TH[E] CREEDS. By A. E. Burn, B.D. *Demy 8vo. 10s. 6d.*

THE PHILOSOPHY OF RELIGION IN ENGLAND AN[D] AMERICA. By Alfred Caldecott, D.D. *Dem[y] 8vo. 10s. 6d.*

University Extension Series

Edited by J. E. SYMES, M.A.,
Principal of University College, Nottingham.

Crown 8vo. Price (with some exceptions) 2s. 6d.

A series of books on historical, literary, and scientific subjects, suitable fo extension students and home-reading circles. Each volume is complete i itself, and the subjects are treated by competent writers in a broad and philo sophic spirit.

THE INDUSTRIAL HISTORY OF ENGLAND. By H. de B. Gibbins, Litt.D., M.A. *Eighth Edition.* Revised. With Maps and Plans. 3s.
A HISTORY OF ENGLISH POLITICAL ECONOMY. By L. L. Price, M.A. *Third Edition.*
PROBLEMS OF POVERTY. By J. A. Hobson, M.A. *Fourth Edition.*
VICTORIAN POETS. By A. Sharp.
THE FRENCH REVOLUTION. By J. E. Symes, M.A.
PSYCHOLOGY. By S. F. Granger, M.A. *Second Edition.*
THE EVOLUTION OF PLANT LIFE: Lower Forms. By G. Massee. Illustrated.
AIR AND WATER. By V. B. Lewes, M.A. Illustrated.
THE CHEMISTRY OF LIFE AND HEALTH. By C. W. Kimmins, M.A. Illustrated.
THE MECHANICS OF DAILY LIFE. By V. P. Sells, M.A. Illustrated.
ENGLISH SOCIAL REFORMERS. By H. de B. Gibbins, Litt.D., M.A. *Second Edition.*
ENGLISH TRADE AND FINANCE IN THE SEVENTEENTH CENTURY. By W. A. S. Hewins, B.A.
THE CHEMISTRY OF FIRE. By M. M. Pattiso Muir, M.A. Illustrated.
A TEXT-BOOK OF AGRICULTURAL BOTANY. B M. C. Potter, M.A., F.L.S. Illustrated. *Secon Edition.* 4s. 6d.
THE VAULT OF HEAVEN. A Popular Introductio to Astronomy. By R. A. Gregory. With numerou Illustrations.
METEOROLOGY. By H. N. Dickson, F.R.S.E., F.R Met. Soc. Illustrated.
A MANUAL OF ELECTRICAL SCIENCE. By Georg J. Burch, M.A., F.R.S. Illustrated. 3s.
THE EARTH. An Introduction to Physiography By Evan Small, M.A. Illustrated.
INSECT LIFE. By F. W. Theobald, M.A. Illustrated.
ENGLISH POETRY FROM BLAKE TO BROWNING By W. M. Dixon, M.A. *Second Edition.*
ENGLISH LOCAL GOVERNMENT. By E. Jenk M.A.
THE GREEK VIEW OF LIFE. By G. L. Dickinsor *Second Edition.*

Methuen's Commercial Series

Edited by H. DE B. GIBBINS, Litt.D., M.A.

COMMERCIAL EDUCATION IN THEORY AND PRACTICE. By E. E. Whitfield, M.A.
An introduction to Methuen's Commercial Series treating the question of Commercial Education fully from both the point of view of the teacher and of the parent.
BRITISH COMMERCE AND COLONIES FROM ELIZABETH TO VICTORIA. By H. de B. Gibbins, Litt.D., M.A. *Third Edition.* 2s.
COMMERCIAL EXAMINATION PAPERS. By H. de B. Gibbins, Litt.D., M.A. 1s. 6d.
THE ECONOMICS OF COMMERCE. By H. de B. Gibbins, Litt.D., M.A. 1s. 6d.
A GERMAN COMMERCIAL READER. By S. E. Bally, With Vocabulary. 2s.
A COMMERCIAL GEOGRAPHY OF THE BRITISH EMPIRE. By L. W. Lyde, M.A. *Third Edition.*
A PRIMER OF BUSINESS. By S. Jackson, M.A *Third Edition.* 1s. 6d.
COMMERCIAL ARITHMETIC. By F. G. Taylo M.A. *Third Edition.* 1s. 6d.
FRENCH COMMERCIAL CORRESPONDENCE. By S E. Bally. With Vocabulary. *Third Edition.* 2s
GERMAN COMMERCIAL CORRESPONDENCE. B S. E. Bally. With Vocabulary. 2s. 6d.
A FRENCH COMMERCIAL READER. By S. E. Bally With Vocabulary. *Second Edition.* 2s.
PRECIS WRITING AND OFFICE CORRESPONDENCE By E. E. Whitfield, M.A. *Second Edition.* 2s.
A GUIDE TO PROFESSIONS AND BUSINESS. By H Jones. 1s. 6d.
THE PRINCIPLES OF BOOK-KEEPING BY DOUBL ENTRY. By J. E. B. M'Allen, M.A. 2s.
COMMERCIAL LAW. By W. Douglas Edwards. 2s
A COMMERCIAL GEOGRAPHY OF FOREIG NATIONS. By F. C. Boon, B.A. 2s.

Classical Translations

Edited by H. F. FOX, M.A., Fellow and Tutor of Brasenose College, Oxford.

ÆSCHYLUS—Agamemnon, Choephoroe, Eumenides. Translated by Lewis Campbell, LL.D. 5s.
CICERO—De Oratore I. Translated by E. N. P. Moor, M.A. 3s. 6d.
CICERO—Select Orations (Pro Milone, Pro Mureno, Philippic II., in Catilinam). Translated by H. E. D. Blakiston, M.A. 5s.
CICERO—De Natura Deorum. Translated by F. Brooks, M.A. 3s. 6d.
CICERO—De Officiis. Translated by G. B. Gardiner, M.A. 2s. 6d.
HORACE—The Odes and Epodes. Translated b A. Godley, M.A. 2s.
LUCIAN—Six Dialogues (Nigrinus, Icaro-Menippus The Cock, The Ship, The Parasite, The Lover c Falsehood). Translated by S. T. Irwin, M.A 3s. 6d.
SOPHOCLES—Electra and Ajax. Translated by E D. A. Morshead, M.A. 2s. 6d.
TACITUS—Agricola and Germania. Translated b R. B. Townshend. 2s. 6d.

Methuen's Junior School-Books.

Edited by O. D. INSKIP, LL.D., and W. WILLIAMSON, B.A.

A CLASS-BOOK OF DICTATION PASSAGES. By W. Williamson, B.A. *Seventh Edition. Crown 8vo.* 1*s.* 6*d.*

THE GOSPEL ACCORDING TO ST. MARK. Edited by A. E. Rubie, M.A., Headmaster of the Royal Naval School, Eltham. With Three Maps. *Crown 8vo.* 1*s.* 6*d.*

A JUNIOR ENGLISH GRAMMAR. By W. Williamson, B.A. With numerous passages for parsing and analysis, and a chapter on Essay Writing. *Crown 8vo.* 2*s.*

A JUNIOR CHEMISTRY. By E. A. Tyler, B.A., F.C.S., Science Master at Framlingham College. With 73 Illustrations. *Crown 8vo.* 2*s.* 6*d.*

School Examination Series

Edited by A. M. M. STEDMAN, M.A. *Crown 8vo.* 2*s.* 6*d.*

FRENCH EXAMINATION PAPERS. By A. M. M. Stedman, M.A. *Twelfth Edition.*
A KEY, issued to Tutors and Private Students only, to be had on application to the Publishers. *Fifth Edition. Crown 8vo.* 6*s. net.*

LATIN EXAMINATION PAPERS. By A. M. M. Stedman, M.A. *Eleventh Edition.*
KEY (*Fourth Edition*) issued as above. 6*s. net.*

GREEK EXAMINATION PAPERS. By A. M. M. Stedman, M.A. *Sixth Edition.*
KEY (*Second Edition*) issued as above. 6*s. net.*

GERMAN EXAMINATION PAPERS. By R. J. Morich. *Fifth Edition.*
KEY (*Second Edition*) issued as above. 6*s. net.*

HISTORY AND GEOGRAPHY EXAMINATION PAPERS. By C. H. Spence, M.A., Clifton College. *Second Edition.*

PHYSICS EXAMINATION PAPERS. By R. E. Steel, M.A., F.C.S.

GENERAL KNOWLEDGE EXAMINATION PAPERS. By A. M. M. Stedman, M.A. *Fourth Edition.*
KEY (*Second Edition*) issued as above. 7*s. net.*

EXAMINATION PAPERS IN ENGLISH HISTORY. By J. Tait Plowden-Wardlaw, B.A. *Crown 8vo.* 2*s.* 6*d.*

Junior Examination Series.

Edited by A. M. M. STEDMAN, M.A. *Fcap. 8vo.* 1*s.*

JUNIOR FRENCH EXAMINATION PAPERS. By F. Jacob, B.A.

JUNIOR LATIN EXAMINATION PAPERS. By C. G. BOTTING, M.A.

JUNIOR ENGLISH EXAMINATION PAPERS. By W. Williamson, B.A., Headmaster West Kent Grammar School, Brockley.

JUNIOR ARITHMETIC EXAMINATION PAPERS. By W. S. Beard, Headmaster Modern School, Fareham.

JUNIOR ALGEBRA EXAMINATION PAPERS. By W. S. Finn, M.A.

Technology—Textbooks of

Edited by W. GARNETT, D.C.L., and PROFESSOR J. WERTHEIMER, F.I.C.
Fully Illustrated.

HOW TO MAKE A DRESS. By J. A. E Wood. *Second Edition. Crown 8vo.* 1*s.* 6*d.*

CARPENTRY AND JOINERY. By F. C. Webber. *Second Edition. Crown 8vo.* 3*s.* 6*d.*

PRACTICAL MECHANICS. By Sidney H. Wells. *Second Edition. Crown 8vo.* 3*s.* 6*d.*

PRACTICAL PHYSICS. By H. Stroud, D.Sc., M.A. *Crown 8vo.* 3*s.* 6*d.*

MILLINERY, THEORETICA AND PRACTICAL. By Clare Hill. *Crown 8vo.* 2*s.*

PRACTICAL CHEMISTRY. By W. French, M.A *Crown 8vo.* Part I. 1*s.* 6*d.*

PART II.—FICTION

Marie Corelli's Novels.

Crown 8vo. 6s. each.

A ROMANCE OF TWO WORLDS. *Twenty-Third Edition.*
VENDETTA. *Nineteenth Edition.*
THELMA. *Twenty-Eighth Edition.*
ARDATH: THE STORY OF A DEAD SELF. *Fourteenth Edition.*
THE SOUL OF LILITH. *Eleventh Edit.*
WORMWOOD. *Twelfth Edition.*
BARABBAS: A DREAM OF THE WORLD'S TRAGEDY. *Thirty-Eighth Edition.*

'The tender reverence of the treatment and the imaginative beauty of the writing have reconciled us to the daring of the conception. This "Dream of the World's Tragedy" is a lofty and not inadequate paraphrase of the supreme climax of the inspired narrative.'—*Dublin Review.*

THE SORROWS OF SATAN. *Forty-Sixth Edition.*

'A very powerful piece of work. . . . The conception is magnificent, and is likely to win an abiding place within the memory of man. . . . The author has immense command of language, and a limitless audacity. . . . This interesting and remarkable romance will live long after much of the ephemeral literature of the day is forgotten. . . . A literary phenomenon . . . novel, and even sublime.'—W. T. STEAD in the *Review of Reviews.*

THE MASTER CHRISTIAN. [*165th Thousand.*

'It cannot be denied that "The Master Christian" is a powerful book; that it is one likely to raise uncomfortable questions in all but the most self-satisfied readers, and that it strikes at the root of the failure of the Churches—the decay of faith—in a manner which shows the inevitable disaster heaping up . . . The good Cardinal Bonpré is a beautiful figure, fit to stand beside the good Bishop in "Les Misérables." It is a book with a serious purpose expressed wit absolute unconventionality and passion . . And this is to say it is a book worth reac ing.'—*Examiner.*

TEMPORAL POWER: A STUDY I SUPREMACY. [*150th Thousand.*

'It is impossible to read such a work a "Temporal Power" without becoming co vinced that the story is intended to conve certain criticisms on the ways of the worl and certain suggestions for the betterme of humanity. . . . The chief characteristi of the book are an attack on convention prejudices and manners and on certa practices attributed to the Roman Churc (the policy of M. Combes makes parts of th novel specially up to date), and the pr pounding of theories for the improveme of the social and political systems. . . . the chief intention of the book was to ho the mirror up to shams, injustice, dishonest cruelty, and neglect of conscience, nothin but praise can be given to that intention.'—*Morning Post.*

Anthony Hope's Novels.

Crown 8vo. 6s. each.

THE GOD IN THE CAR. *Ninth Edition.*

'A very remarkable book, deserving of critical analysis impossible within our limit; brilliant, but not superficial; well considered, but not elaborated; constructed with the proverbial art that conceals, but yet allows itself to be enjoyed by readers to whom fine literary method is a keen pleasure.'—*The World.*

A CHANGE OF AIR. *Sixth Edition.*

'A graceful, vivacious comedy, true to human nature. The characters are traced with a masterly hand.'—*Times.*

A MAN OF MARK. *Fifth Edition.*

'Of all Mr. Hope's books, "A Man of Mark" is the one which best compares with "The Prisoner of Zenda."'—*National Observer.*

THE CHRONICLES OF COUNT ANTONIO. *Fifth Edition.*

'It is a perfectly enchanting story of love and chivalry, and pure romance. The Count is the most constant, desperate, and modest and tender of lovers, a peerle gentleman, an intrepid fighter, a faithf friend, and a magnanimous foe.'—*Guardia*

PHROSO. Illustrated by H. R. MILLA *Sixth Edition.*

'The tale is thoroughly fresh, quick wit vitality, stirring the blood.'—*St. James Gazette.*

SIMON DALE. Illustrated. *Sixth Editio*

'There is searching analysis of huma nature, with a most ingeniously construct plot. Mr. Hope has drawn the contras of his women with marvellous subtlety a delicacy.'—*Times.*

THE KING'S MIRROR. *Fourth Editio*

'In elegance, delicacy, and tact it ran with the best of his novels, while in the wi range of its portraiture and the subtil of its analysis it surpasses all his earli ventures.'—*Spectator.*

QUISANTE. *Third Edition.*

'The book is notable for a very high lite ary quality, and an impress of power a mastery on every page.'—*Daily Chronicle*

W. W. Jacobs' Novels.

Crown 8vo. 3s. 6d. each.

MANY CARGOES. *Twenty-Sixth Edition.*

SEA URCHINS. *Ninth Edition.*

A MASTER OF CRAFT. Illustrated. *Fifth Edition.*

'Can be unreservedly recommended to all who have not lost their appetite for wholesome laughter.'—*Spectator.*

'The best humorous book published for many a day.'—*Black and White.*

LIGHT FREIGHTS. Illustrated. *Four Edition.*

'His wit and humour are perfectly irresi tible. Mr. Jacobs writes of skippers, a mates, and seamen, and his crew are t jolliest lot that ever sailed.'—*Daily News.*

'Laughter in every page.'—*Daily Mail.*

Lucas Malet's Novels.

Crown 8vo. 6s. each.

)LONEL ENDERBY'S WIFE. *Third Edition.*

COUNSEL OF PERFECTION. *New Edition.*

TTLE PETER. *Second Edition.* 3s. 6d.

IE WAGES OF SIN. *Thirteenth Edition.*

IE CARISSIMA. *Fourth Edition.*

IE GATELESS BARRIER. *Fourth Edition.*

'In "The Gateless Barrier" it is at once evident that, whilst Lucas Malet has preerved her birthright of originality, the rtistry, the actual writing, is above even he high level of the books that were born efore.'—*Westminster Gazette.*

THE HISTORY OF SIR RICHARD CALMADY. *Seventh Edition.* A Limited Edition in Two Volumes. *Crown 8vo.* 12s.

'A picture finely and amply conceived. In the strength and insight in which the story has been conceived, in the wealth of fancy and reflection bestowed upon its execution, and in the moving sincerity of its pathos throughout, "Sir Richard Calmady" must rank as the great novel of a great writer.'—*Literature.*

'The ripest fruit of Lucas Malet's genius. A picture of maternal love by turns tender and terrible.'—*Spectator.*

'A remarkably fine book, with a noble motive and a sound conclusion.'—*Pilot.*

Gilbert Parker's Novels.

Crown 8vo. 6s. each.

ERRE AND HIS PEOPLE. *Fifth Edition.*

'Stories happily conceived and finely excuted. There is strength and genius in Mr. Parker's style.'—*Daily Telegraph.*

S. FALCHION. *Fourth Edition.*

'A splendid study of character.'—*Athenæum.*

E TRANSLATION OF A SAVAGE. *Second Edition.*

E TRAIL OF THE SWORD. Illusrated. *Seventh Edition.*

'A rousing and dramatic tale. A book ke this is a joy inexpressible.'—*Daily Chronicle.*

EN VALMOND CAME TO PONTIAC: he Story of a Lost Napoleon. *Fifth Edition.*

'Here we find romance—real, breathing, ving romance. The character of Valmond s drawn unerringly.'—*Pall Mall Gazette.*

AN ADVENTURER OF THE NORTH: The Last Adventures of 'Pretty Pierre.' *Second Edition.*

'The present book is full of fine and moving stories of the great North.'—*Glasgow Herald.*

THE SEATS OF THE MIGHTY. Illustrated. *Twelfth Edition.*

'Mr. Parker has produced a really fine historical novel.'—*Athenæum.*

'A great book.'—*Black and White.*

THE BATTLE OF THE STRONG: a Romance of Two Kingdoms. Illustrated. *Fourth Edition.*

'Nothing more vigorous or more human has come from Mr. Gilbert Parker than this novel.'—*Literature.*

THE POMP OF THE LAVILETTES. *Second Edition.* 3s. 6d.

'Unforced pathos, and a deeper knowledge of human nature than he has displayed before.'—*Pall Mall Gazette.*

Arthur Morrison's Novels.

Crown 8vo. 6s. each.

LES OF MEAN STREETS. *Fifth Edition.*

'A great book. The author's method is mazingly effective, and produces a thrilling nse of reality. The writer lays upon us master hand. The book is simply appalling nd irresistible in its interest. It is humorous so; without humour it would not make the ark it is certain to make.'—*World.*

HILD OF THE JAGO. *Fourth Edition.*

'The book is a masterpiece.'—*Pall Mall zette.*

LONDON TOWN. *Second Edition.*

'This is the new Mr. Arthur Morrison, acious and tender, sympathetic and man.'—*Daily Telegraph.*

CUNNING MURRELL.

'Admirable. . . . Delightful humorous relief . . . a most artistic and satisfactory achievement.'—*Spectator.*

THE HOLE IN THE WALL. *Third Edition.*

'A masterpiece of artistic realism. It has a finality of touch that only a master may command.'—*Daily Chronicle.*

'An absolute masterpiece, which any novelist might be proud to claim.'—*Graphic.*

'"The Hole in the Wall" is a masterly piece of work. His characters are drawn with amazing skill. Extraordinary power.'—*Daily Telegraph.*

Eden Phillpotts' Novels.

Crown 8vo. 6s. each.

LYING PROPHETS.
CHILDREN OF THE MIST.
THE HUMAN BOY. With a Frontispiece. *Fourth Edition.*

'Mr. Phillpotts knows exactly what school-boys do, and can lay bare their inmost thoughts; likewise he shows an all-pervading sense of humour.'—*Academy.*

SONS OF THE MORNING. *Second Edition.*

'A book of strange power and fascination.'—*Morning Post.*

THE STRIKING HOURS. *Second Edition.*

'Tragedy and comedy, pathos and humour, are blended to a nicety in this volume.'—*World.*

'The whole book is redolent of a fresher and ampler air than breathes in the circumscribed life of great towns.'—*Spectator.*

FANCY FREE. Illustrated. *Second E[dition.]*

'Of variety and racy humour ther[e is] plenty.'—*Daily Graphic.*

THE RIVER. *Third Edition.*

'"The River" places Mr. Phillpotts in [the] front rank of living novelists.'—*Punch.*

'Since "Lorna Doone" we have [had] nothing so picturesque as this new roma[nce.]'—*Birmingham Gazette.*

'Mr. Phillpotts's new book is a ma[ster]piece which brings him indisputably [into] the front rank of English novelists.'—[*Pall*] *Mall Gazette.*

'This great romance of the River D[art.] The finest book Mr. Eden Phillpotts [has] written.'—*Morning Post.*

S. Baring-Gould's Novels.

Crown 8vo. 6s. each.

ARMINELL. *Fifth Edition.*
URITH. *Fifth Edition.*
IN THE ROAR OF THE SEA. *Seventh Edition.*
MRS. CURGENVEN OF CURGENVEN. *Fourth Edition.*
CHEAP JACK ZITA. *Fourth Edition.*
THE QUEEN OF LOVE. *Fifth Edition.*
MARGERY OF QUETHER. *Third Edition.*
JACQUETTA. *Third Edition.*
KITTY ALONE. *Fifth Edition.*
NOÉMI. Illustrated. *Fourth Edition.*
THE BROOM-SQUIRE. Illustr[ated.] *Fourth Edition.*
THE PENNYCOMEQUICKS. *T[hird] Edition.*
DARTMOOR IDYLLS.
GUAVAS THE TINNER. Illustr[ated.] *Second Edition.*
BLADYS. Illustrated. *Second Edition.*
DOMITIA. Illustrated. *Second Editi[on.]*
PABO THE PRIEST.
WINIFRED. Illustrated. *Second Edi[tion.]*
THE FROBISHERS.
ROYAL GEORGIE. Illustrated.
MISS QUILLET. Illustrated.

Robert Barr's Novels.

Crown 8vo. 6s. each.

IN THE MIDST OF ALARMS. *Third Edition.*

'A book which has abundantly satisfied us by its capital humour.'—*Daily Chronicle.*

THE MUTABLE MANY. *Second Edition.*

'There is much insight in it, and much excellent humour.'—*Daily Chronicle.*

THE COUNTESS TEKLA. *Third Edition.*

'Of these mediæval romances, which are now gaining ground "The Countess Tekla" is the very best we have seen.'—*Pall Mall Gazette.*

THE STRONG ARM. Illustrated. *S[econd] Edition.*

THE VICTORS.

'Mr. Barr has a rich sense of humo[ur.]'—*Onlooker.*

'A very convincing study of Ame[rican] life in its business and political aspec[ts.]'—*Pilot.*

'Good writing, illuminating sketch[es of] character, and constant variety of scen[e and] incident.'—*Times.*

F. Anstey, Author of 'Vice Versa.' A BAYARD FROM BENGAL. Illustrated by BERNARD PARTRIDGE. *Third Edition. Crown 8vo.* 3*s.* 6*d.*

'A highly amusing story.'—*Pall Mall Gazette.*

'A volume of rollicking irresponsible fun.'—*Outlook.*

'This eminently mirthful narrative.'

'Immensely diverting.'—*Glasgow H[erald.]*

Richard Bagot. A ROMAN MYST[ERY.] *Third Edition. Crown 8vo.* 6*s.*

'An admirable story. The plot is [sensa]tional and original, and the book is [full of] telling situations.'—*St. James's Gaze[tte.]*

ndrew Balfour. BY STROKE OF SWORD. Illustrated. *Fourth Edition.* *Crown 8vo.* 6*s.*

'A recital of thrilling interest, told with unflagging vigour.'—*Globe.*

VENGEANCE IS MINE. Illustrated. *Crown 8vo.* 6*s.*

See also Fleur de Lis Novels.

I. C. Balfour. THE FALL OF THE SPARROW. *Crown 8vo.* 6*s.*

Baring Gould. See page 34.

ane Barlow. THE LAND OF THE SHAMROCK. *Crown 8vo.* 6*s.*

FROM THE EAST UNTO THE WEST. *Crown 8vo.* 6*s.*

THE FOUNDING OF FORTUNES. *Crown 8vo.* 6*s.*

'This interesting and delightful book. Its author has done nothing better, and it is scarcely an exaggeration to say that it would be an injustice to Ireland not to read it.'—*Scotsman.*

See also Fleur de Lis Novels.

obert Barr. See page 34.

A. Barry. IN THE GREAT DEEP. *Crown 8vo.* 6*s.*

eorge Bartram, Author of 'The People of Clopton.' THE THIRTEEN EVENINGS. *Crown 8vo.* 6*s.*

arold Begbie. THE ADVENTURES OF SIR JOHN SPARROW. *Crown 8vo.* 6*s.*

'Mr. Begbie often recalls Stevenson's manner and makes "Sir John Sparrow" most diverting writing. Sir John is inspired with the idea that it is his duty to reform the world, and launches into the vortex of faddists. His experiences are traced with spacious and Rabelaisian humour. Every character has the salience of a type. Entertainingly and deftly written.'—*Daily Graphic.*

F. Benson. DODO: A Detail of the Day. *Crown 8vo.* 6*s.*

THE CAPSINA. *Crown 8vo.* 6*s.*

See also Fleur de Lis Novels.

argaret Benson. SUBJECT TO VANITY. *Crown 8vo.* 3*s.* 6*d.*

Walter Besant. A FIVE YEARS' TRYST, and Other Stories. *Crown 8vo.* 6*s.*

Bloundelle Burton, Author of 'The Clash of Arms.' THE YEAR ONE: A Page of the French Revolution. Illustrated. *Crown 8vo.* 6*s.*

DENOUNCED. *Crown 8vo.* 6*s.*

THE CLASH OF ARMS. *Crown 8vo.* 6*s.*

ACROSS THE SALT SEAS. *Crown 8vo.* 6*s.*

SERVANTS OF SIN. *Crown 8vo.* 6*s.*

THE FATE OF VALSEC. *Crown 8vo.* 6*s.*

'The characters are admirably portrayed. The book not only arrests and sustains the attention, but conveys valuable information in the most pleasant guise.'—*Morning Post.*

See also Fleur de Lis Novels.

Ada Cambridge, THE DEVASTATORS. *Crown 8vo.* 6*s.*

PATH AND GOAL. *Crown 8vo.* 6*s.*

Bernard Capes, Author of 'The Lake of Wine.' PLOTS. *Crown 8vo.* 6*s.*

'The stories are excellently fanciful and concentrated and quite worthy of the author's best work.'—*Morning Leader.*

Weatherby Chesney. JOHN TOPP: PIRATE. *Second Edition. Crown 8vo.* 6*s.*

THE FOUNDERED GALLEON. *Crown 8vo.* 6*s.*

THE BRANDED PRINCE. *Crown 8vo.* 6*s.*

'Always highly interesting and surprising.'—*Daily Express.*

'An ingenious, cleverly-contrived story.'—*Outlook.*

Mrs. W. K. Clifford. A WOMAN ALONE. *Crown 8vo.* 3*s.* 6*d.*

See also Fleur de Lis Novels.

J. Maclaren Cobban. THE KING OF ANDAMAN: A Saviour of Society. *Crown 8vo.* 6*s.*

WILT THOU HAVE THIS WOMAN? *Crown 8vo.* 6*s.*

THE ANGEL OF THE COVENANT. *Crown 8vo.* 6*s.*

E. H. Cooper, Author of 'Mr. Blake of Newmarket.' A FOOL'S YEAR. *Crown 8vo.* 6*s.*

Julian Corbett. A BUSINESS IN GREAT WATERS. *Crown 8vo.* 6*s.*

Marie Corelli. See page 31.

L. Cope Cornford. CAPTAIN JACOBUS: A Romance of the Road. *Cr. 8vo.* 6*s.*

See also Fleur de Lis Novels.

Stephen Crane. WOUNDS IN THE RAIN. *Crown 8vo.* 6*s.*

S. R. Crockett, Author of 'The Raiders,' etc. LOCHINVAR. Illustrated. *Second Edition. Crown 8vo.* 6*s.*

'Full of gallantry and pathos, of the clash of arms, and brightened by episodes of humour and love.'—*Westminster Gazette.*

THE STANDARD BEARER. *Cr. 8vo.* 6*s.*

'Mr. Crockett at his best.'—*Literature.*

B. M. Croker, Author of 'Peggy of the Bartons.' ANGEL. *Third Edition. Crown 8vo.* 6*s.*

'An excellent story. Clever pictures of Anglo-Indian life abound. The heroine is delightful.'—*Manchester Guardian.*

PEGGY OF THE BARTONS. *Crown 8vo.* 6*s.*

A STATE SECRET. *Crown 8vo.* 3*s.* 6*d.*

Hope Dawlish. A SECRETARY OF LEGATION. *Crown 8vo.* 6*s.*

A. J. Dawson. DANIEL WHYTE. *Crown 8vo.* 6*s.*

C. E. Denny. THE ROMANCE OF UPFOLD MANOR. *Crown 8vo.* 6*s.*

Evelyn Dickinson. A VICAR'S WIFE. *Crown 8vo.* 6*s.*

THE SIN OF ANGELS. *Crown 8vo.* 3*s.* 6*d.*

Harris Dickson. THE BLACK WOLF'S BREED. Illustrated. *Second Edition. Crown 8vo.* 6s.

A. Conan Doyle, Author of 'Sherlock Holmes,' 'The White Company,' etc. ROUND THE RED LAMP. *Eighth Edition. Crown 8vo.* 6s.

'The book is far and away the best view that has been vouchsafed us behind the scenes of the consulting-room.'—*Illustrated London News.*

Sara Jeannette Duncan (Mrs. Everard Cotes), Author of 'A Voyage of Consolation.' THOSE DELIGHTFUL AMERICANS. Illustrated. *Third Edition. Crown 8vo.* 6s.

'A rattling picture of American life, bright and good-tempered throughout.'—*Scotsman.*

THE PATH OF A STAR. Illustrated. *Second Edition. Crown 8vo.* 6s.

See also Fleur de Lis Novels.

C. F. Embree. A HEART OF FLAME. *Crown 8vo.* 6s.

G. Manville Fenn. AN ELECTRIC SPARK. *Crown 8vo.* 6s.

ELI'S CHILDREN. *Crown 8vo.* 2s. 6d.

A DOUBLE KNOT. *Crown 8vo.* 2s. 6d.

See also Fleur de Lis Novels.

J. H. Findlater. THE GREEN GRAVES OF BALGOWRIE. *Fourth Edition Crown 8vo.* 6s.

'A powerful and vivid story.'—*Standard.*

'A beautiful story, sad and strange as truth itself.'—*Vanity Fair.*

'A singularly original, clever, and beautiful story.'—*Guardian.*

A DAUGHTER OF STRIFE. *Crown 8vo.* 6s.

See also Fleur de Lis Novels.

Mary Findlater. OVER THE HILLS. *Second Edition. Crown 8vo.* 6s.

BETTY MUSGRAVE. *Second Edition. Crown 8vo.* 6s.

A NARROW WAY. *Third Edition. Crown 8vo.* 6s.

J. S. Fletcher. THE BUILDERS. *Crown 8vo.* 6s.

See also Fleur de Lis Novels.

M. E. Francis. MISS ERIN. *Second Edition. Crown 8vo.* 6s.

Tom Gallon, Author of 'Kiddy.' RICKERBY'S FOLLY. *Crown 8vo.* 6s.

Mary Gaunt. DEADMAN'S. *Crown 8vo.* 6s.

THE MOVING FINGER. *Crown 8vo.* 3s. 6d.

See also Fleur de Lis Novels.

Dorothea Gerard, Author of 'Lady Baby.' THE MILLION. *Crown 8vo.* 6s.

THE CONQUEST OF LONDON. *Second Edition. Crown 8vo.* 6s.

THE SUPREME CRIME. *Cr. 8vo.* 6s.

HOLY MATRIMONY. *Second Edition. Crown 8vo.* 6s.

'The love story which it enshrines is a very pretty and tender one.'—*Mornin Leader.*

'Distinctly interesting.'—*Athenæum.*

THINGS THAT HAVE HAPPENEI *Crown 8vo.* 6s.

R. Murray Gilchrist. WILLOWBRAKI *Crown 8vo.* 6s.

Algernon Gissing. THE KEYS OF TH HOUSE. *Crown 8vo.* 6s.

George Gissing, Author of 'Demos,' 'In t' Year of Jubilee,' etc. THE TOW TRAVELLER. *Second Edition. Crow 8vo.* 6s.

THE CROWN OF LIFE. *Crown 8vo.* 6

Ernest Glanville. THE KLOOF BRID *Crown 8vo.* 3s. 6d.

THE LOST REGIMENT. *Crown 8v* 3s. 6d.

THE DESPATCH RIDER *Crown 8v* 3s. 6d.

THE INCA'S TREASURE. Illustrate *Crown 8vo.* 3s. 6d.

'No lack of exciting incident.'—*Scotsma*

'Most thrilling and exciting.'—*Glasgow Hera*

Charles Gleig. BUNTER'S CRUIS Illustrated. *Crown 8vo.* 3s. 6d.

Julien Gordon. MRS. CLYDE. *Cro 8vo.* 6s.

'A clever picture of many phases feminine and American life.'—*Daily Expre*

'Full of vivacity, with many excruciatin clever and entertaining scenes.'—*Pilot.*

S. Gordon. A HANDFUL OF EXOTI *Crown 8vo.* 3s. 6d.

C. F. Goss. THE REDEMPTION DAVID CORSON. *Third Editi Crown 8vo.* 6s.

E. M'Queen Gray. ELSA. *Crown 8vo.*

MY STEWARDSHIP. *Crown 8vo.* 2s.

A. G. Hales. JAIR THE APOSTAT Illustrated. *Crown 8vo.* 6s.

'An extraordinarily vivid story.'—*Wo*

'Mr. Hales has a vivid pen, and scenes are described with vigour and colour *Morning P*

Lord Ernest Hamilton. MARY HAM TON. *Third Edition. Crown 8vo.* 6

Mrs. Burton Harrison. A PRINCI OF THE HILLS. Illustrated. *Crown* 6s.

'Vigorous, swift, exciting.'—*Outlook.*

'A singularly pleasant story of the Tyro *Morning P*

Robert Hichens, Author of 'Flan etc. THE PROPHET OF BERKEL SQUARE. *Second Edition. Crown* 6s.

'One continuous sparkle. Mr. Hic is witty, satirical, caustic, irresistibly h orous.'—*Birmingham Gazette.*

TONGUES OF CONSCIENCE. *Se Edition. Crown 8vo.* 6s.

FELIX. *Fourth Edition. Crown 8vo.*

'Firm in texture, sane, sincere,

natural. "Felix" is a clever book, and in many respects a true one.'—*Daily Chronicle.*

'A really powerful book.'—*Morning Leader.*

'The story is related with unflagging spirit.'—*World.*

'"Felix" will undoubtedly add to a considerable reputation.'—*Daily Mail.*

See also Fleur de Lis Novels.

ohn Oliver Hobbes, Author of 'Robert Orange.' THE SERIOUS WOOING. *Crown 8vo. 6s.*

'Mrs. Craigie is as brilliant as she ever has been; her characters are all illuminated with sparkling gems of description, and the conversation scintillates with an almost bewildering blaze.'—*Athenæum.*

nthony Hope. See page 32.

Hooper. THE SINGER OF MARLY. *Crown 8vo. 6s.*

iolet Hunt. THE HUMAN INTEREST. *Crown 8vo. 6s.*

J. Cutcliffe Hyne, Author of 'Captain Kettle.' PRINCE RUPERT THE BUCCANEER. With 8 Illustrations. *Second Edition. Crown 8vo. 6s.*

MR. HORROCKS, PURSER. *Crown 8vo. 6s.*

. W. Jacobs. See page 32.

enry James, Author of 'What Maisie Knew.' THE SACRED FOUNT. *Crown 8vo. 6s.*

THE SOFT SIDE. *Second Edition. Crown 8vo. 6s.*

F. Keary. THE JOURNALIST. *Crown 8vo. 6s.*

orence Finch Kelly. WITH HOOPS OF STEEL. *Crown 8vo. 6s.*

on. Emily Lawless. TRAITS AND CONFIDENCES. *Crown 8vo. 6s.*

WITH ESSEX IN IRELAND. *New Edition. Crown 8vo. 6s.*

See also Fleur de Lis Novels.

arry Lawson, Author of 'When the Billy Boils.' CHILDREN OF THE BUSH. *Crown 8vo. 6s.*

'Full of human sympathy and the genuine flavour of a wild, untrammelled, unsophisticated life.'—*Morning Leader.*

'The author writes of the wild, picturesque life 'out back,' with all the affection of a native and the penetrating insight of long observation.'—*Daily Telegraph.*

Lynn Linton. THE TRUE HISTORY OF JOSHUA DAVIDSON, Christian and Communist. *Eleventh Edition. Crown 8vo.* 1s.

rma Lorimer. MIRRY ANN. *Crown 8vo. 6s.*

JOSIAH'S WIFE. *Crown 8vo. 6s.*

arles K. Lush. THE AUTOCRATS. *Crown 8vo. 6s.*

na Lyall. DERRICK VAUGHAN, NOVELIST. *42nd thousand. Crown 8vo.* 3s. 6d.

S. Macnaughtan. THE FORTUNE OF CHRISTINA MACNAB. *Second Edition. Crown 8vo. 6s.*

A. Macdonell. THE STORY OF TERESA. *Crown 8vo. 6s.*

Harold Macgrath. THE PUPPET CROWN. Illustrated. *Crown 8vo. 6s.*

Lucas Malet. See page 33.

Mrs. M. E. Mann. OLIVIA'S SUMMER. *Second Edition. Crown 8vo. 6s.*

'An exceptionally clever book, told with consummate artistry and reticence.'—*Daily Mail.*

'Full of shrewd insight and quiet humour.'—*Academy.*

'Wholly delightful; a very beautiful and refreshing tale.'—*Pall Mall Gazette.*

'The author touches nothing that she does not adorn, so delicate and firm is her hold.'—*Manchester Guardian.*

'A powerful story.'—*Times.*

Richard Marsh. BOTH SIDES OF THE VEIL. *Second Edition. Crown 8vo. 6s.*

THE SEEN AND THE UNSEEN. *Crown 8vo. 6s.*

MARVELS AND MYSTERIES. *Crown 8vo. 6s.*

THE TWICKENHAM PEERAGE. *Second Edition. Crown 8vo. 6s.*

'It is a long time since my Baronite read a novel of such entrancing interest as 'The Twickenham Peerage.' He recommends the gentle reader to get the book. In addition to its breathless interest, it is full of character and bubbling with fun.'—*Punch.*

A. E. W. Mason, Author of 'The Courtship of Morrice Buckler,' 'Miranda of the Balcony,' etc. CLEMENTINA. Illustrated. *Crown 8vo. 6s.*

'A romance of the most delicate ingenuity and humour . . . the very quintessence of romance.'—*Spectator.*

Helen Mathers, Author of 'Comin' thro' the Rye.' HONEY. *Fourth Edition. Crown 8vo. 6s.*

'Racy, pointed, and entertaining.'—*Vanity Fair.*

'Honey is a splendid girl.'—*Daily Express.*

'A vigorously written story, full of clever things, a piquant blend of sweet and sharp.' *Daily Telegraph.*

L. T. Meade. DRIFT. *Crown 8vo. 6s.*

Bertram Mitford. THE SIGN OF THE SPIDER. Illustrated. *Fifth Edition. Crown 8vo.* 3s. 6d.

F. F. Montresor, Author of 'Into the Highways and Hedges.' THE ALIEN. *Second Edition. Crown 8vo. 6s.*

'Fresh, unconventional, and instinct with human sympathy.'—*Manchester Guardian.*

'Miss Montresor creates her tragedy out of passions and necessities elementarily human. Perfect art.'—*Spectator.*

Arthur Morrison. See page 33.

W. E. Norris. THE CREDIT OF THE COUNTY. Illustrated. *Second Edition. Crown 8vo.* 6s.
'A capital novel it is, deftly woven together of the comedy and tragedy of life.'—*Yorkshire Post.*
'It is excellent—keen, graceful, diverting.' —*Times.*
THE EMBARRASSING ORPHAN. *Crown 8vo.* 6s.
HIS GRACE. *Third Edition. Crown 8vo.* 6s.
THE DESPOTIC LADY. *Crown 8vo.* 6s.
CLARISSA FURIOSA. *Crown 8vo.* 6s.
GILES INGILBY. *Illustrated. Second Edition. Crown 8vo.* 6s.
AN OCTAVE. *Second Edition. Crown 8vo.* 6s.
A DEPLORABLE AFFAIR. *Crown 8vo.* 3s. 6d.
JACK'S FATHER. *Crown 8vo.* 2s. 6d.
See also Fleur de Lis Novels.

Mrs. Oliphant. THE TWO MARYS. *Crown 8vo.* 6s.
THE LADY'S WALK. *Crown 8vo.* 6s.
THE PRODIGALS. *Crown 8vo.* 3s. 6d.
See also Fleur de Lis Novels.

Alfred Ollivant. OWD BOB, THE GREY DOG OF KENMUIR. *Fifth Edition. Crown 8vo.* 6s.
'Weird, thrilling, strikingly graphic.'—*Punch.*
'We admire this book . . . It is one to read with admiration and to praise with enthusiasm.'—*Bookman.*
'It is a fine, open-air, blood-stirring book, to be enjoyed by every man and woman to whom a dog is dear.'—*Literature.*

E. Phillips Oppenheim. MASTER OF MEN. *Second Edition. Crown 8vo.* 6s.

Gilbert Parker. See page 33.

James Blythe Patton. BIJLI, THE DANCER. *Crown 8vo.* 6s.

Max Pemberton. THE FOOTSTEPS OF A THRONE. Illustrated. *Second Edition. Crown 8vo.* 6s.
'A story of pure adventure, with a sensation on every page.'—*Daily Mail.*
I CROWN THEE KING. With Illustrations by Frank Dadd and A. Forrestier. *Crown 8vo.* 6s.
'A romance of high adventure, of love and war.'—*Daily News.*

Mrs. F. E. Penny. A FOREST OFFICER. *Crown 8vo.* 6s.

Eden Phillpotts. See page 34.

'Q,' Author of 'Dead Man's Rock.' THE WHITE WOLF. *Second Edition. Crown 8vo.* 6s.
Every story is an accomplished romance in its own way.'—*Scotsman.*
'The poet's vein, the breadth of vision, the touch of mysticism are plain in all.'—*Times.*

R. Orton Prowse. THE POISON OF ASPS. *Crown 8vo.* 3s. 6d.

Richard Pryce. TIME AND TH[E] WOMAN. *Crown 8vo.* 6s.
THE QUIET MRS. FLEMING. *Cro[wn] 8vo.* 3s. 6d.

Walter Raymond, Author of 'Love a[nd] Quiet Life.' FORTUNE'S DARLIN[G]. *Crown 8vo.* 6s.

Edith Rickert. OUT OF THE CYPRE[SS] SWAMP. *Crown 8vo.* 6s.

W. Pett Ridge. LOST PROPERT[Y]. *Second Edition. Crown 8vo.* 6s.
'The story is an interesting and animat[ed] picture of the struggle for life in Lond[on] with a natural humour and tenderness of [its] own.'—*Scotsman*
'A simple, delicate bit of work, whi[ch] will give pleasure to many. Much study [of] the masses has made him, not mad, [but] strong, and—wonder of wonders—cheerf[ul].' —*Times.*
A SON OF THE STATE. *Crown 8[vo.]* 3s. 6d.
SECRETARY TO BAYNE, M.P. *Cro[wn] 8vo.* 6s.

C. G. D. Roberts. THE HEART OF T[HE] ANCIENT WOOD. *Crown 8vo.* 3s. [6d.]

Mrs. M. H. Roberton. A GALLA[NT] QUAKER. Illustrated. *Crown 8vo.*

W. Clark Russell. MY DANISH SWEE[T]HEART. Illustrated. *Fourth Editi[on]. Crown 8vo.* 6s.

Grace Rhys. THE WOOING [OF] SHEILA. *Second Edition. Crown 8vo.*
'A really fine book. A book that deser[ves] to live. Sheila is the sweetest heroine w[ho] has lived in a novelist's pages for man[y a] day. Every scene and every incident [has] the impress of truth. It is a masterly [ro]mance, and one that should be widely r[ead] and appreciated.'—*Morning Leader.*

W. Satchell. THE LAND OF THE LOS[T]. *Crown 8vo.* 6s.

Marshall Saunders. ROSE A CHA[R]LITTE. *Crown 8vo.* 6s.

W. C. Scully. THE WHITE HECATOM[B]. *Crown 8vo.* 6s.
BETWEEN SUN AND SAND. *Cro[wn] 8vo.* 6s.
A VENDETTA OF THE DESE[RT]. *Crown 8vo.* 3s. 6d.

Adeline Sergeant. Author of 'The Stor[y of] a Penitent Soul.' A GREAT LA[DY]. *Crown 8vo.* 6s.
THE MASTER OF BEECHWO[OD]. *Crown 8vo.* 6s.
BARBARA'S MONEY. *Second Editi[on]. Crown 8vo.* 6s.
'Full of life and incident, and Barbar[a is] a delightful heroine.'—*Daily Express.*
'An unusually entertaining story[.'—] *World.*

W. F. Shannon. THE MESS DE[CK]. *Crown 8vo.* 3s. 6d.
JIM TWELVES. *Second Edition. Cro[wn] 8vo.* 3s. 6d.

'Full of quaint humour, wise saws, and deep-sea philosophy.'—*Morning Leader.*
'In "Jim Twelves" Mr. Shannon has created a delightful character.'—*Punch.*
'Bright and lively reading throughout.'—*Telegraph.*

len Shipton. THE STRONG GOD CIRCUMSTANCE. *Crown 8vo.* 6*s.*

N. Stephens. A GENTLEMAN PLAYER. *Crown 8vo.* 6*s.*
See also Fleur de Lis Novels.

H. Strain. ELMSLIE'S DRAG-NET. *Crown 8vo.* 6*s.*

né Stuart. A WOMAN OF FORTY. *Crown 8vo.* 3*s.* 6*d.*
CHRISTALLA. *Crown 8vo.* 6*s.*

chess of Sutherland. ONE HOUR AND THE NEXT. *Third Edition. Crown 8vo.* 6*s.*

nie Swan. LOVE GROWN COLD. *Second Edition. Crown 8vo.* 5*s.*

njamin Swift. SIREN CITY. *Crown 8vo.* 6*s.*
GORDON. *Crown 8vo.* 6*s.*

. Townshend. LONE PINE: A Romance of Mexican Life. *Crown 8vo.* 6*s.*

l Waineman. A HEROINE FROM FINLAND. *Crown 8vo.* 6*s.*
'A lovely tale.'—*Manchester Guardian.*
'A vivid picture of pastoral life in a beautiful and too little known country.'
—*Pall Mall Gazette.*

tor Waite. CROSS TRAILS. *Crown 8vo.* 6*s.*

. Marriott Watson. THE SKIRTS OF HAPPY CHANCE. Illustrated. *Second Edition. Crown 8vo.* 6*s.*

. Wells. THE STOLEN BACILLUS, and other Stories. *Second Edition. Crown 8vo.* 3*s.* 6*d.*
THE PLATTNER STORY AND OTHERS. *Second Edition. Crown 8vo.* 3*s.* 6*d.*
THE SEA LADY. *Crown 8vo.* 6*s.*
'A strange, fantastic tale, a really beautiful idyll.'—*Standard.*
'In literary charm, in inventiveness, in fun and humour, it is equal to the best of Mr. Wells' stories.'—*Daily News.*
'Highly successful farce and plenty of polished satire.'—*Daily Mail.*
TALES OF SPACE AND TIME. *Crown 8vo.* 6*s.*
WHEN THE SLEEPER WAKES. *Crown 8vo.* 6*s.*
THE INVISIBLE MAN. *Crown 8vo.* 6*s.*
LOVE AND MR. LEWISHAM. *Crown 8vo.* 6*s.*

Stanley Weyman, Author of 'A Gentleman of France.' UNDER THE RED ROBE. With Illustratious by R. C. WOODVILLE. *Seventeenth Edition. Crown 8vo.* 6*s.*
'Every one who reads books at all must read this thrilling romance, from the first page of which to the last the breathless reader is haled along. An inspiration of manliness and courage.'—*Daily Chronicle.*

Mrs. C. N. Williamson, Author of 'The Barnstormers.' PAPA. *Second Edition. Crown 8vo.* 6*s.*
'Full of startling adventures and sensational episodes.'—*Daily Graphic.*
THE ADVENTURE OF PRINCESS SLYVIA. *Crown 8vo.* 3*s.* 6*d.*

C. N. and A. M. Williamson. THE LIGHTNING CONDUCTOR: Being the Romance of a Motor Car. Illustrated. *Crown 8vo.* 6*s.*
'A very ingenious and diverting book.'—*Morning Leader.*

Zack, Author of 'Life is Life.' TALES OF DUNSTABLE WEIR. *Crown 8vo.* 6*s.*

X.L. AUT DIABOLUS AUT NIHIL. *Crown 8vo.* 3*s.* 6*d.*

The Fleur de Lis Novels

Crown 8vo. 3*s.* 6*d.*

MESSRS. METHUEN are now publishing a cheaper issue of some of their popular novels in a new and most charming style of binding.

Andrew Balfour.
ARMS!

Jane Barlow.
EEL OF IRISH STORIES.

E. F. Benson.
VINTAGE.

J. Bloundelle-Burton.
E DAY OF ADVERSITY.

Mrs. Caffyn (Iota).
MAULEVERER.

Mrs. W. K. Clifford.
SH OF SUMMER.

L. Cope Cornford.
OF ADVERSITY.

Menie Muriel Dowie.
BROOK OF THE BOUGH.

Mrs. Dudeney.
THE THIRD FLOOR.

Sara Jeannette Duncan.
A VOYAGE OF CONSOLATION.

G. Manville Fenn.
THE STAR GAZERS.

Jane H. Findlater.
RACHEL.

Jane H. and Mary Findlater.
TALES THAT ARE TOLD.

J. S. Fletcher.
THE PATHS OF THE PRUDENT.

Mary Gaunt.
KIRKHAM'S FIND.

Robert Hichens.
BYEWAYS.

Emily Lawless.

HURRISH.
MAELCHO.

W. E. Norris.

MATTHEW AUSTIN.

Mrs. Oliphant.

SIR ROBERT'S FORTUNE.

Mary A. Owen.

THE DAUGHTER OF ALOUETTE.

Mary L. Pendered.

AN ENGLISHMAN.

Morley Roberts.

THE PLUNDERERS.

R. N. Stephens.

AN ENEMY TO THE KING.

Mrs. Walford.

SUCCESSORS TO THE TITLE.

Percy White.

A PASSIONATE PILGRIM.

Books for Boys and Girls

Crown 8vo. 3s. 6d.

THE ICELANDER'S SWORD. By S. Baring-Gould.
TWO LITTLE CHILDREN AND CHING. By Edith E. Cuthell.
TODDLEBEN'S HERO. By M. M. Blake.
ONLY A GUARD-ROOM DOG. By Edith E. Cuthell.
THE DOCTOR OF THE JULIET. By Harry Collingwood.
MASTER ROCKAFELLAR'S VOYAGE. By W. Clark Russell.
SYD BELTON: Or, the Boy who would not go to
By G. Manville Fenn.
THE RED GRANGE. By Mrs. Molesworth.
THE SECRET OF MADAME DE MONLUC. By Author of 'Mdle. Mori.'
DUMPS. By Mrs. Parr.
A GIRL OF THE PEOPLE. By L. T. Meade.
HEPSY GIPSY. By L. T. Meade. 2s. 6d.
THE HONOURABLE MISS. By L. T. Meade.

The Novelist

MESSRS. METHUEN are issuing under the above general title a Monthly Se of Novels by popular authors at the price of Sixpence. Each number is as lon the average Six Shilling Novel. The first numbers of 'THE NOVELIST' ar follows:—

I. DEAD MEN TELL NO TALES. By E. W. Hornung.
II. JENNIE BAXTER, JOURNALIST. By Robert Barr.
III. THE INCA'S TREASURE. By Ernest Glanville.
IV. A SON OF THE STATE. By W. Pett Ridge.
V. FURZE BLOOM. By S. Baring-Gould.
VI. BUNTER'S CRUISE. By C. Gleig.
VII. THE GAY DECEIVERS. By Arthur Moore.
VIII. PRISONERS OF WAR. By A. Boyson Weekes.
IX. *Out of print.*
X. VELDT AND LAAGER: Tales of the Transvaal. By E. S. Valentine.
XI. THE NIGGER KNIGHTS. By F. Norreys Connel.
XII. A MARRIAGE AT SEA. By W. Clark Russell.
XIII. THE POMP OF THE LAVILETTES. By Gilbert Parker.
XIV. A MAN OF MARK. By Anthony Hope.
XV. THE CARISSIMA. By Lucas Malet.
XVI. THE LADY'S WALK. By Mrs. Oliphant.
XVII. DERRICK VAUGHAN. By Edna Lyall..
XVIII. IN THE MIDST OF ALARMS. By Robert Barr.
XIX. HIS GRACE. By W. E. Norris.
XX. DODO. By E. F. Benson.
XXI. CHEAP JACK ZITA. By S. Baring-G
XXII. WHEN VALMOND CAME TO PONTIA Gilbert Parker.
XXIII. THE HUMAN BOY. By Eden Phillp
XXIV. THE CHRONICLES OF COUNT ANT By Anthony Hope.
XXV. BY STROKE OF SWORD. By A Balfour.
XXVI. KITTY ALONE. By S. Baring-Gould.
XXVII. GILES INGILBY. By W. E. Norris.
XXVIII. URITH. By S. Baring-Gould.
XXIX. THE TOWN TRAVELLER. By G Gissing.
XXX. MR. SMITH. By Mrs. Walford.
XXXI. A CHANGE OF AIR. By Anthony
XXXII. THE KLOOF BRIDE. By Ernest Gla
XXXIII. ANGEL. By B. M. Croker.
XXXIV. A COUNSEL OF PERFECTION. By Malet.
XXXV. THE BABY'S GRANDMOTHER. B L. B. Walford.
XXXVI. THE COUNTESS TEKLA. By Rober

Methuen's Sixpenny Library

THE MATABELE CAMPAIGN. By Major-General Baden-Powell.
THE DOWNFALL OF PREMPEH. By Major-General Baden-Powell.
MY DANISH SWEETHEART. By W. Clark Russell.
IN THE ROAR OF THE SEA. By S. Baring-Gould.
PEGGY OF THE BARTONS. By B. M. Croker.
THE GREEN GRAVES OF BALGOWRIE. By Jane H. Findlater.
THE STOLEN BACILLUS. By H. G. Wells.
MATTHEW AUSTIN. By W. E. Norris.
THE CONQUEST OF LONDON. By Dorothea Gerard.
A VOYAGE OF CONSOLATION. By Sara J. Duncan.
THE MUTABLE MANY. By Robert Barr.
BEN HUR. By General Lew Wallace.
SIR ROBERT'S FORTUNE. By Mrs. Oliphant.
THE FAIR GOD. By General Lew Wallace.
CLARISSA FURIOSA. By W. E. Norris.
CRANFORD. By Mrs. Gaskell.
NOEMI. By S. Baring-Gould.
THE THRONE OF DAVID. By J. H. Ingraha
ACROSS THE SALT SEAS. By J. Blou Burton.
THE MILL ON THE FLOSS. By George Eliot
PETER SIMPLE. By Captain Marryat.
MARY BARTON. By Mrs. Gaskell.
PRIDE AND PREJUDICE. By Jane Austen.
NORTH AND SOUTH. By Mrs. Gaskell.
JACOB FAITHFUL. By Captain Marryat.
SHIRLEY. By Charlotte Bronte.
FAIRY TALES RE-TOLD. By S. Baring Gou
THE TRUE HISTORY OF JOSHUA DAVIDSC Mrs. Lynn Linton.